MOTHER INDIA

Books by Katherine Mayo

JUSTICE TO ALL
THE STANDARD BEARERS
THAT DAMN Y
MOUNTED JUSTICE
ISLES OF FEAR
MOTHER INDIA
SLAVES OF THE GODS
SOLDIERS—WHAT NEXT?
THE FACE OF MOTHER INDIA
GENERAL WASHINGTON'S DILEMMA

Mother India

BY KATHERINE MAYO

hb

HARCOURT, BRACE AND CO.

NEW YORK

Printed in the United States of America

To
THE PEOPLES OF INDIA
AND TO
THAT INDIAN FIELD LABORER
WHO ONCE, BY AN ACT OF
HUMANITY, SAVED
MY LIFE

"This is a sketch of the ordinary course of manners, administration, and customs, so far as appeared to me to be possible. . . . A description cannot be so complete but that some one may say that he has on one occasion seen or learned something contrary to it; and consequently when such chatterers talk, my [readers] will recognize that absolute concordance is impossible of attainment."

The *Remonstratie* of Francisco Pelsaert Being the Confidential Report of Francisco Pelsaert, Agent of the Dutch East India Company, stationed in Agra from 1620 to 1627. Lately printed in English, under title of *Jahangir's India.*

Foreword

It would be a great pleasure to thank, by name, the many persons, both Indian and English, who have so courteously ·facilitated my access to information, to records, and to those places and things that I desired to see for myself. But the facts that it was impossible to forecast the conclusions I should reach, and that for these conclusions they are in no way responsible, make it improper to **embarrass** them now by connecting them personally therewith.

For this reason the manuscript of this book has not been submitted to any member of the Government of India, nor to any Briton or Indian connected with official life. It has, however, been reviewed by certain public health authorities of international eminence who are familiar with the Indian field.

I may, on the other hand, express my deep indebtedness to my two friends, Miss M. Moyca Newell and Harry Hubert Field, the one for her constant and invaluable collaboration, the other for a helpfulness, both in India and here, beyond either limit or thanks.

K. M.

BEDFORD HILLS
NEW YORK

[ix]

Table of Contents

Part I

Part II

Part III

[xi]

CONTENTS

Part IV

Part V

List of Illustrations

[xiii]

LIST OF ILLUSTRATIONS

PART I

Introduction

THE BUS TO MANDALAY

Calcutta, second largest city in the British Empire, spread along the Ganges called Hooghly, at the top of the Bay of Bengal. Calcutta, big, western, modern, with public buildings, monuments, parks, gardens, hospitals, museums, University, courts of law, hotels, offices, shops, all of which might belong to a prosperous American city; and all backed by an Indian town of temples, mosques, bazaars and intricate courtyards and alleys that has somehow created itself despite the rectangular lines shown on the map. In the courts and alleys and bazaars many little bookstalls, where narrow-chested, near-sighted, anæmic young Bengali students, in native dress, brood over piles of fly-blown Russian pamphlets.

Rich Calcutta, wide-open door to the traffic of the world and India, traffic of bullion, of jute, of cotton —of all that India and the world want out of each other's hands. Decorous, sophisticated Calcutta, where decorous and sophisticated people of all creeds, all colors and all costumes go to Government House Garden Parties, pleasantly to make their bows to Their Excellencies, and pleasantly to talk good English while they take their tea and ices and listen to the regimental band.

You cannot see the street from Government House

[3]

Gardens, for the walls are high. But if you could, you would see it filled with traffic—motor traffic, mostly—limousines, touring cars, taxis and private machines. And rolling along among them now and again, a sort of Fifth Avenue bus, bearing the big-lettered label, "Kali Ghat."

This bus, if you happen to notice it, proceeds along the parkside past the Empire Theater, the various clubs, St. Paul's Cathedral, past the Bishop's House, the General Hospital, the London Missionary Society's Institution, and presently comes to a stop in a rather congested quarter, which is its destination as advertised.

"Kali Ghat"—"place of Kali"—is the root-word of the name Calcutta. Kali is a Hindu goddess, wife of the great god Siva, whose attribute is destruction and whose thirst is for blood and death-sacrifice. Her spiritual domination of the world began about five thousand years ago, and should last nearly four hundred and thirty-two thousand years to come.

Kali has thousands of temples in India, great and small. This of Calcutta is the private property of a family of Brahmans who have owned it for some three centuries. A round hundred of these, "all sons of one father," share its possession today. And one of the hundred obligingly led me, with a Brahman friend, through the precincts. Let him be called Mr. Haldar, for that is the family's name.

But for his white petticoat-drawers and his white toga, the usual Bengali costume, Mr. Haldar might have been taken for a well-groomed northern Italian gentleman. His English was polished and his manner entirely agreeable.

Five hundred and ninety acres, tax free, constitute the temple holding, he said. Pilgrims from far and near, with whom the shrine is always crowded, make money offerings. There are also priestly fees to collect. And the innumerable booths that shoulder each other up and down the approaches, booths where sweetmeats, holy images, marigold flowers, amulets, and votive offerings are sold, bring in a sound income.

Rapidly cleaving a way through the coming and going mass of the devotees, Mr. Haldar leads us to the temple proper. A high platform, roofed and pillared, approached on three sides by tiers of steps of its own length and width. At one end, a deep, semi-enclosed shrine in which, dimly half-visible, looms the figure of the goddess. Black of face she is, with a monstrous lolling tongue, dripping blood. Of her four hands, one grasps a bleeding human head, one a knife, the third, outstretched, cradles blood, the fourth, raised in menace, is empty. In the shadows close about her feet stand the priests ministrant.

On the long platform before the deity, men and women prostrate themselves in vehement supplication. Among them stroll lounging boys, sucking lollypops fixed on sticks. Also, a white bull-calf wanders, while one reverend graybeard in the midst of it all, squatting cross-legged on the pavement before a great book, lifts up a droning voice.

"He," said Mr. Haldar, "is reading to the worshipers from our Hindu mythology. The history of Kali."

Of a sudden, a piercing outburst of shrill bleating. We turn the corner of the edifice to reach the open courtyard at the end opposite the shrine. Here stand two priests, one with a cutlass in his hand, the other holding a young goat. The goat shrieks, for in the air is that smell that all beasts fear. A crash of sound, as before the goddess drums thunder. The priest who holds the goat swings it up and drops it, stretched by the legs, its screaming head held fast in a cleft post. The second priest with a single blow of his cutlass decapitates the little creature. The blood gushes forth on the pavement, the drums and the gongs before the goddess burst out wildly. "Kali! Kali! Kali!" shout all the priests and the suppliants together, some flinging themselves face downward on the temple floor.

Meantime, and instantly, a woman who waited behind the killers of the goat has rushed forward and fallen on all fours to lap up the blood with her tongue —"in the hope of having a child." And now a second woman, stooping, sops at the blood with a cloth, and thrusts the cloth into her bosom, while half a dozen sick, sore dogs, horribly misshapen by nameless diseases, stick their hungry muzzles into the lengthening pool of gore.

"In this manner we kill here from one hundred and fifty to two hundred kids each day," says Mr. Haldar with some pride. "The worshipers supply the kids."

Now he leads us among the chapels of minor deities

[6]

—that of the little red goddess of smallpox, side by side with her littler red twin who dispenses chicken pox or not, according to humor; that of the five-headed black cobra who wears a tiny figure of a priest beneath his chin, to whom those make offerings who fear snake-bite; that of the red monkey-god, to whom wrestlers do homage before the bout; that to which rich merchants and students of the University pray, before confronting examinations or risking new ventures in trade; that of "the Universal God," a mask, only, like an Alaskan totem. And then the ever-present phallic emblem of Siva, Kali's husband. Before them all, little offerings of marigold blossoms, or of red wads of something in baskets trimmed with shells, both of which may be had at the temple booths, at a price, together with sacred cakes made of the dung of the temple bulls.

Mr. Haldar leads us through a lane down which, neatly arranged in rows, sit scores of more or less naked holy men and mendicants, mostly fat and hairy and covered with ashes, begging. All are eager to be photographed. *Saddhus*—reverend ascetics—spring up and pose. One, a madman, flings himself at us, badly scaring a little girl who is being towed past by a young man whose wrist is tied to her tiny one by the two ends of a scarf. "Husband and new wife," says Mr. Haldar. "They come to pray for a son."

We proceed to the temple burning-ghat. A burning is in progress. In the midst of an open space an oblong pit, dug in the ground. This is now half filled with sticks of wood. On the ground, close by, lies a rather

beautiful young Indian woman, relaxed as though in a
swoon. Her long black hair falls loose around her, a
few flowers among its meshes. Her forehead, her
hands and the soles of her feet are painted red, showing that she is blessed among women, in that she is
saved from widowhood—her husband survives her.
The relatives, two or three men and a ten-year-old boy,
standing near, seem uninterested. Crouching at a distance, one old woman, keening. Five or six beggars
like horse-flies nagging about.

Now they take up the body and lay it on the pile of
wood in the pit. The woman's head turns and one arm
drops, as though she moved in her sleep. She died only
a few hours ago. They heap sticks of wood over her,
tossing it on until it rises high. Then the little boy, her
son, walks seven times around the pyre, carrying a
torch. After that he throws the torch into the wood,
flames and smoke rush up, and the ceremony is done.

"With a good fire everything burns but the navel,"
explains Mr. Haldar. "That is picked out of the ashes,
by the temple attendants, and, with a gold coin provided
by the dead person's family, is rolled in a ball of clay
and flung into the Ganges. We shall now see the
Ganges."

Again he conducts us through the crowds to a point
below the temple, where runs a muddy brook, shallow
and filled with bathers. "This," says Mr. Haldar, "is
the most ancient remaining outlet of the Ganges.
Therefore its virtues are accounted great. Hundreds
of thousands of sick persons come here annually to

bathe and be cured of their sickness just as you see those doing now. Also, such as would supplicate the goddess for other reasons bathe here first, to be cleansed of their sins."

As the bathers finished their ablutions, they drank of the water that lapped their knees. Then most of them devoted a few moments to grubbing with their hands in the bottom, bringing up handfuls of mud which they carefully sorted over in their palms. "Those," said Mr. Haldar, "are looking for the gold coins flung in from the burning-ghat. They hope."

Meantime, up and down the embankment, priests came and went, each leading three or four kids, which they washed in the stream among the bathers and then dragged back, screaming and struggling, toward the temple forecourt. And men and women bearing water-jars, descending and ascending, filled their jars in the stream and disappeared by the same path.

"Each kid," continued Mr. Haldar, "must be purified in the holy stream before it is slain. As for the water-carriers, they bring the water as an offering. It is poured over Kali's feet, and over the feet of the priests that stand before her."

As Mr. Haldar took leave of us, just at the rear of the outer temple wall, I noticed a drain-hole about the size of a man's hand, piercing the wall at the level of the ground. By this hole, on a little flat stone, lay a few marigold flowers, a few rose-petals, a few pennies. As I looked, suddenly out of the hole gushed a flow

[9]

of dirty water, and a woman, rushing up, thrust a cup under it and drank.

"That is our holy Ganges water, rendered more holy by having flowed over the feet of Kali and her priests. From the floor of the shrine it is carried here by this ancient drain. It is found most excellent against dysentery and enteric fever. The sick who have strength to move drink it here, first having bathed in the Ganges. To those too ill to come, their friends may carry it."

So we found our waiting motor and rolled away, past the General Hospital, the Bishop's House, the various Clubs, the Empire Theater, straight into the heart of Calcutta in a few minutes' time.

"Why did you go to Kali Ghat? That is not India. Only the lowest and most ignorant of Indians are Kali worshipers," said an English Theosophist, sadly, next day.

I repeated the words to one of the most learned and distinguished of Bengali Brahmans. His comment was this:

"Your English friend is wrong. It is true that in the lower castes the percentage of worshipers of Kali is larger than the percentage of the worshipers of Vishnu, perhaps because the latter demands some self-restraint, such as abstinence from intoxicants. But hundreds of thousands of Brahmans, everywhere, worship Kali, and the devotees at Kali Ghat will include Hindus of all castes and conditions, among whom are found some of the most highly educated and important personages of this town and of India."

Chapter I

THE ARGUMENT

The area we know as India is nearly half as large as the United States. Its population is three times greater than ours. Its import and export trade—as yet but the germ of the possible—amounted, in the year 1924-25, to about two and a half billion dollars.[1] And Bombay is but three weeks' journey from New York.

Under present conditions of human activity, whereby, whether we will or no, the roads that join us to every part of the world continually shorten and multiply, it would appear that some knowledge of main facts concerning so big and today so near a neighbor should be a part of our intelligence and our self-protection.

But what does the average American actually know about India? That Mr. Gandhi lives there; also tigers. His further ideas, if such he has, resolve themselves into more or less hazy notions more or less unconsciously absorbed from professional propagandists out of one camp or another; from religious or mystical sources; or from tales and travel-books, novels and verses, having India as their scene.

It was dissatisfaction with this status that sent me to India, to see what a volunteer unsubsidized, un-

[1] *Review of the Trade of India in 1924-25*, Department of Commercial Intelligence and Statistics, Calcutta, 1926, p. 51.

committed, and unattached, could observe of common things in daily human life.

Leaving untouched the realms of religion, of politics, and of the arts, I would confine my inquiry to such workaday ground as public health and its contributing factors. I would try to determine, for example, what situation would confront a public health official charged with the duty of stopping an epidemic of cholera or of plague; what elements would work for and against a campaign against hookworm; or what forces would help or hinder a governmental effort to lower infant mortality, to better living conditions, or to raise educational levels, supposing such work to be required.

None of these points could well be wrapped in "eastern mystery," and all concern the whole family of nations in the same way that the sanitary practices of John Smith of 23 Main Street concern Peter Jones at the other end of the block.

Therefore, in early October, 1925, I went to London, called at India Office, and, a complete stranger, stated my plan.

"What would you like us to do for you?" asked the gentlemen who received me.

"Nothing," I answered, "except to believe what I say. A foreign stranger prying about India, not studying ancient architecture, not seeking philosophers or poets, not even hunting big game, and commissioned by no one, anywhere, may seem a queer figure. Especially if that stranger develops an acute tendency to ask questions. I should like it to be accepted that I am neither an idle busybody nor a political agent, but merely an ordinary American citizen seeking test facts to lay before my own people."

To such Indians as I met, whether then or later, I made the same statement. In the period that followed, the introductions that both gave me, coupled with the untiring courtesy and helpfulness alike of Indians and of British, official or private, all over India, made possible a survey more thorough than could have been accomplished in five times the time without such aid.

"But whatever you do, be careful not to generalize," the British urged. "In this huge country little or nothing is everywhere true. Madras and Peshawar, Bombay and Calcutta—attribute the things of one of these to any one of the others, and you are out of court."

Those journeys I made, plus many another up and down and across the land. Everywhere I talked with health officers, both Indian and British, of all degrees, going out with them into their respective fields, city or rural, to observe their tasks and their ways of handling them. I visited hospitals of many sorts and localities, talked at length with the doctors, and studied conditions and cases. I made long sorties in the open country from the North-West Frontier to Madras, sometimes accompanying a district commissioner on his tours of checkered duty, sometimes "sitting in" at village councils of peasants, or at Indian municipal board

meetings, or at court sessions with their luminous parade of life. I went with English nurses into bazaars
and courtyards and inner chambers and over city roofs,
visiting where need called. I saw, as well, the homes
of the rich. I studied the handling of confinements,
the care of children and of the sick, the care and protection of food, and the values placed upon cleanliness. I noted the personal habits of various castes and
grades, in travel or at home, in daily life. I visited
agricultural stations and cattle-farms, and looked into
the general management of cattle and crops. I inves-
tigated the animal sanctuaries provided by Indian
piety. I saw the schools, and discussed with teachers
and pupils their aims and experience. The sittings of
the various legislatures, all-India and provincial, re-
paid attendance by the light they shed upon the mind-
quality of the elements represented. I sought and
found private opportunity to question eminent Indians
—princes, politicians, administrators, religious leaders;
and the frankness of their talk, as to the mental and
physical status and conditions of the peoples of India,
thrown out upon the background of my personal observation, proved an asset of the first value.

And just this excellent Indian frankness finally led
me to think that, after all, there are perhaps certain
points on which—south, north, east and west—you *can*
generalize about India. Still more: that you can generalize about the only matters in which we of the busy
West will, to a man, see our own concern.

John Smith of 23 Main Street may care little

enough about the ancestry of Peter Jones, and still less about his religion, his philosophy, or his views on art. But if Peter cultivates habits of living and ways of thinking that make him a physical menace not only to himself and his family, but to all the rest of the block, then practical John will want details.

"Why," ask modern Indian thinkers, "why, after all the long years of British rule, are we still marked among the peoples of the world for our ignorance, our poverty, and our monstrous death rate? By what right are light and bread and life denied?"

"What this country suffers from is want of initiative, want of enterprise, and want of hard, sustained work," mourns Sir Chimanlal Setalvad.[2] "We rightly charge the English rulers for our helplessness and lack of initiative and originality," says Mr. Gandhi.[3]

Other public men demand: "Why are our enthusiasms so sterile? Why are our mutual pledges, our self-dedications to brotherhood and the cause of liberty so soon spent and forgotten? Why is our manhood itself so brief? Why do we tire so soon and die so young?" Only to answer themselves with the cry: "Our spiritual part is wounded and bleeding. Our very souls are poisoned by the shadow of the arrogant stranger, blotting out our sun. Nothing can be done—nothing, anywhere, but to mount the political platform and faithfully denounce our tyrant until he takes his flight. When Britain has abdicated and gone, then, and not

[2] *Legislative Assembly Debates,* 1925, Vol. VI, No. 6, p. 396.
[3] *Young India,* March 25, 1926, p. 112. This is Mr. Gandhi's weekly publication from which much hereinafter will be quoted.

till then, free men breathing free air, may we turn our minds to the lesser needs of our dear Mother India."

Now it is precisely at this point, and in a spirit of hearty sympathy with the suffering peoples, that I venture my main generality. It is this:

The British administration of India, be it good, bad, or indifferent, has nothing whatever to do with the conditions above indicated. Inertia, helplessness, lack of initiative and originality, lack of staying power and of sustained loyalties, sterility of enthusiasm, weakness of life-vigor itself—all are traits that truly characterize the Indian not only of today, but of long-past history. All, furthermore, will continue to characterize him, in increasing degree, until he admits their causes and with his own two hands uproots them. His soul and body are indeed chained in slavery. But he himself wields and hugs his chains and with violence defends them. No agency but a new spirit within his own breast can set him free. And his arraignments of outside elements, past, present, or to come, serve only to deceive his own mind and to put off the day of his deliverance.

Take a girl child twelve years old, a pitiful physical specimen in bone and blood, illiterate, ignorant, without any sort of training in habits of health. Force motherhood upon her at the earliest possible moment. Rear her weakling son in intensive vicious practices that drain his small vitality day by day. Give him no outlet in sports. Give him habits that make him, by the time he is thirty years of age, a decrepit and querulous old wreck—and will you ask what has sapped the energy of his manhood?

Take a huge population, mainly rural, illiterate and loving its illiteracy. Try to give it primary education without employing any of its women as teachers—because if you do employ them you invite the ruin of each woman that you so expose. Will you ask why that people's education proceeds slowly?

Take bodies and minds bred and built on the lines thus indicated. Will you ask why the death rate is high and the people poor?

Whether British or Russians or Japanese sit in the seat of the highest; whether the native princes divide the land, reviving old days of princely dominance; or whether some autonomy more complete than that now existing be set up, the only power that can hasten the pace of Indian development toward freedom, beyond the pace it is traveling today, is the power of the men of India, wasting no more time in talk, recriminations, and shiftings of blame, but facing and attacking, with the best resolution they can muster, the task that awaits them in their own bodies and souls.

This subject has not, I believe, been presented in common print. The Indian does not confront it in its entirety; he knows its component parts, but avoids the embarrassment of assembling them or of drawing their essential inferences. The traveler in India misses it, having no occasion to delve below the picturesque surface into living things as they are. The British official will especially avoid it—will deprecate its handling by

[17]

others. His own daily labors, since the Reforms of
1919, hinge upon persuasion rather than upon command; therefore his hopes of success, like his orders
from above, impose the policy of the gentle word.
Outside agencies working for the moral welfare of the
Indian seem often to have adopted the method of encouraging their beneficiary to dwell on his own merits
and to harp upon others' shortcomings, rather than to
face his faults and conquer them. And so, in the midst
of an agreement of silence or flattery, you find a sick
man growing daily weaker, dying, body and brain, of
a disease that only himself can cure, and with no one,
anywhere, enough his friend to hold the mirror up
and show him plainly what is killing him.

In shouldering this task myself, I am fully aware
of the resentments I shall incur: of the accusations of
muck-raking; of injustice; of material-mindedness; of
lack of sympathy; of falsehood perhaps; perhaps of
prurience. But the fact of having seen conditions and
their bearings, and of being in a position to present
them, would seem to deprive one of the right to indulge a personal reluctance to incur consequences.

Here, in the beginning of this book, therefore,
stands the kernel of what seems to me the most important factor in the life and future of one-eighth of
the human race. In the pages to come will be found an
attempt to widen the picture, stretching into other
fields and touching upon other aspects of Indian life.
But in no field, in no aspect, can that life escape the
influences of its inception.

Chapter II

"SLAVE MENTALITY"

"Let us not put off everything until Swaraj[1] is attained and thus put off Swaraj itself," pleads Gandhi. "Swaraj can be had only by brave and clean people."[2]

But, in these days of the former leader's waned influence, it is not for such teachings that he gains ears. From every political platform stream flaming protests of devotion to the death to Mother India; but India's children fit no action to their words. Poor indeed she is, and sick—ignorant and helpless. But, instead of flinging their strength to her rescue, her ablest sons, as they themselves lament, spend their time in quarrels together or else lie idly weeping over their own futility.

Meantime the British Government, in administering the affairs of India, would seem to have reached a set rate of progress, which, if it be not seriously interrupted, might fairly be forecast decade by decade. So many schools constructed, so many hospitals; so many furlongs of highway laid, so many bridges built; so many hundred miles of irrigation canal dug; so many markets made available; so many thousand acres of waste land brought under homestead cultivation; so many wells sunk; so much rice and wheat and millet

[1] Self-government.
[2] *Young India,* Nov. 19, 1925, p. 399.

[19]

and cotton added to the country's food and trade resources.

This pace of advance, compared to the huge needs of the country, or compared to like movements in the United States or in Canada, is slow. To hasten it materially, one single element would suffice—the hearty, hard-working and intelligent devotion to the practical job itself, of the educated Indian. Today, however, few signs appear, among Indian public men, of concern for the status of the masses, while they curse the one power which, however little to their liking, is doing practically all of whatever is done for the comfort of sad old Mother India.

The population of all India is reckoned, in round numbers, to be 319,000,000.[3] Setting aside Indian States ruled by Indian princes, that of British India is 247,000,000. Among these peoples live fewer than 200,000 Europeans, counting every man, woman and child in the land, from the Viceroy down to the haberdasher's baby. The British personnel of the Army, including all ranks, numbers fewer than 60,000 men. The British Civilian cadre, inclusive of the Civil Service, the medical men, the engineers, foresters, railway administrators, mint, assay, educational, agricultural and veterinary experts, etc., etc., totals 3,432 men. Of the Indian Police Service, the British membership approximates 4,000. This last figure excludes the subordinate and provincial services, in which the number of Europeans is, however, negligible.

[3] *The Indian Year Book*, Times Press, Bombay, 1926, p. 13.

Representing the British man-power in India today, you therefore have these figures:

Army	60,000
Civil Services	3,432
Police	4,000

$$67,432$$

This is the entire local strength of the body to whose oppressive presence the Indian attributes what he himself describes as the "slave mentality" of 247,000,000 human beings.

But one must not overlook the fact that, back of Britain's day, India was ever either a chaos of small wars and brigandage, chief preying upon chief, and all upon the people; or else she was the flaccid subject of a foreign rule. If, once and again, a native king arose above the rest and spread his sway, the reign of his house was short, and never covered all of India. Again and again conquering forces came sweeping through the mountain passes down out of Central Asia. And the ancient Hindu stock, softly absorbing each recurrent blow, quivered—and lay still.

Many a reason is advanced to account for these things, as, the devitalizing character of the Hindu religion, with its teachings of the nothingness of things as they seem, of the infinitude of lives—dreams all—to follow this present seeming. And this element, beyond doubt, plays its part. But we, as "hard-headed Americans," may, for a beginning, put such matters aside while we consider points on which we shall admit less

[21]

room for debate and where we need no interpreter and no glossary.

The whole pyramid of the Hindu's woes, material and spiritual—poverty, sickness, ignorance, political minority, melancholy, ineffectiveness, not forgetting that subconscious conviction of inferiority which he forever bares and advertises by his gnawing and imaginative alertness for social affronts—rests upon a rock-bottom physical base. This base is, simply, his manner of getting into the world and his sex-life thenceforward.

In the great orthodox Hindu majority, the girl looks for motherhood nine months after reaching puberty [4] —or anywhere between the ages of fourteen and eight. The latter age is extreme, although in some sections not exceptional; the former is well above the average. Because of her years and upbringing and because countless generations behind her have been bred even as she, she is frail of body. She is also completely unlettered, her stock of knowledge comprising only the ritual of worship of the household idols, the rites of placation of the wrath of deities and evil spirits, and the detailed ceremony of the service of her husband, who is ritualistically her personal god.

As to the husband, he may be a child scarcely older than herself or he may be a widower of fifty, when first he requires of her his conjugal rights. In any case, whether from immaturity or from exhaustion, he has small vitality to transmit.

4 Cf. *post.*, p. 44.

The little mother goes through a destructive pregnancy, ending in a confinement whose peculiar tortures will not be imagined unless in detail explained.

The infant that survives the birth-strain—a feeble creature at best, bankrupt in bone-stuff and vitality, often venereally poisoned, always predisposed to any malady that may be afloat—must look to his child-mother for care. Ignorant of the laws of hygiene, guided only by the most primitive superstitions, she has no helpers in her task other than the older women of the household, whose knowledge, despite their years, is little greater than hers. Because of her place in the social system, child-bearing and matters of pro-creation are the woman's one interest in life, her one subject of conversation, be her caste high or low. Therefore, the child growing up in the home learns, from earliest grasp of word and act, to dwell upon sex relations.

Siva, one of the greatest of the Hindu deities, is represented, on highroad shrines, in the temples, on the little altar of the home, or in personal amulets, by the image of the male generative organ, in which shape he receives the daily sacrifices of the devout. The followers of Vishnu, multitudinous in the south, from their childhood wear painted upon their foreheads the sign of the function of generation.[5] And although it is accepted that the ancient inventors of these and kindred emblems intended them as aids to the climbing of spiritual heights, practice and extremely

[5] Fanciful interpretations of this symbol are sometimes given.

[23]

detailed narratives of the intimacies of the gods, preserved in the hymns of the fireside, give them literal
meaning and suggestive power, as well as religious
sanction in the common mind.[6]

"Fools," says a modern teacher of the spiritual sense
of the phallic cult, "do not understand, and they never
will, for they look at it only from the physical side." [7]

But, despite the scorn of the sage, practical observation in India forces one to the conclusion that a religion adapted to the wise alone leaves most of the
sheep unshepherded.

And, even though the sex-symbols themselves were
not present, there are the sculptures and paintings on
temple walls and temple chariots, on palace doors and
street-wall frescoes, realistically demonstrating every
conceivable aspect and humor of sex contact; there are
the eternal songs on the lips of the women of the
household; there is, in brief, the occupation and preoccupation of the whole human world within the child's
vision, to predispose thought.

It is true that, to conform to the International Con-
vention for the Suppression of the Circulation of and
Traffic in Obscene Publications, signed in Geneva on
September 12, 1923, the Indian Legislature duly
amended the Indian Penal Code and Code of Criminal
Procedure; and that this amendment duly prescribes

[6] *Hindu Manners, Customs and Ceremonies,* Abbé J. A. Dubois,
1821. Edited and corrected by H. K. Beauchamp. Clarendon Press,
Oxford, 1924, pp. 111-112, 628-31, etc.
[7] Swami Vivekananda, in *Bhakti Yoga.* For a brief and liberal
discussion of the topic see Chapter XIII in *The Heart of Aryavarta,*
by the Earl of Ronaldshay, Constable & Co., Ltd., London, 1925.

set penalties for "whoever sells, lets to hire, distributes, publicly exhibits . . . conveys . . . or receives profit from any obscene object, book, representation or figure." But its enactment unqualified, although welcome to the Muhammadans, would have wrought havoc with the religious belongings, the ancient traditions and customs and the priestly prerogatives dear to the Hindu majority. Therefore the Indian Legislature, preponderantly Hindu, saddled the amendment with an exception, which reads:[8]

This section does not extend to any book, pamphlet, writing, drawing or painting kept or used *bona fide* for religious purposes or any representation sculptured, engraved, painted or otherwise represented on or in any temple, or on any car used for the conveyance of idols, or kept or used for any religious purpose.

In many parts of the country, north and south, the little boy, his mind so prepared, is likely, if physically attractive, to be drafted for the satisfaction of grown men, or to be regularly attached to a temple, in the capacity of prostitute. Neither parent as a rule sees any harm in this, but is, rather, flattered that the son has been found pleasing.

This, also, is a matter neither of rank nor of special ignorance. In fact, so far are they from seeing good and evil as we see good and evil, that the mother, high caste or low caste, will practice upon her children —the girl "to make her sleep well," the boy "to make

[8] *Indian Penal Code,* Act No. VIII of 1925, Section 292.

[25]

him manly," an abuse which the boy, at least, is apt to
continue daily for the rest of his life.

This last point should be noticed. Highest medical
authority in widely scattered sections attests that practically every child brought under observation, for
whatever reason, bears on its body the signs of this
habit. Whatever opinion may be held as to its physical
effects during childhood, its effect upon early thought-
training cannot be overlooked. And, when constantly
practiced during mature life, its devastation of body
and nerves will scarcely be questioned.

Ancient Hindu religious teachings are cited to prove
that the marriage of the immature has not original
Scriptural sanction. Text is flung against text, in each
recurrence of the argument. Pundits radically disagree.
But against the fog evoked in their dispute stand sharp
and clear the facts of daily usage. Hindu custom demands that a man have a legitimate son at the earliest
possible moment—a son to perform the proper religious ceremonies at and after the death of the father
and to crack the father's skull on the funeral pyre,
according to his caste's ritual. For this reason as well
as from inclination, the beginning of the average boy's
sexual commerce barely awaits his ability. Neither general habit nor public opinion confines that commerce
to his wife or wives.

Mr. Gandhi has recorded that he lived with his
wife, as such, when he was thirteen years old, and
adds that if he had not, unlike his brother in similar
case, left her presence for a certain period each day

women surgeons was once more brought forward as equally applicable after the lapse of years. No one disputed, no one can yet dispute, its continued force. The Englishman who now introduced it into the debate could not bring himself to read its text aloud. But, referring to the bill raising the Age of Consent then under discussion, he concluded his speech thus:

A number of persons . . . have said that this Bill is likely to give rise to agitation. No one dislikes agitation more than I do. I am sick of agitation. But when, Sir, it is a case of the lives of women and children, I can only say, in the words of the Duke of Wellington: "Agitate and be damned!"

In a recent issue of his weekly paper, *Young India,*[4] Mr. Gandhi printed an article over his own name entitled "Curse of Child Marriage." Said Mr. Gandhi:

It is sapping the vitality of thousands of our promising boys and girls on whom the future of our society entirely rests.

It is bringing into existence every year thousands of weaklings—both boys and girls—who are born of immature parenthood.

It is a very fruitful source of appalling child-mortality and still-births that now prevail in our society.

It is a very important cause of the gradual and steady decline of Hindu society in point of (1) numbers, (2) physical strength and courage, and (3) morality.

Not less interesting than the article itself is the reply that it quickly elicits from an Indian correspondent

4 *Young India,* August 26, 1926, p. 302.

whom Mr. Gandhi himself vouches for as "a man occupying a high position in society." This correspondent writes: [5]

> I am very much pained to read your article on "Curse of Child Marriage." . . .
>
> I fail to understand why you could not take a charitable view of those whose opinion differs from you. . . . I think it improper to say that those who insist on child marriage are "steeped in vice." . . .
>
> The practice of early marriage is not confined to any province or class of society, but is practically a universal custom in India. . . .
>
> The chief objection to early marriage is that it weakens the health of the girl and her children. But this objection is not very convincing for the following reasons. The age of marriage is now rising among the Hindus, but the race is becoming weaker. Fifty or a hundred years ago the men and women were generally stronger, healthier and more long-lived than now. But early marriage was then more in vogue. . . . From these facts it appears probable that early marriage does not cause as much physical deterioration as some people believe. . . .

The type of logic employed in the paragraph last quoted is so essentially Indian that its character should not be passed by without particular note. The writer sees no connection between the practice of the grandparents and the condition of the grandchildren, even though he sets both down in black and white on the paper before him.

[5] *Young India,* Sept. 9, 1926, p. 318.

A voice in the wilderness, Mr. Gandhi continues the attack, printing still further correspondence drawn forth by his original article. He gives the letter of a Bengali Hindu lady, who writes: [6]

I don't know how to thank you for your speaking on behalf of the poor girl-wives of our Hindu society. . . . Our women always bear their burden of sorrow, in silence, with meekness. They have no power left in them to fight against any evil whatever.

To this Mr. Gandhi rejoins by adducing from his own knowledge instances in support, such as that of a sixty-year-old educationalist, who, without loss of public respect, has taken home a wife of nine years. But he ends on a rare new note, arraigning India's western-taught women who spend their energies in politics, publicity-seeking, and empty talk, to the utter neglect of the crucial work for India that only they can do: [7]

May women always throw the blame on men and salve their consciences? . . . They may fight, if they like, for votes for women. It costs neither time nor trouble. It provides them with innocent recreation. But where are the brave women who work among the girl-wives and girl-widows, and who would take no rest and leave none for men, till girl-marriage became an impossibility?

It has been the habit, in approaching these matters, to draw a veil before their nakedness and pass quickly

[6] *Ibid.*, Oct. 7, 1926, p. 349.
[7] *Ibid.*

by. Searching missionaries' reports for light out of their long experience, one finds neat rows of dots, marking the silent tombs of the indecorous. For the missionary is thinking, first, of the dovecotes at home whence his money comes, and on whose sitting-room tables his report will be laid; and, second, of the super-sensitive Indians on whose sufferance he depends for whatever measure of success he may attain. Again, lay-men who know the facts have written around rather than about them, swathing the spot in euphemisms, partly to avoid the Indian's resentment at being held up to a disapproval whose grounds he can neither feel nor understand, partly out of respect to the occidental reader's taste.

Yet, to suppress or to veil the bare truth is, in cases such as this, to belie it. For few western readers, with-out plain telling, spade by spade, will imagine the con-ditions that exist.

Given, then, a constructive desire really to under-stand India's problems, it is merely what Mr. Gandhi calls "self-deception, the worst of sins," to beg off from facing the facts in these fundamental aspects of Indian life. And if any one is inclined to bolt the task, let him stop to consider whether he has a right so to humor himself, a right to find it too hard even to speak or to hear of things that millions of little children, and of women scarcely more than children, are this very day enduring in their tormented flesh.

PART II

Interlude

THE GRAND TRUNK ROAD

The Grand Trunk Road, at the Khyber. Black, barren, jagged hills scowl into the chasm that cleaves them. Tribesmen's villages on either side—each house in itself a fortalice, its high fighting towers surrounded by high, blind walls loop-holed for rifles.

"What is your calling?" you ask the master. "What but the calling of my people?" says he. "We are raiders."

They may not shoot across the road, it being the highway of the King-Emperor. But on either side they shoot as they please, the country being their country. Their whole life is war, clan on clan, house on house, man on man, yet, for utter joy, Muslim on Hindu. Hills are bare, food is scarce, and the delight of life is stalking human prey, excelling its cunning.

Two miles of camels, majestic, tail to nose, nose to tail, bearing salt, cotton and sugar from India to Asia, swinging gloriously past two miles of camels, nose to tail, tail to nose, bearing the wares of Asia into India. Armed escorts of Afridi soldiers. Armed posts. Frequent roadside emplacements for three or four sharpshooters with rifles. Barbed wire entanglements. Tribesmen afoot, hawk-nosed, hawk-eyed, carrying two rifles apiece, taking the lay of the land on the

[65]

off-chance. Tramp—tramp—a marching detachment
of the 2nd Battalion Royal Fusiliers—open-faced,
bright-skinned English lads, smart and keen—an incredible sight in that setting. Yet because of them and
them only may the Hindu today venture the Khyber.
Until the Pax Britannica reached so far, few Hindus
came through alive, unless mounted and clad as women.

The Grand Trunk Road rolls South and South—a
broad, smooth river of peace whose waves are un-
thinking humanity. Monkeys of many sorts play along
its sides. Peacocks. Deer. Herds of camels shepherded
by little naked boys entirely competent. Dust of traffic.
White bullocks, almond-eyed, string upon string of
sky-blue beads twisted around their necks and horns,
pulling wains heaped high with cotton for Japan. Villages—villages—villages—true homes of India, scattered, miles apart, across the open country. Each just
a handful of mud-walled huts clustered beside the
hole they took the mud from, now half full of stagnant water in which they wash and bathe and quench
their thirst. In villages such as these live nine-tenths
of all the peoples of India. Hindu or Muhammadan
alike—hard-working cultivators of the soil, simple,
illiterate, peaceful, kindly, save when men steal
amongst them carrying fire.

Sunset. The ghost of a ghost—a thin long veil of
blue, floating twice a man's height above the earth.
Softly it widens, deepens, till all the air is blue and
the tall tree-trunks and the stars themselves show blue
behind it. Now comes its breath—a biting tang of

[66]

smoke—the smoke of all the hearth-fires in all the villages. And this is the hour, this the incense, this the invocation of Mother India, walking among the tree-trunks in the twilight, veiled in the smoke of the hearth-fires of her children, her hands outstretched in entreaty, blue stars shining in her hair.

For the rest, the Grand Trunk is just *Kim*. Read it again, for all of it is true. Zam Zammah still stands in Lahore. Mahbub Ali died three years ago, but his two boys are in England at school. And the Old Lady still travels in her bullock-cart, scolding shrilly through her curtains into the clouds of dust.

Chapter VI

THE EARTHLY GOD

A beautiful Rolls-Royce of His Highness's sending was whirling us along the road from the Guest House to the Palace. My escort, one of the chief officials of the Prince's household, a high-caste orthodox Brahman scholar easily at home in his European dress, had already shown readiness to converse and to explain.

"Let us suppose," I now asked him, "that you have an infant daughter. At what age will you marry her?"

"At five—at seven—but I must surely marry her," he replied in his excellent English, "before she completes her ninth year."

"And if you do not, what is the penalty, and upon whom does it fall?"

"It falls upon me; I am outcasted by my caste. None of them will eat with me or give me water to drink or admit me to any ceremony. None will give me his daughter to marry my son, so that I can have no son's son of right birth. I shall have, in fact, no further social existence. No fellow caste-man will even lend his shoulder to carry my body to the burning-ghat. And my penance in the next life will be heavier still than this."

"Then as to the child herself, what would befall her?"

"The child? Ah, yes. According to our law I must turn her out of my house and send her into the forest alone. There I must leave her with empty hands. Thenceforth I may not notice her in any way. Nor may any Hindu give her food or help from the wild beasts, on penalty of sharing the curse."

"And would you really do that thing?"

"No; for the reason that occasion would not arise. I could not conceivably commit the sin whose consequence it is."

It was noticeable that in this picture the speaker saw no suffering figure save his own.

A girl child, in the Hindu scheme, is usually a heavy and unwelcome cash liability. Her birth elicits the formal condolences of family friends. But not always would one find so ingenuous a witness as that prosperous old Hindu landowner who said to me: "I have had twelve children. Ten girls, which, naturally, did not live. Who, indeed, could have borne that burden! The two boys, of course, I preserved."

Yet Sir Michael O'Dwyer records a similar instance of open speech from his own days of service as Settlement Commissioner in Bharatpur: [1]

The sister of the Maharaja was to be married to a great Punjab Sirdar. The family pressed [the Maharaja being a minor] for the lavish expenditure usual on those occasions—£30,000 to £40,000—and the local members of the State Council supported their view. The Political Agent—the State

[1] *India As I Knew It,* Sir Michael O'Dwyer, Constable & Co., Ltd. London, 1925, p. 102.

[69]

being then under British supervision—and I strongly protested against such extravagance in a year of severe scarcity
and distress. Finally, the matter was discussed in full Council.
I asked the oldest member of the Council to quote precedents
—how much had been sanctioned on similar marriages of the
daughter or sister of a Maharaja in the past. He shook his
head and said there was no precedent. I said, "How can that
be?—the State has been in existence over two hundred years,
and there have been eleven successions without adoption, from
father to son; do you mean to tell me that there were never
any daughters?" The old man hesitated a little, and then said,
"Sahib, you know our customs, surely you know the reason.
There were daughters born, but till this generation they were
not allowed to grow up." And it was so.

But it is fair to remember that infanticide has been
common not with primitive races only but with Greece,
with Rome, with nearly all peoples known to history
save those who have been affected by Christian or
Muhammadan culture. Forbidden in India by Imperial
law, the ancient practice, so easily followed in secret,
seems still to persist in many parts of the country.[2]

Statistical proof in such matters is practically unat-
tainable, as will be realized later in this chapter. But
the statement of the Superintendent of the United
Provinces Census [3] regarding girl children of older
growth is cautious enough to avoid all pitfalls:

I very much doubt whether there is any active dislike of

---

[2] See *Census of India*, Vol. I, Part I, 1921, Appendix VI. See also
The Punjab Peasant in Prosperity and Debt, M. L. Darling, Oxford,
1925, pp. 58-9.

[3] *Census of India*, 1911, Vol. XV, p. 190.

girl babies. . . . But if there is no active dislike, there is unquestionably passive neglect. "The parents look after the son, and God looks after the daughter." The daughter is less warmly clad, she receives less attention when ill, and less and worse food when well. This is not due to cruelty, or even to indifference; it is due simply to the fact that the son is preferred to the daughter and all the care, attention and dainties are lavished on him, whilst the daughter must be content with the remnants of all three. . . . The result is that [the female] death-rate between one and five is almost invariably somewhat higher than the male death-rate.

This attitude toward the unwanted was illustrated in an incident that I myself chanced upon in a hospital in Bengal. The patient, a girl of five or six years, had fallen down a well and sustained a bad cut across her head. The mother, with the bleeding and unconscious child in her arms, had rushed to the hospital for help. In a day or two tetanus developed. Now the child lay at death's door, in agony terrible to see. The crisis was on, and the mother, crouching beside her, a figure of grief and fear, muttered prayers to the gods while the English doctor worked. Suddenly, there at the bedside, stood a man—a Bengali *babu*—some sort of small official or clerk.

"Miss Sahib," he said, addressing the doctor, "I have come for my wife."

"Your wife!" exclaimed the doctor, sternly. "Look at your wife. Look at your child. What do you mean!"

"I mean," he went on, "that I have come to fetch

[71]

my wife home, at once, for my proper marital use."

"But your child will die if her mother leaves her now. You cannot separate them—see!" and the child, who had somehow understood the threat even through her mortal pain, clung to her mother, wailing.

The woman threw herself prostrate upon the floor, clutched his knees, imploring, kissed his feet, and with her two hands, Indian fashion, took the dust from his feet and put it upon her head. "My lord, my lord," she wept, "be merciful!"

"Come away," said he. "I have need of you, I say. You have left me long enough."

"My lord—the child—the little child—my Master!"

He gave the suppliant figure a thrust with his foot. "I have spoken"—and with never another word or look, turning on the threshold, he walked away into the world of sun.

The woman rose. The child screamed.

"Will you obey?" exclaimed the doctor, incredulous for all her years of seeing.

"I dare not disobey," sobbed the woman—and, pulling her veil across her stricken face, she ran after her man—crouching, like a small, weak animal.

The girl, going to her husband by her ninth or twelfth year, or earlier, has little time and less chance to learn from books. But two things she surely will have learned—her duty toward her husband and her duty toward those gods and devils that concern her.

Her duty toward her husband, as of old laid down in the *Padmapurana*,[4] is thus translated:[5]

There is no other god on earth for a woman than her husband. The most excellent of all the good works that she can do is to seek to please him by manifesting perfect obedience to him. Therein should lie her sole rule of life.

Be her husband deformed, aged, infirm, offensive in his manners; let him also be choleric, debauched, immoral, a drunkard, a gambler; let him frequent places of ill-repute, live in open sin with other women, have no affection whatever for his home; let him rave like a lunatic; let him live without honour; let him be blind, deaf, dumb or crippled, in a word, let his defects be what they may, let his wickedness be what it may, a wife should always look upon him as her god, should lavish on him all her attention and care, paying no heed whatsoever to his character and giving him no cause whatsoever for displeasure. . . .

A wife must eat only after her husband has had his fill. If the latter fasts, she shall fast, too; if he touch not food, she also shall not touch it; if he be in affliction, she shall be so, too; if he be cheerful she shall share his joy. . . . She must, on the death of her husband, allow herself to be burnt alive on the same funeral pyre; then everybody will praise her virtue. . . .

If he sing she must be in ecstasy; if he dance she must look at him with delight; if he speak of learned things she must listen to him with admiration. In his presence, indeed, she ought always to be cheerful, and never show signs of sadness or discontent.

[4] The *Puranas,* ancient religious poems, are the Bible of the Hindu peoples.
[5] *Hindu Manners. Customs, and Ceremonies,* pp. 344-9.

Let her carefully avoid creating domestic squabbles on the subject of her parents, or on account of another woman whom her husband may wish to keep, or on account of any unpleasant remark which may have been addressed to her. To leave the house for reasons such as these would expose her to public ridicule, and would give cause for much evil speaking.

If her husband flies into a passion, threatens her, abuses her grossly, even beats her unjustly, she shall answer him meekly, shall lay hold of his hands, kiss them, and beg his pardon, instead of uttering loud cries and running away from the house. . . .

Let all her words and actions give public proof that she looks upon her husband as her god. Honoured by everybody, she shall thus enjoy the reputation of a faithful and virtuous spouse.

The Abbé Dubois found this ancient law still the ،ode of nineteenth-century Hinduism, and weighed its aspect with philosophic care. His comment ran: [6]

A real union with sincere and mutual affection, or even peace, is very rare in Hindu households. The moral gulf which exists in this country between the sexes is so great that in the eyes of a native the woman is simply a passive object who must be abjectly submissive to her husband's will and fancy. She is never looked upon as a companion who can share her husband's thoughts and be the first object of his care and affection. The Hindu wife finds in her husband only a proud and overbearing master who regards her as a fortunate woman to be allowed the honour of sharing his bed and board.

[6] *Hindu Manners, Customs, and Ceremonies,* p. 231.

Photo by M. Moyca Newell

A STURDY MUHAMMADAN MOTHER

(See page iii.)

Photos by M. Moyca Newell

VILLAGES

Above: A Village in Nadia, Bengal

Below: Mauwiye, a village in the United Provinces

In the handling of this point by the modern, Rabin-dranath Tagore, appears another useful hint as to the caution we might well observe in accepting, at their face value to us, the expressions of Hindu speakers and writers. Says Tagore, presenting the Hindu theory: [7]

For the purpose of marriage, spontaneous love is unreliable; its proper cultivation should yield the best results . . . and this cultivation should begin before marriage. Therefore from their earliest years, the husband as an idea is held up before our girls, in verse and story, through ceremonial and worship. When at length they get this husband, he is to them not a person but a principle, like loyalty, patriotism, or such other abstractions. . . .

As to the theory of the matter, let that be what it may. As to the actual practice of the times, material will be recalled from the previous pages of this book bearing upon the likeness of the Hindu husband, as such, to "loyalty," "patriotism," or any impersonal abstraction.

Mr. Gandhi tirelessly denounces the dominance of the old teaching. "By sheer force of a vicious custom," he repeats, "even the most ignorant and worthless men have been enjoying a superiority over women which they do not deserve and ought not to have." [8]

But a creed through tens of centuries bred into weak, ignorant, and fanatical peoples is not to be uprooted in one or two hundred years; neither can it be shaken by the wrath of a single prophet, however reverenced.

[7] *The Book of Marriage,* Keyserling, pp. 112-13.
[8] Quoted in *The Indian Social Reformer,* Oct. 29, 1922, p. 135.

[75]

The general body of the ancient law relating to the status and conduct of women yet reigns practically supreme among the great Hindu majority.

In the Puranic code great stress is laid upon the duty of the wife to her mother-in-law. Upon this foundation rests a tremendous factor in every woman's life. A Hindu marriage does not betoken the setting up of a new homestead; the little bride, on the contrary, is simply added to the household of the groom's parents, as that household already exists. There she becomes at once the acknowledged servant of the mother-in-law, at whose beck and call she lives. The father-in-law, the sister-in-law, demand what they like of her, and, bred as she is, it lies not in her to rebel. The very idea that she possibly could rebel or acquire any degree of freedom has neither root nor ground in her mind. She exists to serve. The mother-in-law is often hard, ruling without mercy or affection; and if by chance the child is slow to bear children, or if her children be daughters, then, too frequently, the elder woman's tongue is a flail, her hand heavy in blows, her revengeful spirit set on clouding her victim's life with threats of the new wife who, according to the Hindu code, may supplant and enslave her.

Not infrequently, in pursuing my inquiry in the rural districts, I came upon the record of suicides of women between the ages of fourteen and nineteen. The commonest cause assigned by the Indian police recorder was "colic pains, and a quarrel with the mother-in-law."

As to the direct relation of wife to husband, as understood in high-class Hindu families today, it has thus been described by that most eminent of Indian ladies, whose knowledge of her sisters of all ranks and creeds is wide, deep, and kind, Miss Cornelia Sorabji: [9]

Chief priestess of her husband, whom to serve is her religion and her delight . . . moving on a plane far below him for all purposes religious, mental and social; gentle and adoring, but incapable of participation in the larger interests of his life. . . . To please his mother, whose chief handmaiden she is, and to bring him a son, these are her two ambitions. . . . The whole idea of marriage in the east revolves simply on the conception of life; a community of interests, companionship, these never enter into the general calculation. She waits upon her husband when he feeds, silent in his presence, with downcast eyes. To look him in the face were bold indeed.

Then says Miss Sorabji, continuing her picture: [10]

When she is the mother of a son, greater respect is hers from the other women in the zenana . . . she has been successful, has justified her existence. The self-respect it gives the woman herself is most marked. She is still a faithful slave to her husband, but she is an entity, a person, in so far as that is possible in a Hindu zenana; she can lift her head above the women who taunted her, her heart above the fear of a rival.

[9] *Between the Twilights,* Cornelia Sorabji, Harper Brothers, London, 1908, pp. 125-32.
[10] *Ibid.,* pp. 45-6.

This general characterization of the wife in the *zenana* of educated, well-to-do, and prominent Hindus finds its faithful echo in one of many similar incidents that came to my notice in humbler fields. For the orthodox Hindu woman, whoever she be, will obey the law of her ancestors and her gods with a pride and integrity unaffected by her social condition.

The woman, in this case, was the wife of a small landowner in a district not far from Delhi. The man, unusually enlightened, sent her to hospital for her first confinement. But he sent her too late, and, after a severe ordeal, the child was born dead.

Again, the following year, the same story was repeated. The patient was brought late, and even the necessary Cæsarean operation did not save the child. Still a third time the *zemindar* appeared, bringing the wife; but now, taught by experience, he had moved in time. As the woman came out of the ether, the young English nurse bent over her, all aglow with the news.

"Little mother, happy little mother, don't you want to see your baby—don't you want to see your boy?"

The head on the pillow turned away. Faintly, slowly the words came back out of the pit of hopeless night:

"Who wants to see—a dead baby! I have seen— too many—too many—dead—dead—" The voice trailed into silence. The heavy eyelids closed.

Then Sister picked up the baby. Baby squealed.

On that instant the thing was already done—so

quickly done that none could measure the time of its doing. The lifeless figure on the bed tautened. The great black eyes flashed wide. The thin arms lifted in a gesture of demand. For the first time in all her life, perhaps, this girl was thinking in the imperative.

"Give me my son!" She spoke as an empress might speak. "Send at once to my village and inform the father of my son that I desire his presence." Utterly changed. Endued with dignity—with self-respect—with importance.

The father came. All the relatives came, heaping like flies into the little family quarters attached, in Indian women's hospitals, to each private room. Ten days they sat there—over a dozen of them, in a space some fifteen by twenty feet square. And on the tenth, in a triumphant procession, they bore home to their village mother and son.

Rich or poor, high caste or low caste, the mother of a son will idolize the child. She has little knowledge to give him, save knowledge of strange taboos and fears and charms and ceremonies to propitiate a universe of powers unseen. She would never discipline him, even though she knew the meaning of the word. She would never teach him to restrain passion or impulse or appetite. She has not the vaguest conception how to feed him or develop him. Her idea of a sufficient meal is to tie a string around his little brown body and stuff him till the string bursts. And so through all his childhood he grows as grew his father before him, back into the mists of time.

[79]

Yet, when the boy himself assumes married life, he will honor his mother above his wife, and show her often a real affection and deference. Then it is that the woman comes into her own, ruling indoors with an iron hand, stoutly maintaining the ancient tradition, and, forgetful of her former misery, visiting upon the slender shoulders of her little daughters-in-law all the burdens and the wrath that fell upon her own young back. But one higher step is perhaps reserved for her. With each grandson laid in her arms she is again exalted. The family line is secure. Her husband's soul is protected. Proud is she among women. Blessed be the gods!

Chapter VII

WAGES OF SIN

The reverse of the picture shows the Hindu widow —the accursed. That so hideous a fate as widowhood should befall a woman can be but for one cause—the enormity of her sins in a former incarnation. From the moment of her husband's decease till the last hour of her own life, she must expiate those sins in shame and suffering and self-immolation, chained in every thought to the service of his soul. Be she a child of three, who knows nothing of the marriage that bound her, or be she a wife in fact, having lived with her husband, her case is the same. By his death she is revealed as a creature of innate guilt and evil portent, herself convinced, when she is old enough to think at all, of the justice of her fate. Miss Sorabji thus treats the subject: [1]

The orthodox Hindu widow suffers her lot with the fierce enjoyment of martyrdom . . . but nothing can minimize the evils of that lot. . . . That she accepts the fact makes it no less of a hardship. For some sin committed in a previous birth, the gods have deprived her of a husband. What is left to her now but to work out his "salvation" and by her prayers and penances to win him a better place in his next genesis? . . . For the mother-in-law, what also is left but the obligation to

[1] *Between the Twilights*, pp. 144-6.

curse? . . . But for this luckless one, her son might still be in the land of the living. . . . There is no determined animosity in the attitude. The person cursing is as much an instrument of Fate as the person cursed. . . . [But] it is all very well to assert no personal animosity toward her whom you hold it a privilege to curse and to burden with every unpleasant duty imaginable. Your practise is apt to mislead.

The widow becomes the menial of every other person in the house of her late husband. All the hardest and ugliest tasks are hers, no comforts, no ease. She may take but one meal a day and that of the meanest. She must perform strict fasts. Her hair must be shaven off. She must take care to absent herself from any scene of ceremony or rejoicing, from a marriage, from a religious celebration, from the sight of an expectant mother or of any person whom the curse of her glance might harm. Those who speak to her may speak in terms of contempt and reproach; and she herself is the priestess of her own misery, for its due continuance is her one remaining merit.

The old French traveler, Bernier, states that the pains of widowhood were imposed "as an easy mode of keeping wives in subjection, of securing their attention in times of sickness, and of deterring them from administering poison to their husbands." [2]

But once, however, did I hear this idea from a Hindu's lips. "We husbands so often make our wives unhappy," said this frank witness, "that we might well

[2] *Travels in the Mogul Empire, A.D. 1656-1668*, François Bernier, Oxford University Press, 1916, pp. 310-11.

INTERIOR OF A HINDU HOUSE

COW-DUNG CAKES

The fuel of India

fear they would poison us. Therefore did our wise ancestors make the penalty of widowhood so frightful —in order that the woman may not be tempted."

In the female wards of prisons in many parts of India I have seen women under sentence for the murder of their husbands. These are perhaps rare mentalities, perhaps hysteria cases. More characteristic are the still-recurring instances of practical *suttee,* where the newly-widowed wife deliberately pours oil over her garments, sets them afire and burns to death, in a connived-at secrecy. She has seen the fate of other widows. She is about to become a drudge, a slave, starved, tyrannized over, abused—and this is the sacred way out—"following the divine law." Committing a pious and meritorious act, in spite of all foreign-made interdicts, she escapes a present hell and may hope for happier birth in her next incarnation.

Although demanded in the scripture already quoted, the practice of burning the widow upon the husband's funeral pyre is today unlawful. But it must be noted that this change represents an exceptional episode; it represents not a natural advance of public opinion, but one of the rare incursions of the British strong hand into the field of native religions. *Suttee* was forbidden by British Governors [3] some twenty-nine years before the actual taking over by the Crown of direct government. That advanced Indian, Raja Ram Mohan Roy, supported the act. But other influential Bengali gentlemen, vigorously opposing, did not hesitate to push

[3] Regulation XVII of 1829.

[83]

their fight for the preservation of the practice even to the court of last resort—the Privy Council in London.

Is it conceivable that, given opportunity, the submerged root of the matter might come again to life and light? In Mr. Gandhi's weekly [4] of November 11, 1926, a Hindu writer declares the impossibility of a widow's remarriage today, without the deathbed permission of the deceased husband. No devout husband will give such permission, the correspondent affirms, and adds: "He will rather fain agree to his wife's becoming *sati* [suttee] if she can."

An inmate of her husband's home at the time of his death, the widow, although she has no legal claim for protection, may be retained there on the terms above described, or she may be turned adrift. Then she must live by charity—or by prostitution, into which she not seldom falls. And her dingy, ragged figure, her bristly, shaven head, even though its stubble be white over the haggard face of unhappy age, is often to be seen in temple crowds or in the streets of pilgrimage cities, where sometimes niggard piety doles her a handful of rice.

As to remarriage, that, in orthodox Hinduism, is impossible. Marriage is not a personal affair, but an eternal sacrament. And it must never be forgotten that the great majority of the Hindus are orthodox to the bone. Whether the widow be an infant and a stranger to the man whose death, she is told, was caused by her sins, or whether she be twenty and of his bed and

[4] *Young India.*

[84]

board, orthodoxy forbids her remarriage. Of recent years, however, the gradual if unrecognized influence of western teaching has aroused a certain response. In different sections of India, several associations have sprung up, having the remarriage of virgin widows as one of their chief purported objects. The movement, however, is almost wholly restricted to the most advanced element of Hindu society, and its influence is, as yet, too fractional appreciably to affect statistics.

The observations on this point made by the Abbé Dubois a century since still, in general, hold good. He saw that the marriage of a small child to a man of sixty and the forbidding of her remarriage after his death must often throw the child, as a widow, into a dissolute life. Yet widow remarriage was unknown. Even were it permitted, says the Abbé, "the strange preference which Brahmins have for children of very tender years would make such a permission almost nominal in the case of their widows." [5]

And one cannot forget, in estimating the effect of the young widow on the social structure of which she is a part, that, in her infancy, she lived in the same atmosphere of sexual stimulus that surrounded the boy child, her brother. If a girl child so reared in thought and so sharpened in desire be barred from lawful satisfaction of desire, is it strange if the desire prove stronger with her than the social law? Her family, the family of the dead husband, will, for their credit's sake, restrain her if they can. And often, per-

[5] *Hindu Manners, Customs and Ceremonies,* p. 212.

[85]

haps most often, she needs no restraint save her own spirit of sacrifice. But the opposite example is frequently commented upon by Indian speakers. Lala Lajpat Rai, Swarajist politician, laments: [6]

The condition of child-widows is indescribable. God may bless those who are opposed to their remarriage, but their superstition introduces so many abuses and brings about so much moral and physical misery as to cripple society as a whole and handicap it in the struggle for life.

Mr. Gandhi acquiescently cites another Indian writer on child marriage and enforced child widowhood, thus: "It is bringing into existence thousands of girl-widows every year who in their turn are a source of corruption and dangerous infection to society." [7]

Talk there is, resolutions passed, in caste and association conventions, as to changing these things of oppression and of scornings. But a virgin widow's remarriage is still a headline event, even to the reform newspapers, while the remarriage of a Hindu widowed wife is still held to be inconceivable.

And here, curiously enough, the very influence that on the one hand most strongly operates to rescue the woman, on the other more widely enslaves her. While British practice and western education tend, at the top of the ladder, to breed discontent with ancient darkness, British public works, British sanitation and agricultural development, steadily raising the economic condition of

[6] Presidential Speech delivered before the Hindu Mahasabha Conference, in Bombay, December, 1925.
[7] *Young India*, Aug. 26, 1926, p. 302.

the lower classes, as steadily breed aspirants to greater
social prestige. Thus the census of 1921 finds restriction in widow remarriage definitely increasing in those
low ranks of the social scale that, by their own code,
have no such inhibition. Hindu caste rank is entirely
independent of worldly wealth; but the first move of
the man of little place, suddenly awakening to a new
prosperity, security, and peace, is to mimic the manners
of those to whom he has looked up. He becomes a
social climber, not less in India than in the United
States, and assumes the shackles of the elect.

Mr. Mukerjea of Baroda, an Indian official observer, thus writes of attempts to break down the custom of obligatory widowhood: [8]

All such efforts will be powerless as long as authoritative
Hindu opinion continues to regard the prohibition of widow
remarriage as a badge of respectability. Amongst the lower
Hindu castes, the socially affluent sections are discountenancing the practice of widow remarriage as actively as any
Brahman.

It was a distinguished Bengali, the Pundit Iswar
Chunder Vidyasagar, who, among Indians, started the
movement for remarriage of virgin widows and supported Government in the enactment of a law legalizing such remarriages. But over him and the fruit of
his work another eminent Indian thus laments: [9]

[8] *Census of India,* 1921, Vol. I, Chapter VII, paragraph 134.
[9] *A Nation in the Making.* Sir Surendranath Banerjea, Oxford
University Press, 1925, pp. 8-9

I well remember the stir and agitation which the movement produced and how orthodox Hindus were up in arms against it. . . . The champion of the Hindu widows died a disappointed man, like so many of those who were in advance of their age, leaving his message unfulfilled. . . . The progress which the movement has made since his death in 1891 has been slow. A new generation has sprung up, but he has found no successor. The mantle of Elijah has not fallen upon Elisha. The lot of the Hindu widow today remains very much the same that it was fifty years ago. There are few to wipe her tears and to remove the enforced widowhood that is her lot. The group of sentimental sympathisers have perhaps increased—shouting at public meetings on the Vidyasagar anniversary day, but leaving unredeemed the message of the great champion of the Hindu widow.

Mr. Gandhi, always true to his light, himself has said: [10]

To force widowhood upon little girls is a brutal crime for which we Hindus are daily paying dearly. . . . There is no warrant in any *shastra* [11] for such widowhood. Voluntary widowhood consciously adopted by a woman who has felt the affection of a partner adds grace and dignity to life, sanctifies the home and uplifts religion itself. Widowhood imposed by religion or custom is an unbearable yoke and defiles the home by secret vice and degrades religion. And does not the Hindu widowhood stink in one's nostrils when one thinks of old and diseased men over fifty taking or rather purchasing girl wives, sometimes one on top of another?

[10] *Young India,* August 5, 1926, p. 276.
[11] Hindu book of sacred institutes.

But this, again, is a personal opinion, rather than a public force. "We want no more of Gandhi's doctrines," one conspicuous Indian politician told me; "Gandhi is a deluded man."

That distinguished Indian, Sir Ganga Ram, C.I.E., C.V.O., with some help from Government has built and endowed a fine home and school for Hindu widows in the city of Lahore. This establishment, in 1926, had over forty inmates. In Bombay Presidency are five Government-aided institutes for widows and deserted wives, run by philanthropic Indian gentlemen. Other such institutions may exist; but, if they do, their existence has escaped the official recorders. I myself saw, in the pilgrim city of Nawadwip, in Bengal, a refuge for widows maintained by local subscription and pilgrims' gifts. It was fourteen years old and had eight inmates—the extent, it appeared, of its intention and capacity.

The number of widows in India is, according to the latest published official computation, 26,834,838.[12]

[12] *Statistical Abstract for British India,* 1914-15 to 1923-24, Government of India Publication, 1925, p. 20.

Chapter VIII

MOTHER INDIA

Row upon row of girl children—little tots all, four, five, six, even seven years old, sitting cross-legged on the floor, facing the brazen goddess. Before each one, laid straight and tidy, certain treasures—a flower, a bead or two, a piece of fruit—precious things brought from their homes as sacrificial offerings. For this is a sort of day-school of piety. These babies are learning texts—"mantrims" to use in worship—learning the rites that belong to the various ceremonies incumbent upon Hindu women. And that is all they are learning; that is all they need to know. Now in unison they pray.

"What are they praying for?" one asks the teacher, a grave-faced Hindu lady.

"What should a woman-child pray for? A husband, if she is not married; or, if she is, then for a better husband at her next re-birth."

Women pray first as to husbands; then, to bear sons. Men must have sons to serve their souls.

Already we have seen some evidence of the general attitude of the Hindu toward this, the greatest of all his concerns, in its prenatal aspect. But another cardinal point that, in any practical survey of Indian competency, can be neither contested nor suppressed, is the

[90]

manner in which the Hindu of all classes permits his much-coveted son to be ushered into the light of day.

We have spoken of women's hospitals in various parts of India. These are doing excellent work, mostly gynecological. But they are few, relatively to the work to be done, nor could the vast majority of Indian women, in their present state of development, be induced to use a hospital, were it at their very door.

What the typical Indian woman wants in her hour of trial is the thing to which she is historically used—the midwife—the *dhai*. And the *dhai* is a creature that must indeed be seen to be credited.

According to the Hindu code, a woman in childbirth and in convalescence therefrom is ceremonially unclean, contaminating all that she touches. Therefore only those become *dhais* who are themselves of the unclean, "untouchable" class, the class whose filthy habits will be adduced by the orthodox Hindu as his good and sufficient reason for barring them from contact with himself. Again according to the Hindu code, a woman in childbirth, like the new-born child itself, is peculiarly susceptible to the "evil eye." Therefore no woman whose child has died, no one who has had an abortion, may, in many parts of India, serve as *dhai*, because of the malice or jealousy that may secretly inspire her. Neither may any widow so serve, being herself a thing of evil omen. Not all of these disqualifications obtain everywhere. But each holds in large sections.

Further, no sort of training is held necessary for the

[91]

work. As a calling, it descends in families. At the death of a *dhai*, her daughter or daughter-in-law may adopt it, beginning at once to practice even though she has never seen a confinement in all her life.[1] But other women, outside the line of descent, may also take on the work and, if they are properly beyond the lines of the taboos, will find ready employment without any sort of preparation and for the mere asking.

Therefore, in total, you have the half-blind, the aged, the crippled, the palsied and the diseased, drawn from the dirtiest poor, as sole ministrants to the women of India in the most delicate, the most dangerous and the most important hour of their existence.

The expectant mother makes no preparations for the baby's coming—such as the getting ready of little garments. This would be taking dangerously for granted the favor of the gods. But she may and does toss into a shed or into a small dark chamber whatever soiled and disreputable rags, incapable of further use, fall from the hands of the household during the year.

And it is into this evil-smelling rubbish-hole that the young wife creeps when her hour is come upon her. "Unclean" she is, in her pain—unclean whatever she touches, and fit thereafter only to be destroyed. In the name of thrift, therefore, give her about her only the unclean and the worthless, whether human or in-animate. If there be a broken-legged, ragged string-cot, let her have that to lie upon; it can be saved in

[1] Cf. Edris Griffin, Health Visitor, Delhi, in *National Health*, Oct., 1925, p. 125.

that same black chamber for the next to need it. Other-wise, make her a little support of cow-dung or of stones, on the bare earthen floor. And let no one waste effort in sweeping or dusting or washing the place till this occasion be over.[2]

When the pains begin, send for the *dhai*. If the *dhai*, when the call reaches her, chances to be wearing decent clothes, she will stop, whatever the haste, to change into the rags she keeps for the purpose, in-fected and re-infected from the succession of diseased cases that have come into her practice. And so, at her dirtiest, a bearer of multiple contagions, she shuts her-self in with her victim.

If there be an air-hole in the room, she stops it up with straw and refuse; fresh air is bad in confine-ments—it gives fever. If there be rags sufficient to make curtains, she cobbles them together, strings them across a corner and puts the patient within, against the wall, still farther to keep away the air. Then, to make darkness darker, she lights the tiniest glim—a bit of cord in a bit of oil, or a little kerosene lamp without a chimney, smoking villainously. Next, she makes a small charcoal fire in a pan beneath the bed or close by the patient's side, whence it joins its poisonous breath to the serried stenches.

The first *dhai* that I saw in action tossed upon this coal-pot, as I entered the room, a handful of some special vile-smelling stuff to ward off the evil eye -

---

[2] *National Health*, 1925, p. 70. See also Maggie Ghose in *Victoria Memorial Scholarship Fund Report*, Calcutta, 1918, p. 153.

[93]

my evil eye. The smoke of it rose thick—also a tongue of flame. By that light one saw her Witch-of-Endor face through its vermin-infested elf-locks, her hanging rags, her dirty claws, as she peered with festered and almost sightless eyes out over the stink-cloud she had raised. But it was not she who ran to quench the flame that caught in the bed and went writhing up the body of her unconscious patient. She was too blind—too dull of sense to see or to feel it.

If the delivery is at all delayed, the *dhai* is expected to explore for the reason of the delay. She thrusts her long-unwashed hand, loaded with dirty rings and bracelets and encrusted with untold living contaminations, into the patient's body, pulling and twisting at what she finds there.[3] If the delivery is long delayed and difficult, a second or a third *dhai* may be called in, if the husband of the patient will sanction the expense, and the child may be dragged forth in detached sections —a leg or an arm torn off at a time.[4]

Again to quote from a medical woman:[5]

One often sees in cases of contracted pelvis due to osteomalacia, if there seems no chance of the head passing down [that the *dhai*] attempts to draw on the limbs, and, if possible, breaks them off. She prefers to extract the child *by main force*, and the patient in such cases is badly torn, often into her bladder, with the resulting large vesico-vaginal fistulae so

[3] *V.M.S.F. Report,* "Improvement of the Conditions of Child-Birth in India," pp. 70 et seq.
[4] Dr. Marion A. Wylie., M.A., M.B., Ch. B., *Ibid.,* p. 85, and *Ibid.,* Appendix V, p. 69.
[5] *Ibid.,* p. 71.

common in Indian women, and which cause them so much misery.

Such labor may last three, four, five, even six days. During all this period the woman is given no nourishment whatever—such is the code—and the *dhai* resorts to all her traditions. She kneads the patient with her fists; stands her against the wall and butts her with her head; props her upright on the bare ground, seizes her hands and shoves against her thighs with gruesome bare feet,[6] until, so the doctors state, the patient's flesh is often torn to ribbons by the *dhai's* long, ragged toe-nails. Or, she lays the woman flat and walks up and down her body, like one treading grapes. Also, she makes balls of strange substances, such as hollyhock roots, or dirty string, or rags full of quince-seeds; or earth, or earth mixed with cloves, butter and marigold flowers; or nuts, or spices—any irritant—and thrusts them into the uterus, to hasten the event. In some parts of the country, goats' hair, scorpions' stings, monkey-skulls, and snake-skins are considered valuable applications.[7]

These insertions and the wounds they occasion commonly result in partial or complete permanent closing of the passage.

If the afterbirth be over five minutes in appearing, again the filthy, ringed and bracelet-loaded hand and

[6] *V.M.S.F. Report,* p. 99, Dr. K. O. Vaughan.
[7] *Ibid.,* pp. 151-2, Mrs. Chowdhri, sub-assistant surgeon.

wrist are thrust in, and the placenta is ripped loose and dragged away.[8]

No clean clothes are provided for use in the confinement, and no hot water. Fresh cow-dung or goats' droppings, or hot ashes, however, often serve as heating agents when the patient's body begins to turn cold.[9]

In Benares, sacred among cities, citadel of orthodox Hinduism, the sweepers, all of whom are "Untouchables," are divided into seven grades. From the first come the *dhais*; from the last and lowest come the "cord-cutters." To cut the umbilical cord is considered a task so degrading that in the Holy City even a sweep will not undertake it, unless she be at the bottom of her kind. Therefore the unspeakable *dhai* brings with her a still more unspeakable servant to wreak her quality upon the mother and the child in birth.

Sometimes it is a split bamboo that they use; sometimes a bit of an old tin can, or a rusty nail, or a potsherd or a fragment of broken glass. Sometimes, having no tool of their own and having found nothing sharp-edged lying about, they go out to the neighbors to borrow. I shall not soon forget the cry: "Hi, there, inside! Bring me back that knife! I hadn't finished paring my vegetables for dinner."

The end of the cut cord, at best, is left undressed, to take care of itself. In more careful and less happy cases, it is treated with a handful of earth, or with charcoal, or with several other substances, including

[8] *V.M.S.F. Report,* p. 86, Dr. M. A. Wylie.
[9] *Ibid.,* p. 152, Miss Vidyabai M. Ram.

cow-dung. Needless to add, a heavy per cent. of such children as survive the strain of birth, die of lock-jaw [10] or of erysipelas.

As the child is taken from the mother, it is commonly laid upon the bare floor, uncovered and unattended, until the *dhai* is ready to take it up. If it be a girl child, many simple rules have been handed down through the ages for discontinuing the unwelcome life then and there.

In the matter of feeding, practice varies. In the Central Provinces, the first feedings are likely to be of crude sugar mixed with the child's own urine.[11] In Delhi, it may get sugar and spices, or wine, or honey. Or, it may be fed for the first three days on something called *gutli*, a combination of spices in which have been stewed old rust-encrusted lucky coins and charms written out on scraps of paper. These things, differing somewhat in different regions, castes and communities, differ more in detail than in the quality of intelligence displayed.

As to the mother, she, as has already been said, is usually kept without any food or drink for from four to seven days from the outset of her confinement; or, if she be fed, she is given only a few dry nuts and dates. The purpose here seems sometimes to be one of

[10] "Ordinarily half the children born in Bengal die before reaching the age of eight years, and only one-quarter of the population reaches the age of forty years. . . . As to the causes influencing infant mortality, 50 per cent. of the deaths are due to debility at birth and 11.4 per cent. to tetanus." *54th Annual Report of the Director of Public Health of Bengal,* pp. 8-10.

[11] *V.M.S.F. Report,* p. 86, Dr. M. A. Wylie.

thrift—to save the family utensils from pollution. But in any case it enjoys the prestige of an ancient tenet to which the economical spirit of the household lends a spontaneous support.[12]

In some regions or communities the baby is not put to the breast till after the third day [13]—a custom productive of dire results. But in others the mother is expected to feed not only the newly born, but her elder children as well, if she have them. A child three years old will not seldom be sent in to be fed at the mother's breast during the throes of a difficult labor. "It cried— it was hungry. It wouldn't have other food," the women outside will explain.

As a result, first, of their feeble and diseased ancestry; second, of their poor diet; and, third, of their own infant marriage and premature sexual use and infection, a heavy percentage of the women of India are either too small-boned or too internally misshapen and diseased to give normal birth to a child, but require surgical aid. It may safely be said that all these cases die by slow torture, unless they receive the care of a British or American woman doctor, or of an Indian woman, British-trained.[14] Such care, even though it be

[12] Edris Griffin, in *National Health,* Oct., 1925, p. 124.
[13] *V.M.S.F. Report,* p. 86.
[14] For the male medical student in India, instruction in gynecology and midwifery is extremely difficult to get, for the reason that Indian women can rarely be persuaded to come to hospitals open to medical men. With the exception of certain extremely limited opportunities, therefore, the Indian student must get his gynecology from books. Even though he learns it abroad, he has little or no opportunity to practice it. Sometimes, it is true, the western-diplomaed Indian doctor will conduct a labor case by sitting on the far side of a heavy curtain calling out advice based on the statements shouted across by the *dhai* who is handling the patient. But this scarcely constitutes "practice" as the word is generally meant.

at hand, is often denied the sufferer, either by the husband or by the elder women of the family, in their devotion to the ancient cults.

Or, even in cases where a delivery is normal, the results, from an Indian point of view, are often more tragic than death. An able woman surgeon, Dr. K. O. Vaughan, of the Zenana Hospital at Srinagar, thus expresses it: [15]

Many women who are childless and permanently disabled are so from the maltreatment received during parturition; many men are without male issue because the child has been killed by ignorance when born, or their wives so mangled by the midwives they are incapable of further childbearing. . . .

I [illustrate] my remarks with a few cases typical of the sort of thing every medical woman practising in this country encounters.

A summons comes, and we are told a woman is in labour. On arrival at the house we are taken into a small, dark and dirty room, often with no window. If there is one it is stopped up. Puerperal fever is supposed to be caused by fresh air. The remaining air is vitiated by the presence of a charcoal fire burning in a pan, and on a *charpoy* [cot] or on the floor is the woman. With her are one or two dirty old women, their clothes filthy, their hands begrimed with dirt, their heads alive with vermin. They explain that they are midwives, that the patient has been in labour three days, and they cannot get the child out. They are rubbing their hands on the floor previous to making another effort. On inspection we find the vulva swollen and torn. They tell us, yes, it is a bad case and they have had to use both feet and hands in their effort to deliver her. . . . Chloroform is given and the child extracted with

[15] *V.M.S.F. Report,* pp. 98-9.

forceps. We are sure to find hollyhock roots which have been pushed inside the mother, sometimes string and a dirty rag containing quince-seeds in the uterus itself. . . .

Do not think it is the poor only who suffer like this. I can show you the homes of many Indian men with University degrees whose wives are confined on filthy rags and attended by these Bazaar *dhais* because it is the custom, and the course for the B.A. degree does not include a little common sense.

Doctor Vaughan then proceeds to quote further illustrations from her own practice, of which the following is a specimen: [16]

A wealthy Hindu, a graduate of an Indian University and a lecturer himself, a man who is highly educated, calls us to his house, as his wife has been delivered of a child and has fever. . . . We find that [the *dhai*] had no disinfectants as they would have cost her about Rs. 3 [one dollar, American], and the fee she will get on the case is only Rs. 1 and a few dirty clothes. The patient is lying on a heap of cast-off and dirty clothes, an old waistcoat, an English railway rug, a piece of water-proof packing from a parcel, half a stained and dirty shirt of her husband's. There are no sheets or clean rags of any kind. As her husband tells me: "We shall give her clean things on the fifth day, but not now; that is our custom."

That woman, in spite of all we could do, died of septicæmia contracted either from the dirty clothing which is saved from one confinement in the family to another [unwashed], or from the *dhai*, who did her best in the absence of either hot water, soap, nail-brush or disinfectants.

[16] *V.M.S.F. Report*, pp. 99-100.

Evidence is in hand of educated, traveled and well-born Indians, themselves holders of European university degrees, who permit their wives to undergo this same inheritance of darkness. The case may be cited of an Indian medical man, holding an English University's Ph.D. and M.D. degrees, considered to be exceptionally able and brilliant and now actually in charge of a government center for the training of *dhais* in modern midwifery. His own young wife being recently confined, he yielded to the pressure of the elder women of his family and called in an old-school *dhai*, dirty and ignorant as the rest, to attend her. The wife died of puerperal fever; the child died in the birth. "When we have the spectacle of even educated Indians with English degrees allowing their wives and children to be killed off like flies by ignorant midwives," says Doctor Vaughan again, "we can faintly imagine the sufferings of their humbler sisters."

But the question of station or of worldly goods has small part in the matter. To this the admirable sisterhood of English and American women doctors unites to testify.

Dr. Marion A. Wylie's words are: [17]

These conditions are by no means confined to the poorest or most ignorant classes. I have attended the families of Rajahs, where many of these practices were carried out, and met with strenuous opposition when I introduced ventilation and aseptic measures.

[17] *Ibid.,* p. 86.

[101]

Sweeper-girl or Brahman, outcaste or queen, there is essentially little to choose between their lots, in that fierce moment for which alone they were born. An Indian Christian lady of distinguished position and attainment, whose character has opened to her many doors that remain to others fast closed, gives the following story of her visit of mercy to a child-princess.

The little thing, wife of a ruling prince and just past her tenth year, was already in labor when her visitor entered the room. The *dhais* were busy over her, but the case was obviously serious, and priestly assistance had been called. Outside the door sat its exponent— an old man, reading aloud from the scriptures and from time to time chanting words of direction deciphered from his book.

"Hark, within, there!" he suddenly shouted. "Now it is time to make a fire upon this woman's body. Make and light a fire upon her body, quick!"

Instantly the *dhais* set about to obey.

"And what will the fire do to our little princess?" quietly asked the visitor, too practiced to express alarm.

"Oh," replied the women, listlessly, "if it be her fate to live, she will live, and there will, of course, be a great scar branded upon her. Or, if it be her fate to die, then she will die"—and on they went with their fire-building.

Out to the ministrant squatting at the door flew the quick-witted visitor. "Holy One," she asked, "are you not afraid of the divine jealousies? You are about to make the Fire-sacrifice—but this is a queen, not a com-

mon mortal. Will not Mother Ganges see and be
jealous that no honor is paid to her?"

The old man looked up, perplexed. "It is true," he
said, "it is true the gods are ever jealous and easily
provoked to anger—but the Book here surely says—"
And his troubled eyes turned to the ancient writ out-
spread upon his knees.

"Have you Ganges water here in the house?" interrupted the other.

"Surely. Dare the house live without it!" answered
the old one.

"Then here is what I am given to say: Let water of
Holy Ganges be put upon bright fire and made thrice
hot. Let it then be poured into a marvel-sack that the
gods, by my hand, shall provide. And let that sack be
laid upon the Maharani's body. So in a united offering—fire and water together—shall the gods be propitiated and their wrath escaped."

"This is wisdom. So be it!" cried the old man. Then
quick ran the visitor to fetch her Bond Street hot-water
bag.

Superstition, among the Indian peoples, knows few
boundary lines of condition or class. Women in general are prone to believe that disease is an evidence of
the approach of a god. Medicine and surgery, driving
that god away, offend him, and it is ill business to offend the Great Ones; better, therefore, charms and
propitiations, with an eye to the long run.

And besides the gods, there are the demons and evil

spirits, already as many as the sands of the sea, to whose number more must not be added.

Among the worst of demons are the spirits of women who died in childbirth before the child was born. These walk with their feet turned backward, haunting lonely roads and the family hearth, and are malicious beyond the rest.

Therefore, when a woman is seen to be about to breathe her last, her child yet undelivered—she may have lain for days in labor for a birth against which her starveling bones are locked—the *dhai*, as in duty bound, sets to work upon precautions for the protection of the family.

First she brings pepper and rubs it into the dying eyes, that the soul may be blinded and unable to find its way out. Then she takes two long iron nails, and, stretching out her victim's unresisting arms—for the poor creature knows and accepts her fate—drives a spike straight through each palm fast into the floor. This is done to pinion the soul to the ground, to delay its passing or that it may not rise and wander, vexing the living. And so the woman dies, piteously calling to the gods for pardon for those black sins of a former life for which she now is suffering.

This statement, horrible as it is, rests upon the testimony of many and unimpeachable medical witnesses in widely separated parts of India. All the main statements in this chapter rest upon such testimony and upon my own observation.

It would be unjust to assume, however, that the

dhai, for all her monstrous deeds, is a blameworthy creature. Every move that she makes is a part of the ancient and accepted ritual of her calling. Did she omit or change any part of it, nothing would be gained; simply the elder women of the households she serves would revile her for incapacity and call in another more faithful to the creed.

Her services include attendance at the time of confinement and for ten days, more or less, thereafter, the approximate interval during which no member of the family will approach the patient because of her uncleanness. During this time the *dhai* does all that is done for the sick woman and the infant. At its end she is expected to clean the defiled room and coat with cow-dung its floor and walls.

She receives her pay in accordance with the sex of the child that was born. These sums vary. A rich man may give her for the entire period of service as much as Rs. 15 (about $5.00) if the child be a son. From the well-to-do the more usual fee is about R. 1 ($.33) for a son and eight annas ($.16) for a daughter. The poor pay the *dhai* for her fortnight's work the equivalent of four or five cents for a son and two to three cents for a daughter. Herself the poorest of the poor, she has no means of her own wherewith to buy as much as a cake of soap or a bit of clean cotton. None are anywhere provided for her. And so, the slaughter goes on.[18]

Various funds subscribed by British charity sustain

[18] *V.M.S.F. Report,* p. 89.

maternal and child-welfare works in many parts of
India, whose devoted British doctors and nurses attempt
to teach the *dhais*. But the task is extremely difficult.
Invariably the *dhais* protest that they have nothing to
learn, in which their clients agree with them. One
medical woman said in showing me her *dhai* class, an
appalling array of decrepit old crones:

"We pay these women, out of a fund from England, for coming to class. We also pay some of them
not to practice, a small sum, but just enough to live on.
They are too old, too stupid and too generally miserable to be capable of learning. Yet, when we beg them
not to take cases because of the harm they do, they say:
'How else can we live? This is our only means to earn
food.' Which is true."

A characteristic incident, freshly happened when it
came to my knowledge, concerned a Public Health
instructor stationed, by one of the funds above mentioned, in the north. To visualize the scene, one must
think of the instructor as what she is—a conspicuously
comely and spirited young lady of the type that under
all circumstances looks *chic* and well-groomed. She had
been training a class of *dhais* in Lahore, and had invited
her "graduates" when handling a difficult case to call
her in for advice.

At three o'clock one cold winter's morning of 1926,
a graduate summoned her. The summons led to the
house of an outcaste, a little mud hut with an interior
perhaps eight by twelve feet square. In the room were
ten people, three generations of the family, all save

[106]

the patient fast asleep. Also, a sheep, two goats, some chickens and a cow, because the owner did not trust his neighbors. No light but a glim in an earthen pot. No heat but that from the bodies of man and beast. No aperture but the door, which was closed.

In a small alcove at the back of the room four cot beds, planted one upon another, all occupied by members of the family. In the cot third from the ground lay a woman in advanced labor.

"*Dhai* went outside," observed Grandmother, stirring sleepily, and turned her face to the wall.

Not a moment to be lost. No time to hunt up the *dhai*. By good luck, the cow lay snug against the cot-pile. So our trig little English lady climbs up on the back of the placid and unobjecting cow, and from that vantage point successfully brings into the world a pair of tiny Hindus—a girl and a boy.

Just as the thing is over, back comes the *dhai*, in a rage. She had been out in the yard, quarreling with the husband about the size of the coin that he should lay in her palm, on which to cut the cord—without which coin already in her possession no canny *dhai* will operate.

And this is merely an ordinary experience.

"Our Indian conduct of midwifery undoubtedly should be otherwise than it is," said a group of Indian gentlemen discussing the whole problem as it exists in their own superior circle, "but is it possible, do you think, that enough English ladies will be found to come out and do the work inclusively?"

[107]

A fractional percentage of the young wives are now found ready to accept modern medical help. But it is from the elder women of the household that resistance both determined and effective comes.

Says Dr. Agnes C. Scott, M.B., B.S., of the Punjab, one of the most distinguished of the many British medical women today giving their lives to India: [19]

An educated man may desire a better-trained woman to attend on his wife, but he is helpless against the stone wall of ignorance and prejudice built and kept up by the older women of the *zenana* who are the real rulers of the house.

Dr. K. O. Vaughan says upon this point: [20]

The women are their own greatest enemies, and if any one can devise a system of education and enlightenment for grandmother, great-grandmother and great-great-grandmother which will persuade them not to employ the ignorant, dirty Bazaar *dhai*, they will deserve well of the Indian nation. In my opinion that is an impossible task.

And another woman surgeon adds: [21]

Usually a mother-in-law or some ancient dame superintends the confinement, who is herself used to the old traditions and insists on their observance. . . . It has been the immemorial custom that the management of a confinement is the province of the leading woman of the house, and the men are powerless to interfere.

[19] *V.M.S.F. Report*, p. 91. Cf. Sir Patrick Hehir, *The Medical Profession in India*, Henry Frowde & Hodder and Stoughton, London, 1923, pp. 125-31.
[20] *Ibid.*, p. 101.
[21] *Ibid.*, p. 71.

Thus arises a curious picture—the picture of the man who has since time immemorial enslaved his wife, and whose most vital need in all life, present and to come, is the getting of a son; and of this man, by means none other than the will of his willing slave, balked in his heart's desire! He has thought it good that she be kept ignorant; that she forever suppress her natural spirit and inclinations, walking ceremonially, in stiff harness, before him, her "earthly god." She has so walked, obedient from infancy to death, through untold centuries of merciless discipline, while he, from infancy to death, through untold centuries, has given himself no discipline at all. And now their harvests ripen in kind: hers a death-grip on the rock of the old law, making her dead-weight negative to any change, however merciful; his, a weakness of will and purpose, a fatigue of nerve and spirit, that deliver him in his own house, beaten, into the hands of his slave.

Of Indian babies born alive about 2,000,000 die each year. "Available statistics show," says the latest Census of India, "that over forty per cent. of the deaths of infants occur in the first week after birth, and over sixty per cent. in the first month." [22]

The number of still births is heavy. Syphilis and gonorrhea are among its main causes, to which must be added the sheer inability of the child to bear the strain of coming into the world.

Vital statistics are weak in India, for they must largely depend upon illiterate villagers as collectors.

[22] *Census of India,* 1921, Vol. I, Part I, p. 132.

If a baby dies, the mother's wail trails down the darkness of a night or two. But if the village be near a river, the little body may just be tossed into the stream, without waste of a rag for a shroud. Kites and the turtles finish its brief history. And it is more than probable that no one in the village will think it worth while to report either the birth or the death. Statistics as to babies must therefore be taken as at best approximate.

It is probable, however, in view of existing conditions, that the actual figures of infant mortality, were it possible to know them, would surprise the western mind rather by their smallness than by their height. "I used to think," said one of the American medical women, "that a baby was a delicate creature. But experience here is forcing me to believe it the toughest fabric ever made, since it ever survives."

Chapter IX

BEHIND THE VEIL

The chapters preceding have chiefly dealt with the Hindu, who forms, roughly, three-quarters of the population of India. The remaining quarter, the Muhammadans, differ considerably as between the northern element, whose blood contains a substantial strain of the old conquering Persian and Afghan stock, and the southern contingent, who are, for the larger part, descendants of Hindu converts retaining in greater or less degree many of the qualities of Hindu character.

In some respects, Muhammadan women enjoy great advantages over their Hindu sisters. Conspicuous among such advantages is their freedom from infant marriage and from enforced widowhood, with the train of miseries evoked by each. Their consequent better inheritance, supported by a diet greatly superior to that of the Hindu, brings them to the threshold of a maturity sturdier than that of the Hindu type. Upon crossing that threshold the advantage of Muhammadan women of the better class is, however, forfeit. For they pass into practical life-imprisonment within the four walls of the home.

Purdah, as this system of women's seclusion is called, having been introduced by the Muslim conquerors and by them observed, soon came to be regarded by higher caste Hindus as a hall-mark of social prestige. These, therefore, adopted it as a matter of mode. And today, as a consequence of the growing prosperity of the country, this mediaeval custom, like the interdiction of remarriage of virgin widows among the Hindus, seems to be actually on the increase. For every woman at the top of the scale whom western influence sets free, several humbler but prospering sisters, socially ambitious, deliberately assume the bonds.

That view of women which makes them the proper loot of war was probably the origin of the custom of *purdah*. When a man has his women shut up within his own four walls, he can guard the door. Taking Indian evidence on the question, it appears that in some degree the same necessity exists today. In a part of India where *purdah* but little obtains, I observed the united request of several Hindu ladies of high position that the Amusement Club for English and Indian ladies to which they belong reduce the minimum age required for membership to twelve or, better, to eleven years. This, they frankly said, was because they were afraid to leave their daughters of that age at home, even for one afternoon, without a mother's eye and accessible to the men of the family.

Far down the social scale the same anxiety is found. The Hindu peasant villager's wife will not leave her girl child at home alone for the space of an hour, being practically sure that, if she does so, the child will be ruined. I dare not affirm that this condition everywhere obtains. But I can affirm that it was brought to my attention by Indians and by Occidentals, as regulating daily life in widely separated sections of the country.

No typical Muhammadan will trust another man in his *zenana,* simply because he knows that such liberty would be regarded as opportunity. If there be a handful of Hindus of another persuasion, it is almost or quite invariably because they are reflecting some part of the western attitude toward women; and this they do without abatement of their distrust of their fellowmen. Intercourse between men and women which is both free and innocent is a thing well-nigh incredible to the Indian mind.

In many parts of India the precincts of the *zenana,* among better-class Hindus, are therefore closed and the women cloistered within. And the cloistered Muhammadan women, if they emerge from their seclusion, do so under concealing veils, or in concealing vehicles. The Rolls-Royce of a Hindu reigning prince's wife may sometimes possess dark window-glasses, through which the lady looks out at ease, herself unseen. But the wife of a prosperous Muhammadan cook, if she go out on an errand, will cover herself from the crown of the head downward in a thick cotton shroud, through whose scant three inches of mesh-covered eye-space she peers half-blinded.

I happened to be present at a *"purdah* party"—a party for veiled ladies, attended by ladies only—in a private house in Delhi when tragedy hovered nigh. The Indian ladies had all arrived, stepping heavily swathed from their close-curtained motor cars. Their hostess, wife of a high English official, herself had met them on her threshold; for, out of deference to the custom of the *purdah,* all the men servants had been banished from the house, leaving Lady —— alone to conduct her guests to the dressing room. There they had laid aside their swathings. And now, in all the grace of their native costumes, they were sitting about the room, gently conversing with the English ladies invited to meet them. The senior Indian lady easily dominated her party. She was far advanced in years, they said, and she wore long, light blue velvet trousers, tight from the knee down, golden slippers, a smart little jacket of silk brocade and a beautifully embroidered Kashmir shawl draped over her head.

We went in to tea. And again Lady ——, singlehanded, except for the help of the English ladies, moved back and forth, from pantry to tea-table, serving her Indian guests.

Suddenly, from the veranda without, arose a sound of incursion—a rushing—men's voices, women's voices, loud, louder, coming close. The hostess with a face of dismay dashed for the door. Within the room panic prevailed. Their great white mantles being out of reach, the Indian ladies ran into the corners, turning their backs, while the English, understanding their plight, stood before them to screen them as best might be.

Meantime, out on the veranda, more fracas had arisen—then a sudden silence and a whir of retreating

TWO EMINENT INDIANS

Left to right: Dr. Kiroth Bose, director of the model village of Asrapur. Miss Mona Bose, principal of the Victoria School for Girls, Lahore. Both ladies have received the Kaisar-i-Hind Medal for Public Service to India. (*See* page 138.)

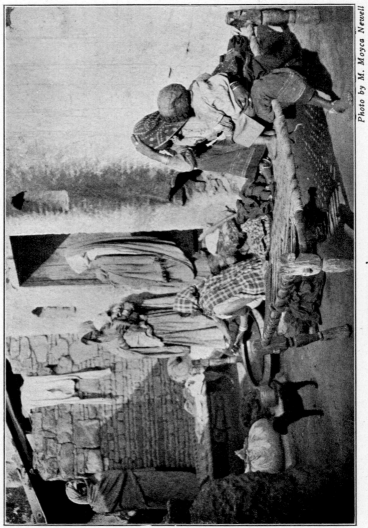

A LAUNDRY-MAN'S HOUSE. DELHI

wheels. Lady —— returned, panting, all apologies and relief.

"I am *too* sorry! But it is all over now. Do forgive it! Nothing shall frighten you again," she said to the trembling Indian ladies; and, to the rest of us: "It was the young Roosevelts come to call. They didn't know!"

It was in the talk immediately following that one of the youngest of the Indian ladies exclaimed:

"You find it difficult to like our *purdah*. But we have known nothing else. We lead a quiet, peaceful, protected life within our own homes. And, with men as they are, we should be miserable, terrified, outside."

But one of the ladies of middle age expressed another mind: "I have been with my husband to England," she said, speaking quietly to escape the others' ears. "While we were there he let me leave off *purdah*, for women are respected in England. So I went about freely, in streets and shops and galleries and gardens and to the houses of friends, quite comfortable always. No one frightened or disturbed me and I had much interesting talk with gentlemen as well as ladies. Oh, it was wonderful—a paradise! But here—here there is nothing. I must stay within the *zenana*, keeping strict *purdah*, as becomes our rank, seeing no one but the women, and my husband. We see nothing. We know nothing. We have nothing to say to each other. We quarrel. It is *dull*. But they," nodding surreptitiously toward the oldest woman, "will have it so. It is only because of our hostess that such as she would come here today. More they would never consent to. And they know how to make life horrible for us in each household, if we offer to relax an atom of the *purdah* law."

Then, looking from face to face, one saw the illustration of the talk—the pretty, blank features of the novices; the unutterable listlessness and fatigue of those of the speaker's age; the sharp-eyed, iron-lipped authority of the old.

The report of the Calcutta University Commission says: [1]

All orthodox Bengali women of the higher classes, whether Hindu or Muslim, pass at an early age behind the *purdah*, and spend the rest of their lives in the complete seclusion of their homes, and under the control of the eldest woman of the household. This seclusion is more strict among the Musalmans than among the Hindus. . . . A few westernised women have emancipated themselves, . . . [but] they are regarded by most of their countrywomen as denationalised.

Bombay, however, practices but little *purdah*, largely, no doubt, because of the advanced status and liberalizing influence of the Parsi ladies; and in the Province of Madras it is as a rule peculiar only to the Muhammadans and the wealthy Hindus. From two Hindu gentlemen, both trained in England to a scientific profession, I heard that they themselves had insisted that their wives quit *purdah*, and that they were bringing up their little daughters in a European school. But their wives, they added, unhappy in what seemed

[1] Vol. II, Part I, pp. 4-5.

to them too great exposure, would be only too glad to resume their former sheltered state. And, viewing things as they are, one can scarcely escape the conclusion that much is to be said on that side. One frequently hears, in India and out of it, of the beauty of the sayings of the Hindu masters on the exalted position of women. One finds often quoted such passages as the precept of Manu:

> Where a woman is not honoured
> Vain is sacrificial rite.

But, as Mr. Gandhi tersely sums it up: "What is the teaching worth, if their practice denies it?" [2]

One consequence of *purdah* seclusion is its incubation of tuberculosis. Dr. Arthur Lankester [3] has shown that among the *purdah*-keeping classes the mortality of women from tuberculosis is terribly high. It is also shown that, among persons living in the same locality and of the same habits and means, the men of the *purdah*-keeping classes display a higher incidence of death from tuberculosis than do those whose women are less shut in.

The Health Officer for Calcutta declares in his report for 1917:

In spite of the improvement in the general death-rate of the city, the death-rate amongst females is still more than 40 per cent. higher than amongst males. . . . Until it is real-

[2] Statement to the author, Sabarmati, Ahmedabad, March 17, 1926.
[3] *Tuberculosis in India,* Arthur Lankester, M.D., Butterworth & Co., London, 1920, p. 140.

ised that the strict observance of the *purdah* system in a large city, except in the case of the very wealthy who can afford spacious homes standing in their own grounds, necessarily involves the premature death of a large number of women, this standing reproach to the city will never be removed.

Dr. Andrew Balfour, Director of the London School of Hygiene and Tropical Medicine, in pointing out how perfectly the habits of the Indian peoples favor the spread of the disease, speaks of "the system by which big families live together; the *purdah* custom relegating women to the dark and dingy parts of the house; the early marriages, sapping the vitality of thousands of the young; the pernicious habit of indiscriminate spitting." [4] These, added to dirt, bad sanitation, confinement, lack of air and exercise, make a perfect breeding-place for the White Death. Between nine hundred thousand and one million persons, it is estimated, die annually of tuberculosis in India. [5]

It has been further estimated that forty million Indian women, Muhammadan and Hindu, are today in *purdah*. [6] In the opinion, however, of those experienced officers whom I could consult, this estimate, if it is intended to represent the number of women kept so strictly cloistered that they never leave their apartments nor see any male save husband and son, is probably three times too high. Those who never see the outer world, from their marriage day till the day of

[4] *Health Problems of the Empire*, Dr. Andrew Balfour and Dr. H. H. Scott, Collins, London, 1924, p. 286.
[5] *Ibid.*, p. 285.
[6] *India and Missions*, The Bishop of Dornakal.

their death, number by careful estimate of minimum
and maximum between 11,250,000 and 17,290,000
persons.

As to the mental effect of the *purdah* system upon
those who live under it, one may leave its characterization to Indian authorities.

Says Dr. N. N. Parakh, the Indian physician:[7]

> Ignorance and the *purdah* system have brought the women
> of India to the level of animals. They are unable to look
> after themselves, nor have they any will of their own. They
> are slaves to their masculine owners.[8]

Said that outstanding Swarajist leader, Lala Lajpat
Rai, in his Presidential address to the Hindu Mahasabha Conference held in Bombay in December, 1925:

> The great feature of present-day Hindu life is passivity.
> "Let it be so" sums up all their psychology, individual and
> social. They have got into the habit of taking things lying
> down. They have imbibed this tendency and this psychology
> and this habit from their mothers. It seems as if it was in
> their blood. . . . Our women labour under many handicaps.
> It is not only ignorance and superstition that corrode their
> intelligence, but even physically they are a poor race. . . .
> Women get very little open air and almost no exercise. How
> on earth is the race, then, to improve and become efficient?
> A large number of our women develop consumption and die
> at an early age. Such of them as are mothers, infect their
> children also. Segregation of cases affected by tuberculosis is

---

[7] *Legislative Assembly Debates,* Vol. III, Part I, p. 881.
[8] Cf., however, *ante,* pp. 77, 80, 109, 116, etc.

almost impossible. . . . There is nothing so hateful as a quarrelsome, unnecessarily assertive, impudent, ill-mannered woman, but even if that were the only road which the Hindu woman must traverse in order to be an efficient, courageous, independent and physically fit mother, I would prefer it to the existing state of things.

At this point, the practical experience of a school-mistress, the English principal of a Calcutta girls' college, may be cited. Dated eight years later than the Report of the Calcutta Health Officer already quoted, it concerns the daughters of the most progressive and liberal of Bengal's families.[9]

They dislike exercise and take it only under compulsion. They will not go into the fresh air if they can avoid doing so. The average student is very weak. She needs good food, exercise, and often remedial gymnastics. The chest is contracted, and the spine often curved. She has no desire for games. . . . We want the authority . . . to compel the student to take those remedies which will help her to grow into a woman.

But the introduction of physical training as a help to the bankrupt physiques of Hindu girls is thus far only a dream of the occidental intruder. Old orthodoxy will not have it so.

The Hindu father is prone to complain that he does not want his daughter turned into a *nautch* girl. She has to be married into one of a limited number of families; and there

[9] Sister Mary Victoria, Principal of the Diocesan College for Girls, *Fifth Quinquennial Review of the Progress of Education in Bengal*, paragraphs 521-4.

is always a chance of one of the old ladies exclaiming, "This girl has been taught to kick her legs about in public. Surely such a shameless one is not to be brought into our house!" [10]

"It is, indeed, only among the orthodox," says the authority quoting this testimony, "that this kind of objection is taken. But the orthodox are the majority." [11]

Under the caption, "Thou Shalt Do No Murder," the Oxford Mission of Calcutta printed, in its weekly journal of February 20, 1926, an editorial beginning as follows:

A few years ago we published an article with the above heading in which was vividly described by a woman writer the appalling destruction of life and health which was going on in Bengal behind the *purdah* and in *zenanas* amongst the women herded there. We thought that the revelations then made, based on the health officer's reports, would bring to us a stream of indignant letters demanding instant reform. The effect amongst men folk was entirely *nil*. Apparently not a spark of interest was roused. An article condemning the silly credulity of the use of charms and talismans at once evokes criticism, and the absurdities of superstition are vigorously defended even by men who are graduates. But not a voice was raised in horror at the fact that for every male who dies of tuberculosis in Calcutta five females die.

Yet among young western-educated men a certain abstract uneasiness begins to appear concerning things as they are. After they have driven the Occident out of India, many of them say, they must surely take up

___

[10] The Inspectress for Eastern Bengal, *Calcutta University Commission Report*, Vol. II, Part I, p. 23.
[11] *Ibid.*, p. 24.

this matter of women. Not often, however, does one find impatience such as that of Abani Mohan Das Gupta, of Calcutta, expressed in the journal just quoted.

I shudder to think about the condition of our mothers and sisters in the "harem." . . . From early morn till late at night they are working out the same routine throughout the whole of their lives without a murmur, as if they are patience incarnate. There are many instances where a woman has entered the house of her husband at the time of the marriage and did not leave it until death had carried her away. They are always in harness as if they have no will or woe but only to suffer—suffer without any protest. . . . I appeal to young Indians to unfurl their flag for the freedom of women. Allow them their right. . . . Am I crying in the wilderness?

Bengal is the seat of bitterest political unrest—the producer of India's main crop of anarchists, bomb-throwers and assassins. Bengal is also among the most sexually exaggerated regions of India; and medical and police authorities in any country observe the link between that quality and "queer" criminal minds—the exhaustion of normal avenues of excitement creating a thirst and a search in the abnormal for gratification. But Bengal is also the stronghold of strict *purdah*, and one cannot but speculate as to how many explosions of eccentric crime in which the young politicals of Bengal have indulged were given the detonating touch by the unspeakable flatness of their *purdah*-deadened home lives, made the more irksome by their own half-digested dose of foreign doctrines.

[122]

Chapter X

WOMAN THE SPINSTER

Less than 2 per cent. of the women of British India are literate in the sense of being able to write a letter of a few simple phrases, and read its answer, in any one language or dialect. To be exact, such literates numbered, in 1921, eighteen to the thousand.[1] But in the year 1911 they numbered only ten to the thousand. And, in order to estimate the significance of that increase, two points should be considered: first, that a century ago literate women, save for a few rare stars, were practically unknown in India; and, second, that the great body of the peoples, always heavily opposed to female education, still so opposes it, and on religio-social grounds.

Writing in the beginning of the nineteenth century, the Abbé Dubois said:[2]

The social condition of the wives of the Brahmins differ very little from that of the women of other castes. . . . They are considered incapable of developing any of those higher mental qualities which would make them more worthy of consideration and also more capable of playing a useful part in life. . . . As a natural consequence of these views, female education is altogether neglected. A young girl's mind

[1] *India in 1924-25*, L. F. Rushbrook Williams, C.B.E., p. 276.
[2] *Hindu Manners, Customs and Ceremonies*, pp. 336-7.

[123]

remains totally uncultivated, though many of them have good abilities. . . . It would be thought a disgrace to a respectable woman to learn to read; and even if she had learnt she would be ashamed to own it.

This was written of the Hindu. But Islam in India has also disapproved of the education of women, which, therefore, has been held by the vast majority of both creeds to be unnecessary, unorthodox, and dangerous.

In the year 1917, the Governor-General of India in Council appointed a commission to inquire and recommend as to the status of the University of Calcutta and of tributary educational conditions in Bengal. This commission comprised eminent British educators from the faculties of the Universities of Leeds, Glasgow, Manchester, and London, allied with eminent Indian professionals. Bengal, the field of inquiry, has long stood distinguished among all other provinces of British India for its thirst for learning. The testimonies accumulated by the Commission during its three years' work may consequently be taken as not unkindly reflecting the wider Indian horizon.

With regard to the education of women, it is therefore of interest to find Mr. Brajalal Chakravarti, Secretary of the Hindu Academy at Daulatpur, affirming: [3]

It is strictly enjoined in the religious books of the Hindus that females should not be allowed to come under any influence outside that of the family. For this reason, no system of

[3] *Calcutta University Commission Report,* Vol. XII, p. 414.

school and college education can be made to suit their requirements. . . . Women get sufficient moral and practical training in the household and that is far more important than the
type of education schools can give.

Another of the Commission's witnesses, Mr. Hari-
das Goswamy, Head Master of the High School at
Asansol, amplified the thought, saying: [4]

It is not wise to implant in [girls] by means of education
tastes which they would not have an opportunity to gratify in
their after life, and thus sow the seeds of future discontent
and discord.

And Mr. Rabindra Mohan Dutta,[5] member of the
faculty of the University itself, even while deploring
that "darkness of ignorance and superstition" which, he
asserts, puts the women of India "in continual conflict
and disagreement with their educated husbands, brothers or sons," would yet follow the orthodox multitude,
genuinely fearful of importing into the Indian home,
from the distaff side,

the spirit of revolutionary and rationalistic iconoclasm condemning all our ancient institutions that are the outcome of a
long past and are part of our flesh and blood as it were.

When, however, the topic of women's education
comes up for discussion in Indian political bodies,
speakers arise on the side of change. In the Delhi Leg-

[4] *Ibid.,* p. 426.
[5] *Ibid.,* p. 422.

islative Assembly, Dr. Hari Singh Gour [6] denounces the sequestration and suppression of women. And Munshi Iswar Saran,[7] member for the cities of the United Provinces, points out, in a spirit of ridicule, that it is

. . . the sin of this *Kali Yuga* [Age of Destruction] that youngsters receive education and then decline to be ordered about by their elders. . . . Such is our foolhardiness that we have started giving education to our girls. . . . If this is going on, I ask whether you believe that you will be able to dictate to your daughters?

I recall the heat with which a wealthy young Hindu of my acquaintance, but just returned from an English university, asserted that he would never, never take an Indian bride, because he would not tie himself to "a wife of the tenth century." And among western-educated Indians in the higher walks of life, the desire for similarly educated wives sometimes rises even to a willingness to accept such brides with dowries smaller than would otherwise be exacted.

But this factor, though recognizable, is as yet small. Bombay, perhaps, gives its women more latitude than does any other province. Yet its Education Report asserts: [8]

Educated men desire educated wives for their sons and presumably educate their daughters with the same object in view,

---

[6] *Legislative Assembly Debates,* 1921, Vol. I, Part I, p. 363.
[7] *Ibid.,* 1922, Vol. II, Part II, p. 1631.
[8] Quoted in *Progress of Education in India,* 1917-22, Eighth Quinquennial Review, pp. 129-30.

but they generally withdraw them from school on any manifestation of a desire to . . . push education to any length which might interfere with or delay marriage.

The Report of the Central Provinces affirms: *

Even those parents who are not averse to their daughters' being literate consider that the primary course is sufficient, and that after its completion girls are too old to be away from their homes.

And Assam adds: *

[Parents] send their girls to school in order to enable themselves to marry them better and occasionally on easier terms. But as soon as a suitable bridegroom is available the girl is at once placed in the seclusion of the *purdah.*

Certainly the great weight of sentiment remains intact in its loyalty to ancient conditions. To disturb them were to risk the mould of manhood. The metaphor of Dr. Brajendranath Seal, M.A., Ph.D., Professor of Mental and Moral Science in Calcutta University, implies the dreaded risk: "Man," writes this Hindu philosopher, "is a home-brew in the vat of woman the brewster, or, as the Indian would put it, a home-spun in the loom of woman the spinster." [9]

On such general grounds, says the Calcutta University Commission,[10] is the feeling against women's education "very commonly supported by the men, even by

* *Ibid.*
[9] *Calcutta University Commission Report,* Vol. XII, p. 62.
[10] *Ibid.,* Vol. II, Part I, p. 5.

those who have passed through the whole course of western education." If the child be sent to school at all, it is more often to put her in a safe place out of the family's way, rather than to give her instruction for which is felt so faint a need and so great a distrust.

To use the words of Mr. B. Mukherjee, M.A., F.R.E.S.: [11]

The strict social system which makes the marriage of a girl religiously compulsory at the age of twelve or so also puts an end to all hope of continuing the education of the ordinary Hindu girl beyond the [marriageable] age.

It is estimated that over 73 per cent. of the total number of girls at school are withdrawn before they achieve literacy, and in the year 1922, in the great Bengal Presidency, out of every hundred girls under instruction but one was studying above the primary stage.[12]

Such small advance as has been achieved, in the desperately up-hill attempt to bestow literacy upon the women of India, represents, first and foremost, a steady and patient effort of persuasion on the part of the British Government; second, the toil of British and American missionaries; and, third, the ability of the most progressive Indians to conceive and effect the transmission of thought into deed. But it is estimated that, without a radical change in performance on the part of the Indians themselves, ninety-five more years

[11] *Calcutta University Commission Report,* Vol. XII, p. 440.
[12] *Progress of Education in Bengal,* J. W. Holme, M.A., Sixth Quinquennial Review.

of such combined effort will be required to wrest from hostility and inertia the privilege of primary education for as much as 12 per cent. of the female population.[13]

The Seva Sadan Society, pioneer Indian women's organization to provide poor women and girls with training in primary teaching and useful work, was started in 1908, in Poona, near Bombay. By the latest report at hand, it has about a thousand pupils. This society's success shows what the happier women of India could do for the rest, were they so minded. But its work is confined wholly to Bombay Presidency; and unfortunately, it has no counterpart, says the official report, in any other part of India.

As will be shown in another chapter, the administration of education as a province of Government has of late years rested in Indian hands.

In 1921-2, British India possessed 23,778 girls' schools, inclusive of all grades, from primary schools to arts and professional colleges. These schools contained in the primary stage 1,297,643 pupils, only 24,555 in the Middle Schools and a still smaller number—5,818—in the High Schools.[14]

"Although," says the report, "the number of girls who proceed beyond the primary stage is still lamentably small—30,000 in all India out of a possible school-going population of fifteen millions—still it

[13] Cf. *Village Schools in India,* Mason Olcott, Associated Press, Calcutta, 1926, p. 90.
[14] The figures in this paragraph are drawn from *Progress of Education in India,* 1917-22, Vol. II.

shows an increase of thirty per cent. over the attendance in 1917." [15]

In Bombay Presidency, in 1924-5 only 2.14 per cent. of the female population was under instruction of any kind,[16] while in all India, in 1919, .9 per cent. of the Hindu female population, and 1.1 per cent. of the Muhammadan females, were in school.[17]

"It would be perfectly easy to multiply schools in which little girls would amuse themselves in preparatory classes, and from which they would drift away gradually during the lower primary stage. The statistical result would be impressive, but the educational effect would be *nil* and public money would be indefensibly wasted." [18]

But, in the fight for conserving female illiteracy, as in those for maintaining the ancient midwifery and for continuing the cloistering of women, the great constant factor on the side of Things-As-They-Were will be found in the elder women themselves. Out of sheer loyalty to their gods of heaven and their gods of earth they would die to keep their daughters like themselves.

As that blunt old Sikh farmer-soldier, Captain Hira Singh Brar, once said, speaking from his seat in the Legislative Assembly on a measure of reform: [19]

[15] *Progress of Education in India,* Vol. I, p. 135.
[16] *Bombay,* 1924-25, Government Central Press, Bombay, 1926, pp. XV-XVI.
[17] *Progress of Education in India,* 1917-22, Vol. I, p. 126.
[18] *Ibid.,* pp. 138-9.
[19] *Legislative Assembly Debates,* 1925, Vol. V, Part III, p. 2830.

So many Lalas and Pandits get up on the platforms and say, "Now the time has come for this reform and that." But what happens? When they go home and when we meet them next morning they say, "What can we do? We are helpless When we went back home, our ladies would not allow us to do what we wanted to do. They say they do not care what we talk, but they would not allow us to act accordingly."

Abreast of these priestesses of ancient custom in preserving the illiteracy of women, stands another mighty influence—that of economic self-interest; a man must marry his daughter or incur an earthly and eternal penalty that few will face. He can rarely marry her without paying a dowry so large that it strains his resources; to which must be added the costs of the wedding—costs so excessive that, as a rule, they plunge him deep into debt. This heavy tax he commonly incurs before his daughter reaches her teens. Why, then, should he spend still more money on her, to educate her; or why, if he be poor and can use her labor, should he go without her help and send her to school, since she is so early to pass forever into another man's service? The idea has been expressed by Rai Harinath Ghosh, Bahadur,[20] fellow of Calcutta University:

People naturally prefer to educate their boys, well knowing that in future they will make them happy and comfortable in their old age, and glorify their family, whilst the girls, after marriage, will be at the mercy of others.

[20] *Calcutta University Commission Report,* Vol. XII, p. 425.

To the average Indian father, of whatever estate, this range of reasoning appears conclusive. And so the momentous opportunities of the motherhood of India continue to be intrusted to the wisdom and judgment of illiterate babies.

Given such a public sentiment toward even rudimentary schooling for girl children, the facts as to more advanced learning may be easily surmised. Mr. Mohini Mohan Bhattacharjee, of the Calcutta University faculty, expressed it in these words: [21]

The higher education of Indian women . . . may almost be said to be beyond the scope of practical reform. No Hindu or Muhammadan woman of an orthodox type has ever joined a college or even read up to the higher classes in a school. The girls who receive university education are either Brahmo [22] or Christian. . . . The time is far distant when the University will be called upon to make arrangements for the higher education of any large or even a decent number of girls in Bengal.

By the latest available report, the women students in arts and professional colleges, in all British India, numbered only 961. But a more representative tone than that of Mr. Bhattacharjee's rather deprecatory words is heard in the frank statement of Rai Sati Chandra Sen, Bahadur: [23]

[21] *Calcutta University Commission Report,* Vol. XII, p. 411.
[22] The Brahmo or Brahmo Samaj is a sect numbering 6,388 persons, as shown in the *Census of India* of 1921, p. 119.
[23] *Calcutta University Commission Report,* Vol. XII, p 449.

Amongst advanced communities in the West, where women are almost on a footing of equality with men and where every woman cannot expect to enter upon married life, high education may be a necessity to them. But . . . the western system . . . is not only unsuitable, but also demoralising to the women of India . . . and breaks down the ideals and instincts of Indian womanhood.

There remains, then, the question of education after marriage. Under present conditions of Indian thought, this may be dismissed with a word—"impracticable." [24] Directly she enters her husband's home, the little wife, whatever her rank, is at once heavily burdened with services to her husband, to her mother-in-law and to the household gods. Child-bearing quickly overwhelms her and she has neither strength nor leave for other activities. Further, she must be taught by women, if taught at all, since women, only, may have access to her. And so you come to the snake that has swallowed his tail.

For, as we have just seen, the ban that forbids literacy to the women of India thereby discourages the training of women teachers who might break the ban. Those who have such training barely and feebly suffice for the schools that already exist. *Zenana* teaching has thus far languished, an anaemic exotic—a failure, in an undesiring soil.

Returning to the conviction of the uselessness of spending good money on a daughter's education, this

[24] The Seva Sadan Society in Bombay has among its pupils a certain percentage of married women of the laboring class who come for two or three hours' instruction daily.

should not be supposed a class matter. Nobles and rich men share the sentiment with their lesser compatriots.

The point is illustrated in Queen Mary's College in Lahore. This institution was founded years ago by two English ladies who saw that the fractional percentage of Indian girls then receiving education came chiefly if not wholly from the low castes, whilst the daughters of princes, the wives and mothers of princes to come, the future regents, perhaps, for minor sons, were left in untouched darkness. The undertaking that the two ladies began enlisted the approval of Government. The reigning princes, spurred on by the visit of Queen Mary to India, subscribed a certain sum. This sum Government tripled. Suitable buildings were erected and equipped, and there the liberality of the princes practically ceased.

For, as will be found in every direction in which the trait can be expressed, the raising of a building as a monument to his name, be it school, hospital, or what not, interests the wealthy Indian; but for its maintenance in service he can rarely if ever be induced to give one penny. In this case it was necessary, in order to combat initial indifference, to present schooling practically free. Today, the charges have been advanced to stand approximately thus: day scholars, junior, $1.50 per month; senior, $3.00 per month; boarding scholars, $10 to $20 per month, inclusive of all tuition, board, laundry, and ordinary medical treatment.

These terms contemplate payment only for the time actually spent at college. And still some of the fathers are both slow and disputatious over the settlement of accounts. "You send a bill of two rupees [$.66] for stationery, all used up in your school by my two daughters in only two months. I consider this bill excessive. They should not be allowed to use so much costly material; it is not right. It should not be paid," protests one personage; and the representative of another conducts a three weeks' correspondence of inquiry, remonstrance, and reproach over a charge for two yards of ribbon to tie up a little girl's bonnie black locks.

Partly because of the original policy of nominal charges adopted by Government to secure an entering wedge, partly because of their traditional dissociation of women and letters, the rich men of India as a whole remain today still convinced at heart that, if indeed their daughters are to be schooled at all, then Government should give them schooling free of charge.

Queen Mary's College, a charming place, with classrooms, dormitories, common rooms and gardens suitably and attractively designed, is staffed by British ladies of university training. The curriculum is planned to suit the needs of the students. Instruction is given in the several languages of the pupils—Arabic, Urdu, Hindi, etc., and, against the girls' pleas, native dress is firmly required—lest the elders at home take fright of a contagion of western ideas. Throughout the school's varied activities, the continuous effort is to teach cleanliness of habit; and marks are given not only on scholarship but on helpfulness, tidiness, truthfulness, and the sporting spirit.

[135]

Outdoor games in the gardens are encouraged to the utmost possible degree, and a prettier sight would be hard to find than a score or so of these really lovely little gazelle-eyed maidens playing about in their floating gauzes of blue and rose and every rainbow hue.

"They have not ginger enough for good tennis," one of the teachers admits, "but then, they have just emerged from the hands of grandmothers who think it improper for little girls even to walk fast. Do you see that lively small thing in pink and gold? When she first came, two terms ago, she truly maintained that her 'legs wouldn't run.' Now she is one of the best at games.

"But what a pity it is," the teacher continues, "to think of the life of dead passivity to which, in a year or two at best, they will all have relapsed!"

"Will they carry into that after-life much of what they have learned here?" I ask.

"Think of the huge pervading influence that will encompass them! The old palace *zenana,* crowded with women bowed under traditions as fixed as death itself! Where would these delicate children find strength to hold their own alone, through year upon year of that ancient, changeless, smothering domination? Our best hope is that they may, somehow, transmit a little of tonic thought to their children; that they may send their daughters to us; and that so, each generation adding its bit, the end may justify our work."

Queen Mary's is the only school in all India instituted especially for ladies of rank. Not unnaturally, therefore, some of the new Indian officials, themselves without rank other than that which office gives, covet the social prestige of enrolling their daughters in Queen Mary's. The question of enrollment rests as yet with an English Commissioner, and the Commissioner lets the young climbers in. With the result that the princes, displeased, are sending fewer of their children than of yore.

"Shall our daughters be subjected to the presence of daughters of *babus*—of upstart Bengali politicians!" they exclaim, leaving no doubt as to the reply.

And some of the resident faculty, mindful of the original purpose of the school, anxiously question:

"Is it wise to drive away the young princesses? Their future influence is potentially so much further-reaching than that of other women, however intelligent. Should we not strain all points to get and to hold them?"

But to this question, when asked direct, the Commissioner himself replied:

"In British India we are trying to build a democracy. As for the Native States, undoubtedly it would be well to educate the future *Maharanis;* I say to their fathers, the Princes: 'If you want to keep for your daughters a school for their own rank, it can easily be done— but not on Government funds. You must pay for the school yourselves.' But this, invisible as the cost would be to men of their fortunes, they are not apt to do."

Another center of interest in Lahore is the Victoria School, occupying the palace of a grandson of the

[137]

famous Ranjit Singh, in the heart of the old city, just off the bazaar. The head of this institution is an extremely able Indian lady, Miss K. M. Bose, of the third generation of an Indian Christian family. Miss Bose's firm and powerful character, her liberal and genial spirit, her strong influence and fine mind, indicate the possibilities of Indian womanhood set free.

In Victoria School are five hundred girl pupils. "Some are rich, some poor," says Miss Bose, "but all are of good caste, and all are daughters of the leading men of the city. If we took lower caste children here, it would increase expense to an impossible degree. The others would neither sit nor eat with them. Separate classes would have to be maintained, an almost double teaching staff employed, and so on through innumerable embarrassments.

" 'The tuition fees?' Merely nominal; we Indians will not pay for the education of our daughters. In days but just gone by, the richest refused to pay even for lesson books. Books, teaching, and all, had at first to be given free, or we should have got no pupils. This school is maintained by Government grant and by private subscriptions from England."

Many rooms on many floors honeycomb the old barren rabbit-warren of a palace, each chamber filled with children, from mites of four or five in Montessori classes up to big, hearty Muhammadan girls of fifteen or sixteen, not yet given in marriage. Like Queen Mary's, this is a strict *purdah* school. The eye of man may not gaze upon it. When it is necessary to introduce some learned pundit to teach his pundit's specialty, he is separated from the class he teaches by a long, deep, thick, and wholly competent curtain. And he is chosen, not only for learning, but also for tottering age.

"I am responsible for these schools," says the Commissioner, smiling ruefully, "and yet, being a man, I may never inspect them!"

Work, in Victoria School, is done in six languages—Urdu, Persian, Hindi, Punjabi, and Sanskrit, with optional English.

"We give no books to the children until they can really read," says Miss Bose. "Otherwise they merely memorize, learning nothing." [25] And the whole aim and hope of the scheme is to implant in the girls' minds something so definitely applicable to their future life in the *zenana* that some part of it may endure alive through the years of dark and narrow things so soon to come.

Reading, writing, arithmetic enough to keep simple household accounts; a little history; sewing—which art, by the way, is almost unknown to most of the women of India; a little drawing and music; habits of cleanliness and sanitary observance—both subjects of incredible difficulty; first aid, to save themselves and their future babies as far as may be from the barbari-

[25] The Muslim Indian boy may be letter-perfect in long sections of the Arabic Koran without understanding one word that he speaks; similarly the young Hindu, so both English and Indian teachers testify, easily learns by rote whole chapters of text whose words are mere meaningless sounds to his mind.

ties of the domestic code—these are the main studies in this practical institution. Added to them is simple cooking, especially cooking for infants and invalids, using always the native type of stove and utensils; and the handling and serving of food, with particular emphasis on keeping it clean and off the floor.

"Their cooking, in later life, they would never by nature do with their own hands, but would leave entirely to filthy servants, whence come much sickness and death," says the instructress. "Our effort here is to give them a conviction of the use and beauty of **cleanliness and order in all things.**"

Miss L. Sorabji, the Indian lady-principal of the Eden High School for girls at Dacca, thus discreetly suggests the nature of the teacher's struggle: [26]

Undesirable home influences are a great hindrance to progress. Unpunctuality, sloth, untidiness, carelessness regarding the laws of health and sanitation, untruthfulness, irresponsibility, absence of any code of honour, lack of home discipline, are some of the difficulties we have to contend with in our schools. Character-building is what is most needed.

And—the patient upbuilding of a public opinion that, eventually, may create and sustain a genuine and practical Indian movement toward self-help.

At present one beholds a curious spectacle: the daughters of rich landlords; of haughty Brahman plutocrats; of militant nationalist politicians, ferocious

[26] *Calcutta University Commission Report,* Vol. XII, p. 453.

denouncers of the white man and all his works, fed and lodged by the dimes and sixpences of dear old ladies in Illinois and Derbyshire, and taught the a-b-c of responsible living by despised Christians and outcaste apostates.

PART III

Interlude

THE BRAHMAN

Rattling south by rail, out of Bengal into Madras. Square masses of elephant-colored rock piled up to build rectangular hills, sitting one upon another in segments, like Elephant Gods on pedestals.—Miles and more miles of it.

On and on. Then a softer country, where the earth is orange and the only trees are small-topped palms scratched long across the sky like penstrokes ending in a splutter.

Much cultivation, rice fields marked off in slips and fragments by hand-high earth-ridges to hold the precious water. Little dark people with cherry-colored garments, almost black people, with big, bristling mops of curly black hair, drawing water out of wells as they drew it a thousand years ago, or threshing grain under the circling feet of bullocks. Stands of sugar cane, high and four-square. Small clay villages, each small clay house eclipsed under a big round palm-leaf roof like a candle-snuffer. Flocks of orange-colored goats. Patches of orange, on the ground—palm-nuts for betel chewing, spread out to dry. Big orange hawks with proud, white heads. Orange afterglow of sunset, flooding orange over the stubble fields of rice. An orange

[145]

world, punctuated by black human bodies with cherry-colored splashes.

Madras, citadel of Brahmanic Hinduism. Citadel also of the remnant of the ancient folk, the dark-skinned Dravidians. Brahmanic Hinduism broke them, cast them down and tramped upon them, commanded them in their multi-millions to be pariahs, outcasts, ignorant and poor. Then came the Briton, for whatever reason, establishing peace, order, and such measure of democracy as could survive in the soil.

Gradually the Dravidian raised his eyes, and then, most timidly, his head. With him, also, the multitudes of the low castes of the Brahman's world. And now all these, become an Anti-Brahman party, had developed strength enough, for the time at least, to snatch from the Brahman his political majority in the Legislative Council of Madras Presidency.[1] Which, in itself, constituted an epoch in Indian history.

With one of these low-caste men become rich, respected and politically powerful, I sat in private conference, in the city of Madras. A little, vivacious person he was, full of heat and free of tongue. "Will you draw me your picture of the Brahman?" I asked. He answered—and these are his actual words, written down at the moment:

"Once upon a time, when all men lived according to their choice, the Brahman was the only fellow who applied himself to learning. Then, having become

[1] In the fall elections of 1926, the Brahmans regained the majority in the Legislative Council of Madras Presidency.

[146]

WAITING FOR THE ENGLISH SISTER

(*See* page 161.)

Photo by M. Moyca Newell

AN UNTOUCHABLE

Carrying Night-soil in Bombay

learned, and being by nature subtle-minded, he secretly laid hold upon the sacred books, and secretly wrote into those books false texts that declared him, the Brahman, to be lord over all the people. Ages passed. And gradually, because the Brahman only could read and because he gave out his false texts that forbade learning to others, the people grew to believe him the Earthly God he called himself and to obey him accordingly. So in all Hindu India he ruled the spirit of man, and none dared dispute him, not till England came with schools for all.

"Now, here in this Province, Madras, we fight the Brahman. But still he is very strong, because the might of thousands of years breaks slowly, and he is as shrewd as a host of demons. He owns the press, he sways the bench, he holds eighty per cent. of the public offices, and he terrorizes the people, especially the women. For we are all superstitious and mostly illiterate. The 'Earthly God' has seen to that. Also, he hates the British, because they keep him from strangling us. He makes much 'patriotic' outcry, demanding that the British go. And we—we know that if they go now, before we have had time to steady ourselves, he will strangle us again and India will be what it used to be, a cruel despotism wielded by fat priests against a mass of slaves, because our imaginations are not yet free from him. Listen:

"Each Hindu in India pays to the Brahman many times more than he pays to the State. From the day of his birth to the day of his death, a man must be feeding the Earthly God. When a child is born, the Brahman must be paid; otherwise, the child will not prosper. Sixteen days afterward, to be cleansed of 'birth pollution,' the Brahman must be paid. A little later, the child must be named; and the Brahman must be paid. In the third month, the baby's hair must be clipped; and the Brahman must be paid. In the sixth month, we begin to feed the child solids; and the Brahman must be paid. When the child begins to walk, the Brahman must be paid. At the completion of the first year comes the birthday ceremony and the Brahman must be paid. At the end of the seventh year the boy's education begins and the Brahman must be paid well. In well-to-do families he performs the ceremony by guiding golden writing-sticks placed in the boy's hand; and the sticks also go to the Brahman.

"When a girl reaches her first birthday, her seventh, or her ninth, or when a boy is one and a half, or two years old, or anywhere up to sixteen, comes the betrothal, and big pay to the Brahman. Then, when puberty comes, or earlier, if the marriage is consummated earlier, rich pay to the Brahman. At an eclipse, the Brahman must be paid heavily. And so it goes on. When a man dies, the corpse can be removed only after receiving the blessing of the Brahman, for which he is paid. At the cremation, again a lot of money must be paid to many Brahmans. After cremation, every month for a year, the dead man's son must hold a feast for Brahmans—as great a feast as he can—and give them clothes, ornaments. food and whatever would be dear to the dead. For whatever a Brahman eats, drinks or uses is enjoyed by the dead. Thereafter, once a year, during the son's life, he must repeat this observance.

"All such ceremonies and many more the Brahman calls his 'vested rights,' made so by religious law. Whoever neglects them goes to eternal damnation. During the performance of each rite we must wash the Brahman's feet with water and then we must drink some of that water from the palm of our hand. The Brahman is indolent, produces nothing, and takes to no calling but that of lawyer or government official. In this Province he numbers one and a half million and the rest of us, over forty-one millions, feed him.

"Now do you understand that, until we others are able to hold our own in India, we prefer a distant King beyond the sea, who gives us peace, justice, something back for our money and a chance to become free men, to a million and a half masters, here, who eat us up, yet say our very touch would pollute them?"

Chapter XI

LESS THAN MEN

The conundrums of India have a way of answering themselves, when one looks close.

Long and easily we have accepted the catchword "mysterious India." But "mystery," as far as matters concrete are concerned, remains such only as long as one persists in seeking a mysterious cause for the phenomena. Look for a practical cause, as you would do in any bread-and-butter country not labeled "inscrutable," and your mystery vanishes in smoke.

"Why, after so many years of British rule, do we remain 92 per cent. illiterate?" reiterates the Hindu politician, implying that the blame must be laid at the ruler's door.

But in naming his figure, he does not call to your attention a fact which, left to yourself, you would be slow to guess: he does not tell you that of the 247,-000,000 inhabitants of British India, about 25 per cent. —60,000,000—have from time immemorial been specially condemned to illiteracy, even to sub-humanity, by their brother Indians. Surely, if there be a mystery in India, it lies here—it lies in the Hindu's ability anywhere, under any circumstances, to accuse any man, any society, any nation, of "race prejudice," so long as he can be reminded of the existence in India of sixty million fellow Indians to whom he violently denies the common rights of man.[1]

In the beginning, it is explained, when the light-skinned ancestors of the present Hindus first came to India, they found there a darker, thicker-featured native race, the Dravidians, builders of the great temples of the South. And the priests of the newcomers desired that the blood of their people be not mixed with the native stock, but be kept of one strain. So they declared Dravidians to be unclean, "untouchable."

Then the old lawmakers, gradually devising the caste system, placed themselves at the head thereof, under the title of "earthly gods"—Brahmans. Next beneath them they put the Kshattryas, or fighting men; after the fighters, the Vaisyas, or cultivators, upon whom the two above look down; and finally, the fourth division, or Sudra caste, born solely to be servants to the other three. Of these four divisions, themselves today much subdivided, was built the frame of Hindu society. Outside and below all caste, in a limbo of scorn earned by their sins of former existences, must forever grovel the Untouchables.

[1] Indian politicians have for some time been directing a loud and continuous fire upon the British Home Government for not finding means to coerce the Government of the Union of South Africa into a complaisant attitude toward British Indian immigrants in that country. It is worthy of note that of the original 130,000 British Indian immigrants to South Africa, one-third were "Untouchables," mostly from Madras Presidency, whose condition in India is indicated in this chapter, and who would find themselves again in such status, were they to return to Hindu India. The British Indians in South Africa in 1922 numbered, as shown in the official Year-Book, a little over 161,000. This figure includes a later immigration of 10,000 traders, and the natural increase of the combined body.

A quotation from the rule by which the unfortunates were nailed to their fate will suffice to show its nature; the *Bhagavata*,[2] treating of the murder of a Brahman, decrees:

Whoever is guilty of it will be condemned at his death to take the form of one of those insects which feed on filth. Being reborn long afterwards a Pariah [Untouchable], he will belong to this caste, and will be blind for more than four times as many years as there are hairs on the body of a cow. He can, nevertheless, expiate his crime by feeding forty thousand Brahmins.

Thus, at one sweep, is explained the Untouchable's existence as such; are justified the indignities heaped upon him; is emphasized his unspeakable degradation; and is safeguarded the oppressor from the wrath of him oppressed. Even as the Hindu husband, by the horrors imposed upon widowhood, is safeguarded from a maddened wife's revolt.

If a Brahmin kills a Sudra,[3] it will suffice to efface the sin altogether if he recites the *gayatri* [a prayer] a hundred times,

continues the scripture, by opposites driving home its point.

Leaving the ancient roots of things, and coming down to the year 1926 A.D., we find the orthodox Hindu rule as to Untouchables to be roughly this:

[2] Chief of the eighteen *Puranas*, sacred books of India. The translation here given is that of the Abbé Dubois, *Hindu Manners, Customs and Ceremonies*, p. 558.

[3] A member of the fourth division, lowest Hindu caste, yet far above the Untouchable.

Regarded as if sub-human, the tasks held basest are reserved for them; dishonor is associated with their name. Some are permitted to serve only as scavengers and removers of night soil; some, through the ignorance to which they are condemned, are loathsome in their habits; and to all of them the privilege of any sort of teaching is sternly denied. They may neither possess nor read the Hindu scriptures. No Brahman priest will minister to them; and, except in rarest instances, they may not enter a Hindu temple to worship or pray. Their children may not come to the public schools. They may not draw water from the public wells; and if their habitation be in a region where water is scarce and sources far apart, this means, for them, not greater consideration from others, but greater suffering and greater toil.

They may not enter a court of justice; they may not enter a dispensary to get help for their sick; they may stop at no inn. In some provinces they may not even use the public road, and as laborers or agriculturists, they are continually losers, in that they may not enter the shops or even pass through the streets where shops are, but must trust to a haphazard chain of hungry go-betweens to buy or sell their meager wares. Some, in the abyss of their degradation, are permitted no work at all. These may sell nothing, not even their own labor. They may only beg. And even for that purpose they dare not use the road, but must stand far off, unseen, and cry out for alms from those who pass. If alms be given, it must be tossed on the ground, well away from

[153]

the road, and when the giver is out of sight and the roads empty then, and not till then, the watcher may creep up, snatch, and run.

Some, if not all, pollute, beyond caste men's use, any food upon which their shadow falls. Food, after such defilement, can only be destroyed.

Others, again, exude "distance pollution" as an effluvium from their unhappy bodies. If one of these presumes to approach and linger by a highroad, he must measure the distance to the highroad. If it be within two hundred yards, he must carefully place on the road a green leaf weighted down with a handful of earth, thereby indicating that he, the unclean, is within pollution distance of that point. The passing Brahman, seeing the signal, halts and shouts. The poor man forthwith takes to his heels, and only when he has fled far enough calls back, "I am now two hundred yards away. Be pleased to pass."

Still others—the Puliahs of the Malabar Coast—have been forbidden to build themselves huts, and permitted to construct for houses nothing better than a sort of leaf awning on poles, or nests in the crotches of big trees. These may approach no other type of humanity. Dubois recorded that, in his day, a Nair (high-caste Hindu) meeting a Puliah on the road, was entitled to stab the offender on the spot.[4] Today the Nair would hesitate. But still, today, the Puliah may approach no caste man nearer than sixty or ninety feet.

[4] *Hindu Manners, Customs and Ceremonies,* pp. 60-1. See also *Three Voyages of Vasco da Gama,* Gaspar Correa, Hakluyt Society. London, 1869, p. 155.

Under such conditions of preordained misery, certain communities among the Untouchables have developed a business in the practice of crime. These communities specialize, one in pocket-picking, another in burglary, yet others in forging, in highway robbery, in murder, etc., often combining their special trade with prostitution as a second industry. Scattered all over India and known as the Criminal Tribes, they number today about four and a half million persons.

Now it must not be forgotten that the matter of Untouchability, like almost all other Hindu concerns, is woven, warp and woof, into the Hindu religion; and that the Hindus are a tremendously religiose people. To quote the words of that prominent Indian, Sir Surendranath Banerjea: [5]

You cannot think of a social question affecting the Hindu community that is not bound up with religious considerations; and when divine sanction, in whatever form, is invoked in aid of a social institution, it sits enthroned in the popular heart with added firmness and fixity, having its roots in sentiment rather than in reason.

And dire experience shows to what lengths of blood-drenched madness the people can be goaded by a whisper that their caste is threatened or that insult is offered to their gods. That this was from the beginning understood by Government, is shown in an unequivocal clause in the Queen's Proclamation of December 2, 1858:

[5] *A Nation in Making,* London, Humphrey Milford, 1925, p. 396.

We do strictly charge and enjoin all those who may be in authority under us that they abstain from all interference with the religious belief or worship of our subjects, on pain of our highest displeasure.

Nevertheless the immediate impulse of the Briton in India was to espouse the cause of the social victim. The Directors of the East India Company, as early as 1854, recommended that "no boy be refused admission to a Government school or college on ground of caste," and stuck to the principle until their authority was sunk in that of the Crown. Thenceforward it was continually reaffirmed, yet pushed with a caution that might seem faint-hearted to one unfamiliar with the extreme delicacy of the ground. Little or nothing was to be gained in any attempt to impose a foreign idea, by force, on unready and non-understanding millions.

Nor must the workings of caste be confused with snobbery. A man's caste is the outward sign of the history of his soul. To break caste by infringing any one of the multitudinous caste laws brings down an eternal penalty. If, as a Hindu, in obeying these laws, you inflict suffering upon another, that is merely because his soul-history has placed him in the path of pain. You have no concern in the matter; neither will he, thinking as a good Hindu, blame you. For both you and he are working out your god-appointed destiny.

Today almost all that can be accomplished by civil law for the Untouchable has been secured. Government has freely opened their way, as far as Govern-

[156]

ment can determine, to every educational advantage
and to high offices. And Government's various land-
development and coöperative schemes, steadily increasing, have provided tremendous redeeming agencies and
avenues of escape.

But for Provincial Governments to pass legislation
asserting the rights of every citizen to enjoy public
facilities, such as public schools, is one thing; to enforce
that legislation over enormous countrysides and
through multitudinous small villages without the co-
operation and against the will of the people, is another.
Witness that paragraph in the Madras Government
Order of March 17, 1919, reading:

> Children of Panchamas [Untouchables] are admitted only
> into 609 schools out of 8,157 in the Presidency, although the
> regulations state that no boy is to be refused admission merely
> on the ground of caste.

Yet, rightly read, the announcement proclaims a
signal advantage won. Six hundred and nine schools in
a most orthodox province admitting outcastes, as
against only twelve times that number who refuse!

In the Bombay Legislative Council, one day in
August, 1926, they were discussing a resolution to
coerce local boards to permit Untouchables to send
their children to schools, to draw water from public
wells, and to enjoy other common rights of citizenship.
Most of the Hindu members approved in principle.
"But if the resolution is put into effect we would be
faced with a storm of opposition," demurred one mem-

ber, representative of many others. "Orthodox opinion is too strong, and while I sympathize with the resolution I think that . . . given effect, it may have disastrous effect." [6] And he submits that the path of wisdom, for friends of the Untouchables, is not to ask for action, but, instead, to content themselves with verbal expressions of sympathy, such as his own.

A second Hindu member, with characteristic nimbleness, pitchforks the load toward shoulders broad enough to bear it: [7]

I think the British Government have followed a very timid policy in this presidency. They have refused to take part in any social legislation. Probably, being an alien Government, they were afraid that they would be accused of tampering with the religion of the various communities. In spite of the Proclamation of Queen Victoria about equality between the different classes and communities, Government have not given practical effect to it.

It remains, however, to a Muhammadan, Mr. Noor Mahomed, of Sind, to strike the practical note: [8]

I think the day will not be distant when the people who are placed by the tyranny of the higher classes into the lower grade of society . . . will find themselves driven to other religious folds. There will then be no reason at all for the Hindu society to complain that Mahomedan or Christian missionaries are inducing members of depressed classes to change

[6] *Bombay Legislative Council Debates,* 1926, Vol. XVIII, Part IX, p. 717.
[7] *Ibid.,* p. 728.
[8] *Ibid.,* August 5, p. 721.

the religion of their birth. . . . If the Hindu society refuses to allow other human beings, fellow creatures at that, to attend public schools, and if . . . the president of a local board representing so many lakhs [9] of people in this House refuses to allow his fellows and brothers the bare elementary human right of having water to drink, what right have they to ask for more rights from the bureaucracy? . . . Before we accuse people coming from other lands, we should see how we ourselves behave toward our own people. . . . How can [we] ask for greater political rights when [we ourselves] deny elementary rights of human beings?

Regulations may prevail to bring the outcaste to the school door, but his courage may not suffice to get him across the threshold, for his self-assertion was done to death centuries ago. So that his admission to the school will mean, at best, permission to sit on the veranda and pick up from that distance whatever he can by his unaided ears.

Says the Village Education Commission: [10]

Speaking generally, it is still the case that the caste man not only does nothing for the enlightenment of the outcaste, but puts positive obstacles in his way, knowing that if he is enlightened he can no longer be exploited. Outcastes who have the temerity to send their children to school—even if the school be in their quarter, so that there can be no complaint of defiling caste children by contact—find themselves subject to such violence and threatening that they yield and

[9] A lakh is one hundred thousand.
[10] *Village Education in India,* London, Oxford University Press, 1922, p. 21.

[159]

withdraw their children. If the outcastes want not only education but Christian teaching, the persecution, for a time, is
all the fiercer, for the caste people are afraid that if the outcastes become Christians they will no longer be available for
menial service.

An exceedingly small percentage of the outcastes
are yet in school, but he of their number who pursues
education past all the dragons that bar the door is
likely to be one of the best of his kind. And, in spite
of his immemorial history of degradation, the seed of
the power to rise is not dead within him. The Nama-
sudras of Bengal, an Untouchable class there numbering about 1,997,500, have, under the encouragement
of the new light, made a vigorous, steady, and successful fight for self-elevation, and have organized to support schools of their own. By the last report they had
in Bengal over 49,000 children under tuition, of whom
1,025 had reached the High School and 144 the Arts
Colleges,[11] where, because of caste feeling, Government has been obliged to set aside special hostels for
their lodging. This community is rapidly raising its
status.

In the Punjab, where Government irrigation work
is destroying many ancient miseries, appears evidence
of a weakening of the ban that bars the outcaste from
the common schools; although some of the Punjab
municipalities have displayed a genius in tricking these
most needy of their citizens out of the privileges of

[11] *Progress of Education in Bengal,* Sixth Quinquennial Review,
p. 83.

education.[12] Bombay's educational reports also indicate a significant advance in the percentage of Untouchables receiving tuition, largely under mission auspices. And the net results point to some interesting surmises.

Thus, the "depressed classes" have begun holding annual conferences of delegates to air their wrongs and to advance their rights. Their special representatives, now appointed to legislatures and to local bodies, grow more and more assertive. Their economic situation, under Government's steady effort, is, in some communities, looking up. With it their sense of manhood is developing in the shape of resentment of the degradation to which until now they have bowed. Among them a few men of power and parts are beginning to stand out.

Finally, their women, as Christian converts, furnish the main body of Indian teachers for the girls of India of all castes, and of trained nurses for the hospitals; both callings despised and rejected by the superior castes, both necessitating education, and both carrying the possibility of increasing influence.

The first time that I, personally, approached a realizing sense of what the doctrine of Untouchability means, in terms of man's inhumanity to man, was during a visit to a child-welfare center in a northerly Indian city.

The place was crowded with Indian women who had brought their babies to be examined by the English

[12] Cf. *Report on the Progress of Education in the Punjab*, 1924-25, Lahore, 1926, p. 71.

professional in charge, a trained public health nurse. Toward her their attitude was that of children toward a wise and loving mother—confiding, affectionate, trusting. And their needs were inclusive. All morning I had been watching babies washed and weighed and examined, simple remedies handed out, questions answered, advice and friendly cautions given, encouragement and praise. Just now I happened to be looking at a matronly high-caste woman with an intelligent, clean-cut face. She was loaded with heavy gold and silver jewelry and wore a silken mantle. She sat down on the floor to show her baby, unrolling him from the torn fragment of an old quilt, his only garment. This revealed his whole little body caked in a mass of dry and half-dry excreta.

"She appears unconcerned," I remarked to the Sister. The Sister replied:

"We try to get such women to have napkins for their babies, but they won't buy them, they won't wash them themselves, and they won't pay washers to wash them, although they are quite able to do so. This woman is well born. Her husband is well educated—a technical man—and enjoys a good salary. Sometime it may please her to hang that bit of quilt out in the sun in her courtyard, and, when it is dry, to brush off what will come off. That's all. This, incidentally, helps explain why infantile diarrhæa spreads through the families in a district. They will make no attempt whatever to keep things clean."

As the Sister spoke, a figure appeared before the

open doorway—a young woman so graceful and with a face so sweet and appealing as to rivet attention at once. She carried an ailing baby on her arm, but came no farther—just stood still beyond the doorway, wistfully smiling. The Sister, looking up, smiled back.

"Why does she not come in?" I asked.

"She dare not. If she did, all these others would go. She is an Untouchable—an outcaste. She herself would feel it wicked to set her foot upon that sill."

"She looks at least as decent as they," I remarked.

"Untouchables may be as intelligent as any one else—and you see for yourself that they couldn't be dirtier," said the Sister. "But such is the custom of India. Since we can't alter it, we just plod on, trying to help them all, as best we can."

And so the gentle suppliant waited outside, among a crowd of others of her kind, till Sister could go to them, bringing to this one ointment for baby's eyes, to that one a mixture for baby's cough, and hearing the story of another.

But they might not bring their little ones in, to the mercy of the warm bath, as the other women were doing at will. They might not come to the sewing class. They might not defile the scales by laying their babies in its basket, to see what the milk-dole was doing. For they were all horrible sinners in aeons past, deserving now neither help nor sympathy while they worked out their curse.

[163]

Chapter XII

BEHOLD, A LIGHT!

Much is said of the inferiority of character that has resulted from the Untouchables' long degradation. But evidence of the survival of virtues, through all the crushing of the centuries, is by no means lacking. The Mahars, for example, outcastes used by caste villagers as are the Palers of Madras, practically as slaves [1] and for the basest tasks, are now employed by Government as couriers. In that capacity they are said to be entirely trustworthy, transporting hundreds of rupees without abstracting the smallest coin. The Dheds, Untouchables from whom, in the Bombay region, most Britons' servants are drawn, and whom few high caste Indians would tolerate near their persons, are, as a rule, honest, sober, and faithful.

As to the rating of converts to Christianity—there are now about five million of them—opinions differ; but in any case the fact stands that these converts are set free, as far as they can grasp freedom, from caste bonds. The faces of the Hindus are fixed against them, to be sure. But of the converts of the third generation many experienced persons are found to say that they are the hope of India.

[1] *Joint Select Committee on the Government of India Bill,* 1919, Vol. II, *Minutes of Evidence,* p. 188, Rai Bahadur K. V. Reddi: "They are the slaves of the Nation."

So much, thus far, Britain, greatly aided by the Christian Missions, has accomplished for the outcaste, by patient, up-hill work, teaching, persuading, encouraging, on either side of the social gulf. And the last few years have seen the rise of new portents in the sky.

One of these is the tendency, in the National Social Conference and in Hindu political conventions, to declare openly against the oppression of the outcaste. But these declarations, though eloquent, have as yet borne little fruit other than words. A second phenomenon is the appearance of Indian volunteer associations partially pledged against Untouchability. These include the Servants of India,[2] avowedly political; Lord Sinha's society for the help of the outcastes of Bengal and Assam; the Brahmo Samaj, and others. Their work, useful where it touches, is sporadic, and infinitesimal compared to the need, but notable in comparison with the nothingness that went before.

For no such conception is native to India. "All our Indian social work of today," the most distinguished of the Brahmo Samaj leaders said to me, "is frankly an imitation of the English and an outgrowth of their influence in the land." Again and again I heard the gist of that statement from the lips of thoughtful Indians, in frank acknowledgment of the source of the budding change.

"The curse of Untouchability prevails to this day in all parts of India," said Sir Narayan Chandravarkar,[3]

---

[2] *A Brief Account of the Work of the Servants of India Society*, Aryabhushan Press, Poona, 1924, pp. 60-1.

[3] Hindu reformer, Judge of the High Court of Bombay, quoted in *India in 1920*, p. 155.

adding, "with the liberalizing forces of the British Government, the problem is leaping into full light. Thanks to that Government, it has become . . . an all-India problem."

Mr. Gandhi has been less ready to acknowledge beneficent influence from such a source—has, in fact, described the whole administrative system in India as "vile beyond description." But for the last five years his own warfare on Untouchability has not flagged even though his one unfaltering co-worker therein has been the British Government, aided preëminently by the Salvation Army. In its course he reprinted from the Indian vernacular press a learned Brahman pundit's recent statement on the subject, including this passage: [4]

Untouchability is a necessity for man's growth.

Man has magnetic powers about him. This *sakti* [5] is like milk. It will be damaged by improper contacts. If one can keep musk and onion together, one may mix Brahmans and Untouchables.

It should be enough that Untouchables are not denied the privileges of the other world.

Says Mr. Gandhi, in comment on the pundit's creed: [6]

If it was possible to deny them the privileges of the other world, it is highly likely that the defenders of the monster would isolate them even in the other world.

[4] *Young India,* July 29, 1926, p. 268. Mr. Gandhi's phrase quoted a few lines above will be found in *Gandhi's Letters on Indian Affairs,* Madras, V. Narayanah and Co., p. 121.
[5] Energy, or the power of the Supreme personified.
Young India, July 29, 1926.

"Among living Indians," says Professor Rushbrook Williams,[7] "Mr. Gandhi has done most to impress upon his fellow countrymen the necessity for elevating the depressed classes. . . . When he was at the height of his reputation, the more orthodox sections of opinion did not dare to challenge his schemes."

But today the defenders of Untouchability are myriad, and, though Mr. Gandhi lives his faith, but few of his supporters have at any time cared to follow him so far.

On January 5, 1925, a mass meeting of Hindus was held in Bombay to protest against Mr. Gandhi's "heresy" in attacking Untouchability. The presiding officer, Mr. Manamohandas Ramji, explained that Untouchability rests on a plane with the segregation of persons afflicted with contagious diseases. Later he interpreted the speaker who pointedly suggested lynching for "heretics" who "threaten the disruption of Hindu society," to mean only that Hindus are "prepared to sacrifice their lives for the Hindu religion in order to preserve its ancient purity." The meeting closed after appointing a committee specially to undermine Mr. Gandhi's propaganda.

And it is fair to say that the discussions of Untouchability evoked by successive introductions of the subject in the great Hindu conventions show mainly by the heat of the system's defenders that ground has been won.

"You saw," said Mr. Gandhi, "the squabble that

7 *India in 1924-25,* p. 264.

arose over it, in the Hindu *Mahasabha*.[8] But Untouchability is going, in spite of all opposition, and going fast. It has degraded Indian humanity. The 'Untouchables' are treated as if less than beasts. Their very shadow defiles in the name of God. I am as strong or stronger in denouncing Untouchability as I am in denouncing British methods imposed on India. Untouchability for me is more insufferable than British rule. If Hinduism hugs Untouchability, then Hinduism is dead and gone." [9]

Meantime another and a curious development has come to the Untouchables' aid. With the rapid Indianization of Government services, with the rapid concessions in Indian autonomy that have characterized British administration since the World War, an intense jealousy has arisen between the Hindu three-quarters and the Muhammadan fourth of the population. This subject will be treated elsewhere. Here it will suffice merely to name it as the reason why the Untouchables, simply because of numbers, have suddenly become an object of solicitude to the Hindu world. Sir T. W. Holderness, writing in 1920, put the point thus: [10]

The "depressed classes" in India form a vast multitude. . . . A question that is agitating Hinduism at the present moment is as to whether these classes should be counted as

[8] A hot and disorderly demonstration directed against those who would relax the pains of the Untouchables had persisted in the session of this great Hindu Convention of 1926.

[9] Verbal statement to the author. Revised by Mr. Gandhi.

[10] *Peoples and Problems of India,* Revised Edition, London, Williams and Norgate, 1920, pp. 101-2.

Hindus or not. Ten years ago the answer would have been emphatically in the negative. Even now the conservative feeling of the country is for their exclusion. But the conscience of the more advanced section of the educated Hindus is a little sensitive on the point. It is awkward to be reminded by rival Muhammadan politicians that more than one-third of the supposed total Hindu population is not accepted by Hindus as a part of themselves, is not allowed the ministration of Brahman priests, is excluded from Hindu shrines. It is obviously desirable, in presence of such an argument, to claim the "depressed castes" as within the pale of Hinduism. But if they are to be so reckoned, logic demands that they should be treated with greater consideration than at present. Educated Hindus see this, and the uplifting of these castes figures prominently on the programmes of Indian social conferences. But the stoutest-hearted reformer admits to himself that the difficulties in the way of effective action in this matter are great, so strong is the hold that caste has on the Indian mind.

But here a fresh element comes in—another disturbing fruit of the intrusion of the West—a likelihood that, stimulated by the strange new foreign sympathy, the Untouchable may not much longer leave his religious status to be determined at the leisure and pleasure of the Hindu caste man. Islam, utterly democratic, will readily receive him into full partnership in the fold. Christianity not only invites him, but will educate and help him. The moment he accepts either Islam or Christianity, he is rid of his shame. The question, then, is chiefly a question of how long it takes a man, ages oppressed, to summon courage, spirit, and energy to stand up and shake off the dust.

[69]

In the autumn of 1917, the then Secretary of State for India, Mr. Montagu, chief advocate of the speedy Indianization of the Government, sat in Delhi receiving deputations from such elements of the Indian peoples as were moved to address him on that subject. All sorts and conditions of men appeared, all sorts of documentary petitions were submitted, all sorts of angles and interests. Among these, not meanly represented, loomed an element new on the Indian political stage— the Untouchables, awake and assertive, in many organized groups entreating the Secretary's attention.

Without one divergent voice they deprecated the thought of Home Rule for India. To quote them at length would be repetition. Their tenor may be sufficiently gathered from two excerpts.

The Panchama Kalvi Abivirthi-Abimana Sanga, a Madras Presidency outcastes' association,[11] "deprecates political change and desires only to be saved from the Brahmin, whose motive in seeking a greater share in the Government is . . . that of the cobra seeking the charge of a young frog."

The Madras Adi Dravida Jana Sabha, organized to represent six million Dravidian aborigines of Madras Presidency, said: [12]

The caste system of the Hindus stigmatises us as untouchables. . . . Caste Hindus could not, however, get on without our assistance. We supplied labour and they enjoyed the fruit,

[11] *Addresses Presented in India to His Excellency the Viceroy and the Right Honourable the Secretary of State for India,* London, 1918, p. 87.
[12] *Ibid.,* pp. 60-1.

giving us a mere pittance in return. Our improvement in the social and economic scale began with and is due to the British Government. The Britishers in India—Government officers, merchants, and last, but not least, Christian missionaries—love us, and we love them in return. Though the general condition of the community is still very low, there are some educated men amongst us. But these are not allowed to rise in society on account of the general stigma attached by the Hindus to the community. The very names by which these people refer to us breathe contempt.

We need not say that we are strongly opposed to Home Rule. We shall fight to the last drop of our blood any attempt to transfer the seat of authority in this country from British hands to so-called high caste Hindus who have ill-treated us in the past and would do so again but for the protection of British laws. Even as it is, our claims, nay, our very existence, is ignored by the Hindus; and how will they promote our interests if the control of the administration passes into their hands?

"We love them," said these spokesmen of the out-caste—and the expression strikes home with a certain shock. But one is forced to remember that the sorrows of these particular under-dogs have never before, in all their dim centuries of history, elicited from any creature a thought or a helping hand. Here is a tale, as told to me, to show that even the degradation of ages cannot kill that in a man which lifts up his heart to his friend.

It concerns a command of Madrassi Sappers—coal-black Dravidians from around Bangalore—Untouchables all, or almost all. And it happened in the World War, at the taking of Kut.

"The river," said the witness, "is about three hundred yards wide at that point and swift. Our job was to cross in pontoons in the dim first gray of the morning, hoping to surprise the Turk. The duty of the sappers was to take the boats up the night before, under cover of darkness, and to make them ready; then to stand back while the combatant troops rowed themselves across.

"The sappers did their job. But just as the moment came to embark our men, the Turk waked up and opened fire. Our surprise was a washout. But we carried on, all the same.

"Now, the troops could lie flat in the bottom of the boats, but their rowers must sit on the thwarts and pull—three hundred yards, slantwise, in point-blank rifle range. Why, they hadn't a chance!

"What happened? What but those little Madrassis, pushing forward, all eagerness, begging: 'Sahibs, you want rifles over there. *Rifles*, Sahibs, *rifles!* We are only sappers. Let *us* row!'

"So the troops, rushing down, sprang into the boats and stretched flat. And the sappers jumped into the thwarts and pulled. And then—the Turk's machine-guns!

"When the boats came back, out of seventy rowers scarcely a man was left unhurt and many were dead. But those little sapper fellows ashore, they swarmed down, hove their dead out on the bank, jumped into their places, and, as each boat filled with men, shoved off into their comrades' fate. That is how the rifles got over to Kut. And those were coal-black Dravidians, mind you—'Untouchables,' unless they had turned Christian—which a fair lot of them had."

When the Prince of Wales sailed to India, late in 1921, Mr. Gandhi, then at the height of his popularity, proclaimed to the Hindu world that the coming visit was "an insult added to injury," and called for a general boycott.[13]

Political workers obediently snatched up the torch, rushing it through their organizations, and the Prince's landing in Bombay became thereby the signal for murderous riot and destruction. No outbreak occurred among the responsible part of the population, nor along the line of progress, which was, of course, well guarded. But in the remoter areas of the city, hooliganism ran on for several days, with some fifty killings and four hundred woundings, Indian attacking Indian, while arson and loot played their ruinous part.

Meanwhile the Prince, seemingly unmoved by the first unfriendly reception of all his life, proceeded to carry out his officially arranged programme in and about the city. On the evening of November 22 it was scheduled that he should depart for the North.

As he left Government House on the three- or four-mile drive to the Bombay railway station, his automobile ran unguarded save for the pilot police car that went before. Where it entered the city, however, a

[13] *Gandhi's Letters on Indian Affairs*, pp. 96-7.

cordon of police lined the streets on both sides. And behind that cordon pressed the people—the common poor people of the countryside in their uncountable thousands; pressed and pushed until, with the railway station yet half a mile away, the police line bent and broke beneath the strain.

Instantly the crowd surged in, closing around the car, shouting, fighting each other to work nearer— nearer still. What would they do? What was their temper? God knew! Gandhi's hot words had spread among them, and God alone, now, could help. Some reached the running-boards and clung. Others shoved them off, for one instant to take their places, the next themselves to be dragged away. And what was this they shouted? At first nothing could be made of it, in the bedlam of voices, though those charged with the safety of the progress strained their ears to catch the cries.

Then words stood out, continuously chanted, and the words were these:

"*Yuvaraj Maharaj ki jai!*" "Hail to the Prince!" And: "Let me see my Prince! Let me see my Prince! Let me only see my Prince just once before I die!"

The police tried vainly to form again around the car. Moving at a crawl, quite unprotected now, through an almost solid mass of shouting humanity, it won through to the railway station at last.

There, within the barriers that shut off the platform of the royal train, gathered the dignitaries of the Province and the City, to make their formal farewells. To these His Royal Highness listened, returning due acknowledgments. Then, clipping short his own last word, he turned suddenly to the aide beside him.

"How much time left?"

"Three minutes, sir," replied the aide.

"Then drop those barriers and let the people in"—indicating the mobs outside.

"Our hearts jumped into our mouths," said the men who told me the tale, "but the barriers, of course, went down."

Like the sweep of a river in flood the interminable multitudes rolled in—and shouted and adored and laughed and wept, and, when the train started, ran alongside the royal carriage till they could run no more.

After which one or two super-responsible officials went straight home to bed.

So the Prince of Wales moved northward. And as he moved, much of his wholesome influence was lost, through the active hostility of the Indian political leader.

But if Gandhi's exhortations traveled, so did the news of the Prince's aspect—traveled far and fast, as such things do amongst primitive peoples.

And when he turned back from his transit of the Great North Gate—the Khyber Pass itself—a strange thing awaited him. A swarm of Untouchables, emboldened by news that had reached them, clustered at the roadside to do him reverence.

[175]

"Government *ki jai!*" "Hail to the Government!" they shouted, with cheers that echoed from the barren hills.

And when the Prince slowed down his car to return their greetings, they leapt and danced in their excitement.

For nowhere in all their store of memory or of legend had they any history of an Indian magnate who had noticed an Untouchable except to scorn him. And here was a greater than all India contained—the son of the Supreme Power, to them almost divine, who deigned not only to receive but even to thank them for their homage! Small wonder that their spirits soared, that their eyes saw visions, that their tongues laid hold upon mystic words.

"Look! Look!" they cried to one another. "Behold, the Light! the Light!"

And such was their exaltation that many of them somehow worked through to Delhi to add themselves to the twenty-five thousand of their kind who there awaited the Prince's coming. The village people from round about flocked in to join them—the simple people of the soil who know nothing of politics but much of friendship as shown in works. And all together haunted the roadside, waiting and hoping for a glimpse of his face.

At last he came, down the Grand Trunk Road, toward the Delhi Gate. And in the center of the hosts of the Untouchables, one, standing higher than the rest, unfurled a flag.

[176]

"Yuvaraj Maharaj ki jai! Raja ke Bete ki jai!"
"Hail to the Prince! Hail to the King's Son!" they all shouted together, to burst their throats. And the Prince, while the high-caste Indian spectators wondered and revolted within themselves at his lack of princely pride, ordered his car stopped.

Then a spokesman ventured forward, to offer in a humble little speech the love and fealty of the sixty millions of the Unclean and to beg the heir to the throne to intercede for them with his father the King Emperor, never to abandon them into the hands of those who despised them and would keep them slaves.

The Prince heard him through. Then—whether he realized the magnitude of what he did, or whether he acted merely on the impulse of his natural friendly courtesy toward all the world—he did an unheard-of thing. He stood up—stood up, for them, the "worse than dogs," spoke a few words of kindness, looked them all over, slowly, and so, with a radiant smile, gave them his salute.

No sun that had risen in India had witnessed such a sight. As the car started on, moving slowly not to crush them, they went almost mad. And again their eastern tongues clothed their thought. "Brother—that word was truth that our brothers brought us. Behold, the Light is there indeed! The Light—the Glory—on his face!"

Chapter XIII

GIVE ME OFFICE OR GIVE ME DEATH

Education, some Indian politicians affirm, should be driven into the Indian masses by compulsory measures. "England," they say, "introduced compulsory education at home long ago. Why does she not do so here? Because, clearly, it suits her purpose to leave the people ignorant."

To this I took down a hot reply from the lips of the Raja of Panagal, then anti-Brahman leader of Madras Presidency.

"Rubbish!" he exclaimed. "What did the Brahmans do for our education in the five thousand years before Britain came? I remind you: They asserted their right to pour hot lead into the ears of the low-caste man who should dare to study books. All learning belonged to them, they said. When the Muhammadans swarmed in and took us, even that was an improvement on the old Hindu régime. But only in Britain's day did education become the right of all, with state schools, colleges, and universities accessible to all castes, communities, and peoples."

"[The Brahmans] saw well enough," says Dubois,[1] "what a moral ascendancy knowledge would give them over the other castes, and they therefore made a mys-

[1] *Hindu Manners. Customs and Ceremonies*, p. 376.

[178]

Photo by M. Moyca Newell

THE UNTOUCHABLE

"Just stood in the doorway." (*See* page 163.)

tery of it by taking all possible precautions to prevent other classes from obtaining access to it."

But the Brahmans, whatever their intellectual achievement in earliest times, rested quiescent upon these laurels through the succeeding centuries. They were content, while denying light to the remainder of their world, to abide, themselves, in the ever-fading wisdom of the ever-dimmer past. Says the Abbé Dubois again, writing in the beginning of the nineteenth century: [2]

I do not believe that the Brahmins of modern times are, in any degree, more learned than their ancestors of the time of Lycurgus and Pythagoras. During this long space of time many barbarous races have emerged from the darkness of ignorance, have attained the summit of civilization, and have extended their intellectual researches . . . yet all this time the Hindus have been perfectly stationary. We do not find amongst them any trace of mental or moral improvement, any sign of advance in the arts and sciences. Every impartial observer must, indeed, admit that they are now very far behind the peoples who inscribed their names long after them on the roll of civilized nations.

This was written some half-century before the British Crown assumed the government of India.

During that fifty years a new educational movement sprang up in the land. The design of Warren Hastings and later of the East India Company, impelled by the British Parliament, had been to advance Indian culture, as such, toward a native fruition. It remained for

[2] *Ibid.*, pp. 376-7.

a private citizen, one David Hare, an English merchant domiciled in India, to start the wheels turning
the opposite way.

David Hare, no missionary, but an agnostic, was a
man with a conviction. Under its impulse he gave himself and his all to "the education and moral improvement of the natives of Bengal." Parallel to him worked
the famous Hindu, Raja Ram Mohan Roy, a solitary
soul fired to action by the status of his own people in
the intellectual and social-ethical world. And these two,
one in purpose, at length joined to create a secular
Hindu College, whose object they announced as "the
tuition of the sons of respectable Hindoos in the English and Indian language and in the literature and
science of Europe and Asia."

The project, however, only roused the wrath and
distrust of the orthodox Hindu. This was in 1817.

A year later three Baptist missionaries, Carey,
Marshman and Ward, founded a still-extant school
near Calcutta. In 1820 the Anglican Church opened a
college. In 1830 Alexander Duff, again with the help
of Ram Mohan Roy, instituted a fourth college for the
giving of western science to India. A network of primitive vernacular schools at that time existed throughout
Bengal, but it was Raja Ram Mohan Roy himself who
continuously urged upon the British authorities the
necessity, if "the improvement of the native population" were contemplated, of doing away with the old
code and system, of teaching western sciences, and of

[180]

conducting such teachings in the English language.[3]

While these influences were still combating the earlier attitude of the British with its basic tenet that Indian education should run along Indian lines, came a new force into the field—one Thomas Babington Macaulay, to be Chairman of a Committee of Public Instruction. Lord Macaulay declared, and with tremendous vigor, on the side of the western school. In the name of honor and of humanity the full light of western science must, he felt, be given to the Indian world. And he demanded,[4] with fervor, to know by what right, when

. . . we can patronise sound philosophy and true history, we shall countenance, at the public expense, medical doctrines, which would disgrace an English farrier,—astronomy, which would move laughter in girls at an English boarding school,—history, abounding with kings thirty feet high, and reigns thirty thousand years long,—and geography, made up of seas of treacle and seas of butter? . . . What we spend on the Arabic and Sanskrit colleges is not merely a dead loss to the cause of truth; it is bounty money paid to raise up champions of error.

This new advocate, welcomed with acclaim by a few modernist Hindus facing the condemnation of their community, finally cast the expenditures of public educational monies from oriental into western channels. Departments of Public Instruction were now set up in

[3] *A Biographical Sketch of David Hare,* Peary Chand Mittra, Calcutta, 1877, Raja Ram Mohan Roy's Letter to Lord Amherst.
[4] *Minute on Education,* T. B. Macaulay, Feb. 2, 1835.

each province and practical steps taken to stimulate private effort in the establishment of schools and colleges.

All this was done with a definitely stated object—to give into the hands of the peoples the key to health and prosperity and social advance, and to rouse them to "the development of the vast resources of their country, . . . and gradually, but certainly, confer upon them all the advantages which accompany the healthy increase of wealth and commerce." [5]

It should not, however, be understood either that Government now discouraged oriental learning as such or that it excluded the vernacular. On the contrary, it insisted on the proper teaching of the vernacular in all schools, looking forward to the day when that vehicle should achieve a development sufficient to convey the ideas of modern science.[6] Meantime, it chose to teach in English rather than in either of the two classic Indian languages, for the reasons that any one of the three would have to be learned as a new language by all save the most exceptional students, and that the necessary books did not exist in either eastern tongue.

Centers of teaching now gradually multiplied. In the thirty years following 1857, five universities were established—in Calcutta, Bombay, Madras, Lahore, and Allahabad. Aside from literacy courses, instruction in

[5] Despatch of Sir Charles Wood, 1854.
[6] See *Calcutta University Commission Report*, Vol. I, Chapter III; and Vol. II, Chapter XVIII; also *The Educational Despatch of 1854.*

practical, non-literary branches was urged upon the attention of all minded to learn.

But the difficulty then as now was that commerce, scientific agriculture, forestry, engineering, teaching, none of these avenues for service smiled to Indian ambition. India as a national entity was ever an unknown concept to the Indian. And thought for the country at large holds little or no part in native ethical equipment.

This last-named fact, damaging as it is from our viewpoint, should be thoughtfully taken as a fact and not as an accusation. It is the logical fruit of the honestly held doctrines of fate and transmigration and of the consequent egocentric attitude.

For present purposes, the history of modern India's educational progress may be passed over, to reach statistics of today.

In 1923-4 thirteen universities of British India put forth a total of 11,222 graduates. Of these, 7,822 took their degrees in arts and sciences, 2,046 in law, 446 in medicine, 140 in engineering, 546 in education, 136 in commerce, and 86 in agriculture. At the same time, the universities showed an enrollment of 68,530 undergraduates, not dissimilarly apportioned.[7] The high figures consistently stand opposite the arts and law courses, while such vital subjects as agriculture, hygiene and sanitation, surgery, obstetrics, veterinary science and commerce, under whatever aegis offered, still attract few disciples.

For example, the agricultural school maintained by

[7] *Statistical Abstract for British India,* 1914-15 to 1923-24, p. 279.

the American Presbyterian Mission near Allahabad, although equipped to receive two hundred scholars, had in 1926 only fifty men in residence.

"We don't care to be coolies," the majority say, turning away in disgust when they find that the study of agriculture demands familiarity with soil and crops.

"If," says the director, "we could guarantee our graduates a Government office, we should be crowded."

I heard of few technical schools, anywhere in India, that are pressed for room.

The representative Indian desires a university Arts degree, yet not for learning's sake,[8] but solely as a means to public office. To attain this vantage-ground he will grind cruelly hard, driven by the whip and spur of his own and his family's ambition, and will often finally wreck the poor little body that he and his forebears have already so mercilessly maltreated.

Previous chapters have indicated the nature of this maltreatment. One of its consequences is to be seen in the sudden mental drooping and failure—the "fading," as it has come to be called, that so frequently develops in the brilliant Indian student shortly after his university years.

Meantime, if, when he stands panting and exhausted, degree in hand, his chosen reward is not forthcoming, the whole family's disappointment is bitter, their sense of injury and injustice great.

[8] Cf. Mr. Thyagarajaiyer (Indian), Census Superintendent of Mysore, *Census of India,* Vol. I, p. 182: "The pursuit of letters purely as a means for intellectual growth is mostly a figment of the theorists."

Then it is that the young man's poverty of alternatives stands most in his light and in that of Mother India. A land rich in opportunities for usefulness pleads for the service of his brain and his hands, but tradition and "pride" make him blind, deaf and callous to the call.

As Sir Gooroo Dass Banerjee mildly states it: [9]

The caste system . . . has created in the higher castes a prejudice against agricultural, technological, and even commercial pursuits.

The university graduate in these latter days may not be a high-caste man. But if he is not, all the more is he hungry to assume high-caste customs, since education's dearest prize is its promise of increased *izzat*—prestige. Whatever their birth, men disappointed of office are therefore apt flatly to refuse to turn their energies in other directions where their superior knowledge and training would make them infinitely useful to their less favored brothers. Rather than take employment which they consider below their newly acquired dignity, they will sponge forever, idle and unashamed, on the family to which they belong.

"I am a Bachelor of Arts," said a typical youth, simply; "I have not been able to secure a suitable post since my graduation two years ago, so my brother is supporting me. He, having no B.A., can afford to work for one-third the wages that my position compels me to expect."

[9] *Calcutta University Commission Report,* Vol. III, p. 161.

[185]

Nor had the speaker the faintest suspicion that he might be presenting himself in an unflattering light. Even the attempt to capture a degree is held to confer distinction. A man may and does write after his name, "B.A. Plucked" or "B.A. Failed," without exciting the mirth of his public.[10]

A second case among those that came to my personal attention was that of a young university graduate, disappointed of Government employment, who petitioned an American business man for relief.

"Why do you fellows always persist in pushing in where you're not needed, and then being affronted and outraged because there's no room?" asked the American, with American bluntness. "How can you possibly all be Government clerks? Why on earth don't any of you ever go home to your villages, teach school, or farm, or do sanitation and give the poor old home town a lift, out of what you've got? Couldn't you make a living there all right, while you did a job of work?"

"Doubtless," replied the Indian, patiently. "But you forget. That is beneath my dignity now. I am a B.A. Therefore, if you will not help me, I shall commit suicide."

And he did.

Lord Macaulay, over ninety years ago, observed the same phenomenon in the attitude of the Indian edu-

[10] The terms are actually used in common parlance as if in themselves a title, like M.A. or Ph.D.—as: "The school . . . is now under an enthusiastic B.A. plucked teacher." *Fifteenth Annual Report of the Society for the Improvement of the Backward Classes. Bengal & Assam,* Calcutta, 1925, p. 12.

cated at Government expense. Regarding a petition presented to his committee by a body of ex-students of the Sanskrit College, he says: [11]

The petitioners stated that they had studied in the college ten or twelve years; that they had made themselves acquainted with Hindoo literature and science; that they had received certificates of proficiency; and what is the fruit of all this! . . . "We have but little prospect of bettering our condition . . . the indifference with which we are generally looked upon by our countrymen leaving no hope of encouragement and assistance from them." They therefore beg that they may be recommended . . . for places under the Government, not places of high dignity or emolument, but such as may just enable them to exist. "We want means," they say, "for a decent living, and for our progressive improvement, which, however, we cannot obtain without the assistance of Government, by whom we have been educated and maintained from childhood." They conclude by representing, very pathetically, that they are sure that it was never the intention of Government, after behaving so liberally to them during their education, to abandon them to destitution and neglect.

The petition amounts to a demand for redress brought against a Government that has inflicted upon them the injury of a liberal education. "And," comments Macaulay:

I doubt not that they are in the right . . . [for] surely we might, with advantage, have saved the cost of making these persons useless and miserable; surely, men may be

11 *Minute on Education,* Feb. 2, 1835.

[187]

brought up to be burdens to the public . . . at a somewhat smaller charge to the State.

Sanskrit scholars of a century ago or B.A.'s of today, whether plucked or feathered, the principle remains the same, though the spirit has mounted from mild complaint to bitterness.

All over India, among politicians and intelligentsia, Government is hotly assailed for its failure to provide offices for the yearly output of university graduates. With rancor and seeming conviction, Indian gentlemen of the highest political leadership hurl charges from this ground.

"Government," they repeat, "sustains the university. Government is responsible for its existence. What does it mean by accepting our fees for educating us and then not giving us the only thing we want education for? Cursed be the Government! Come, let us drive it out and make places for ourselves and our friends."

Nor is there anywhere that saving humor of public opinion whose Homeric laugh would greet the American lad, just out of Yale or Harvard or Leland Stanford, who should present his shining sheepskin as a draft on the Treasury Department, and who should tragically refuse any form of work save anti-government agitation if the draft were not promptly cashed.

Chapter XIV

WE BOTH MEANT WELL

Between the years 1918 and 1920, compulsory education laws for primary grades were, indeed, enacted in the seven major provinces of India. This was largely the effect of an Indian political opinion which saw, in principle, at least, the need of a literate electorate in a future democracy.

The laws, however, although operative in some few localities, are permissive in character and have since remained largely inactive [1]—a result partly due to the fact that the period of their passage was the period of the "Reforms." "Dyarchy" came in, with its increased Indianization of Government. Education itself, as a function of Government, became a "transferred subject" passing into the hands of Indian provincial ministers responsible to elected legislative councils. The responsibility, and with it the unpopularity to be incurred by enforcement of unpopular measures, had

[1] For example: "The Bengal Legislature . . . passed an Act introducing the principle of compulsory primary education in May, 1919; but it does not appear that a single local authority in the province has availed itself of the option for which the Act provides"—"Primary Education in Bengal," London *Times,* Educational Supplement, Nov. 13, 1926, p. 484.

A recent official report prepared by Mr. Govindbhai H. Desai, Naib Dewan of Baroda, by order of the reigning prince, shows that although that state has had compulsory education for twenty years, its proportion of literacy is less than that of the adjoining British districts where education began much earlier than in Baroda, but where compulsion scarcely exists.

now changed sides. The Indian ministers, the Indian municipal boards, found it less easy to shoulder the burden than it had been to blame their predecessors in burden-bearing. No elected officer, anywhere, wanted either to sponsor the running up of budgets or to dragoon the children of a resentful public into schools undesired.

Compulsory education, moreover, should mean free education. To build schools and to employ teachers enough to care for all the children in the land without charge would mean money galore—which must be taxed out of the people.

In one province—the Punjab—the Hindu element in the Legislature tried to meet one aspect of the crux by saddling the compelling act with a by-law exempting from school attendance all "Untouchables," otherwise known as "depressed classes." This idea, pleasant as it was for the élite, withered in the hands of unsympathetic British authority. As with the Maharajas,[2] so at the other end of the social scale, it would sanction no class monopoly of public education.

Thus Government spoke. But negative weapons, ever India's most effective arms, remained unblunted. How two Punjab cities used them is revealed as follows:[3]

The percentage of boys of compulsory age at school has risen with the introduction of compulsion in Multan from

[2] See *ante*, p. 137.
[3] *Progress of Education in India*, Eighth Quinquennial Review, Vol. I, p. 108.

27 to 54 and in Lahore from 50 to 62. Since no provision has been made at either place for the education of the children belonging to the depressed classes and no proceedings have yet been taken against any defaulting parent, it is improbable that a much higher percentage of attendance can be expected in the near future.

Showing that there are more ways than one to keep the under-dog in his kennel!

In all British India, the total number of primary schools, whether for boys or girls, was, by latest official report,[4] 168,013. Their pupils numbered approximately 7,000,000. But there are in British India about thirty-six and a half million children of primary school age,[5] 90 per cent. of whom are scattered in groups averaging in school attendance forty children each.[6] The education of these children presents all the difficulties that beset education of difficult folk in other difficult countries, plus many that are peculiar to India alone, while offsetting advantages are mainly conspicuous by their absence.[7]

We of America have prided ourselves upon our own educational efforts for the Philippines, and in India that performance is frequently cited with wistful respect. Parallels of comparison may therefore be of interest.

We recall that in the Philippines our educational work has been seriously burdened by the fact that the

[4] *Statistical Abstract for British India, 1914-15 to 1923-24,* p. 263.
[5] *Ibid.,* p. 24.
[6] *Progress of Education in India 1917-22,* Vol. II, p. 119.
[7] Cf. *Village Education in India,* pp. 176-7.

islanders speak eighty-seven dialects [8] and have no common tongue. Against this, set the two hundred and twenty-two vernaculars spoken in India,[9] with no common tongue.

In the Philippines, again, no alphabet or script aside from our own is used by the natives. In India fifty different scripts are employed, having anywhere from two hundred to five hundred characters each; and these are so diverse as to perplex or defeat understanding between dialects.

In the Philippines and in India alike, little or no current literature exists available or of interest to the masses, while in both countries many dialects have no literature at all. In the Philippines and in India alike, therefore, lack of home use of the shallow-rooted knowledge gained in the school produces much loss of literacy—much wastage of cost and effort.

In the Philippines, no social bars exist—no caste distinctions except the distinction between *cacique* and *tao*—rich man and poor man—exploiter and exploited. In India something like three thousand castes [10] split into mutually repellent groups the Hindu three-quarters of the population.

In the Philippines, whatever may be said of the quality of the native teachers, especially as instructors in English, their good will suffices to carry them, both men and women, from the training schools into little

[8] *Population of the Philippine Islands in 1916,* H. Otley Beyer, Manila, 1917, pp. 19-20.
[9] *Census of India, 1921,* Vol. I, Part I, p. 193.
[10] *Oxford History of India,* p. 37.

and remote villages and to keep them there, for two or three years at least, delving on their job. In India, on the contrary, no educated man wants to serve in the villages. The villages, therefore, are starved for teachers.

In the Philippines the native population hungers and thirsts after education and is ready to go all lengths to acquire it, while rich Filipinos often give handsomely out of their private means to secure schools for their own localities. In India, on the contrary, the attitude of the masses toward education for boys is apathy. Toward education for girls it is nearer antagonism, with a general unwillingness on the part of masses and classes alike to pay any educational cost.

The British Administration in India has without doubt made serious mistakes in its educational policies. As to the nature of these mistakes, much may be learned by reading the Monroe Survey Board's report [11] on education in the Philippine Islands. The policies most frequently decried as British errors in India are the very policies that we ourselves, and for identical reasons, adopted and pursued in our attempt to educate our Filipino charges. Nothing is easier than to criticize from results backward, though even from that vantage-point conclusions vary.

Queen Victoria, in 1858, on the assumption by the Crown of the direct Government of India, proclaimed the royal will that: [12]

[11] *A Survey of the Educational System of the Philippines,* Manila Bureau of Printing, 1925.
[12] Foreshadowed in Lord Hardinge's Resolution of 1844

So far as may be, our subjects, of whatever race or creed, be freely and impartially admitted to office in our service, the duties of which they may be qualified by their education, ability, and integrity duly to discharge.

Similarly President McKinley, in his instructions to the Hon. William H. Taft, as President of the first Philippines Commission, laid down that: [13]

The natives of the islands . . . shall be afforded the opportunity to manage their own local affairs to the fullest extent of which they are capable, and . . . which a careful study of their capacities and observation of the workings of native control show to be consistent with the maintenance of law, order, and loyalty.

On both congeries of peoples the effect of these pronouncements was identical. Their small existing intelligentsia, ardently desiring office, desired, therefore, that type of education which prepares for office-holding.

Britain, as we have seen, began with another idea—that of developing Indian education on native lines. But under Indian pressure she soon abandoned her first policy; [14] the more readily because, counting without the Indian's egocentric mentality, she believed that by educating the minds and pushing forward the men already most cultivated she would induce a process of "infiltration," whereby, through sympathetic native

[13] Letter from the Secretary of War, Washington, April 7, 1900.
[14] *The Heart of Aryavarta,* the Earl of Ronaldshay, London, 1925, Chapters II and III.

[194]

channels, learning converted into suitable forms would rapidly seep down through the masses.

America, on her side, fell at once to training Filipino youths to assume those duties that President McKinley had indicated. At the same time, we poured into the empty minds of our young Asiatics the history and literature of our own people, forgetting, in our ingenuous altruism, the confusion that must result.

Oblivious of the thousand years of laborious nation-building that linked Patrick Henry to the Witenagemot, drunk with the new vocabulary whose rhythm and thunder they loved to roll upon their nimble tongues, but whose contents they had no key to guess, America's new charges at one wild leap cleared the ages and perched triumphant at Patrick Henry's side: "Give us liberty or give us death!"

"Self-government is not a thing that can be 'given' to any people. . . . No people can be 'given' the self-control of maturity," said President Wilson,[15] commenting on the situation so evoked. But such language found no lodgment in brains without background of racial experience. For words are built of the life-history of peoples.

And between the Filipino who had no history, and the Hindu, whose creative historic period, as we shall see, is effectively as unrelated to him as the period of Pericles is unrelated to the modern New York Greek,

[15] *Constitutional Government in the United States,* Woodrow Wilson, New York, 1908, pp. 52-3.

there was little to choose, in point of power to grasp the spirit of democracy.

Schools and universities, in the Philippines and in India, have continued to pour the phrases of western political-social history into Asiatic minds. Asiatic memories have caught and held the phrases, supplying strange meanings from their alien inheritance. The result in each case has been identical. "All the teaching we have received . . . has made us clerks or platform orators," said Mr. Gandhi.[16]

But Mr. Gandhi's view sweeps further still:[17]

The ordinary meaning of education is a knowledge of letters. To teach boys reading, writing and arithmetic is called primary education. A peasant earns his bread honestly. He has ordinary knowledge of the world. He knows fairly well how he should behave towards his parents, his wife, his children and his fellow villagers. He understands and observes the rules of morality. But he cannot write his own name. What do you propose to do by giving him a knowledge of letters? Will you add an inch to his happiness? . . .

It now follows that it is not necessary to make this education compulsory. Our ancient school system is enough. . . . We consider your [modern] schools to be useless.

On such views as this, the Swarajist leader Lala Lajpat Rai makes caustic comment:[18]

[16] Statement to the author, Ahmedabad, March, 1926.
[17] *Indian Home Rule*, M. K. Gandhi, Ganesh & Co., Madras, 1924, pp. 97-8, 100, 113.
[18] *The Problem of National Education in India*, George Allen and Unwin, London, 1920, pp. 79-80.

There are some good people in India who do, now and then, talk of the desirability of their country leading a retired, isolated, and self-contained life. They pine for good old days and wish them to come back. They sell books which contain this kind of nonsense. They write poems and songs full of soft sentimentality. I do not know whether they are idiots or traitors. I must warn my countrymen most solemnly and earnestly to beware of them and of that kind of literature. . . . The country must be brought up to the level of the most modern countries . . . in thought and life.

But whose shoulder is being put to the wheel in the enormous task of bringing 92 per cent. of the populace of British India—222,000,000 Indian villagers—"up to the level of the most modern countries," even in the one detail of literacy? Who is going to do the heavy a-b-c work of creating an Indian electorate on whose intelligence the work of a responsible government can be based?

A little while ago a certain American Mission Board, being well replenished in means from home and about to embark on a new period of work, convened a number of such Indian gentlemen as were strongest in citizenship and asked their advice as to future efforts. The Indian gentlemen, having consulted together, proposed that all higher education (which is city work), and also the administration of all funds, be at once turned over to them, the Indians.

"Does that, then, mean that you see no more use for Americans in India?"

[197]

"By no means! You Americans, of course, will look after the villages."

"To you, perhaps, it sounds dubious," said a British Civil Servant of thirty years' experience, to whom I submitted my doubts, "but we who have spent our lives in the work know that the answer is this: We must just plod along, giving the people more and yet more education, as fast as we can get them to take it, until education becomes too general to arrogate to itself, as it does today, a distinction by rights due only to ability and character."

Chapter XV

"WHY IS LIGHT DENIED?"

The illiteracy of India is sometimes attributed to her poverty—a theory as elusive as the famous priority dispute between the hen and the egg. But Indian political critics are wont to charge the high illiteracy rate to the inefficiency, even to the deliberate purpose, of the sovereign power. Thus, Lala Lajpat Rai, the Swaraj political leader, refers to the Viceregal Government as having "so far refused even elementary instruction in the three R's to our masses." [1] And Mr. Mahomed Ali Jinnah [2] accusingly asks, "Why is light denied?"

But, before subscribing to the views of either of these legislative leaders, before accepting either India's poverty or Britain's greed as determining the people's darkness, it may be well to remember the two points recently examined, and to record a third.

First, of British India's population of two hundred

---

[1] In 1923-24, India's total expenditure of public funds on education, including municipal, local, Provincial and Central Government contributions, reached 19.9 crores of rupees, or $66,333,300. This sum is much too small for the work to be done. Nevertheless, when taken in relation to the total revenue of British India it compares not unfavorably with the educational allotments of other countries. See *India in 1924-25,* p. 278; and *Statistical Abstract for British India,* p. 262.

[2] Leader of the Nationalist party in the Legislature of 1925-26.

and forty-seven million persons, about 50 per cent. are women. The people of India, as has been shown, have steadfastly opposed the education of women. And the combined efforts of the British Government, the few other-minded Indians, and the Christian missions, have thus far succeeded in conferring literacy upon less than 2 per cent. of the womankind. Performing the arithmetical calculation herein suggested, one arrives at an approximate figure of 121,000,000, representing British India's illiterate women.

Secondly, reckoned in with the population of British India [3] are sixty million human beings called "Untouchables." To the education of this element the great Hindu majority has ever been and still is strongly, actively and effectively opposed. Subtracting from the Untouchables' total their female half, as having already been dealt with in the comprehensive figure, and assuming, in the absence of authoritative figures, 5 per cent. of literacy among its males, we arrive at another 28,500,000, representing another lot of Indians condemned to illiteracy by direct action of the majority will.

Now, neither with the inhibition of the women nor with the inhibition of the Untouchables has poverty anything whatever to do. As to the action of Government, it has displayed from the first, both as to women and as to outcastes, a steadfast effort in behalf of the inhibited against the dictum of their own people.

Expressed in figures, the fact becomes clearer:

[3] *Census of India 1921*, Vol. I, Part I, p. 225.

Illiterate female population of
    British India 121,000,000
Illiterate male Untouchables . . 28,500,000
                                    —————————

                                     149,500,000
Total population of British
    India 247,000,000
Percentage of the population of
    British India kept illiterate
    by the deliberate will of the
    orthodox Hindu 60.53%

Apart from these two factors appears, however, a third of significance as great, to appreciate whose weight one must keep in mind that the total population of British India is 90 per cent. rural—village folk.

As long, therefore, as the villages remain untaught, the all-India percentage of literacy, no matter what else happens, must continue practically where it is today—hugging the world's low-record line.

But to give primary education to one-eighth of the human race, scattered over an area of 1,094,300 square miles, in five hundred thousand little villages, obviously demands an army of teachers.

Now, consider the problem of recruiting that army when no native women are available for the job. For the village school ma'am, in the India of today, does not and cannot exist.

Consider the effect on our own task of educating the children of rural America, from Canada to the Gulf, from the Atlantic to California, if we were totally debarred from the aid of our legions of women and girls.

No occidental country has ever faced the attempt to educate its masses under this back-breaking condition. The richest nation in the world would stand aghast at the thought.

As for the reason why India's women cannot teach India's children, that may be re-stated in few words. Indian women of child-bearing age cannot safely venture, without special protection, within reach of Indian men.

It would thus appear clear that if Indian self-government were established tomorrow, and if wealth tomorrow rushed in, succeeding poverty in the land, India, unless she reversed her own views as to her "Untouchables" and as to her women, must still continue in the front line of the earth's illiterates.

As to the statement just made concerning women's unavailability as teachers in village schools, I have taken it down, just as it stands, in the United Provinces, over the Punjab, in Bengal and Bombay Presidencies, and across Madras, from the lips of Hindu and Muhammadan officials and educators, from Christian Indian educators and clergy, from American and other Mission heads, and from responsible British administrators, educational, medical, and police. So far as I know, it is nowhere on official record, nor has it been made the subject of important mention in the legislatures. It is one of those things that, to an Indian, is a natural matter of course. And the white man administering India has deliberately adopted the policy of keeping silence on such points—of avoiding surface irritations, while he delves at the roots of the job.

"I should not have thought of telling you about it," said an Indian gentleman of high position, a strong nationalist, a life-long social reformer. "It is so apparent to us that we give it no thought. Our attitude toward women does not permit a woman of character and of marriageable age to leave the protection of her family. Those who have ventured to go out to the villages to teach—and they are usually Christians—lead a hard life, until or unless they submit to the incessant importunities of their male superiors; and their whole career, success and comfort are determined by the manner in which they receive such importunities. The same would apply to women nurses. An appeal to departmental chiefs, since those also are now Indians, would, as a rule, merely transfer the seat of trouble. The fact is, we Indians do not credit the possibility of free and honest women. To us it is against nature. The two terms cancel each other."

The Calcutta University Commission, made up, as will be recalled, of British, Muhammadan, and Hindu professional men, the latter distinguished representatives of their respective communities, expressed the point as follows: [4]

The fact has to be faced that until Bengali men generally learn the rudiments of respect and chivalry toward women

[4] *Report,* Vol. II, Part I, p. 9.

who are not living in *zenanas*, anything like a service of women teachers will be impossible.

If the localizing adjective "Bengali" were withdrawn, the Commission's statement would, it seems, as fairly apply to all India. Mason Olcott [5] is referring to the whole field when he says:

On account of social obstacles and dangers, it is practically impossible for women to teach in the villages, unless they are accompanied by their husbands.

Treating of the "almost desperate condition" of mass education in rural parts, for lack of women teachers, the late Director of Public Instruction of the Central Provinces says: [6]

The general conditions of *mofussil* [rural] life and the Indian attitude toward professional unmarried women are such that life for such as are available is usually intolerable.

"No Indian girl can go alone to teach in rural districts. If she does, she is ruined," the head of a large American Mission college in northern India affirmed. The speaker was a widely experienced woman of the world, characterized by as matter-of-fact a freedom from ignorance as from prejudice. "It is disheartening to know," she went on, "that not one of the young women that you see running about this campus, between classroom and classroom, can be used on the

[5] *Village Schools in India*, p. 196.
[6] *The Education of India*, Arthur Mayhew, London, Faber and Gwyer, 1926, p. 268.

great job of educating India. Not one will go out into the villages to answer the abysmal need of the country. Not one dare risk what awaits her there, for it is no risk, but a certainty. And yet these people cry out to be given *self*-government!" [7]

"Unless women teachers in the *mofussil* are provided with protected residences, and enabled to have elderly and near relatives living with them, it is more than useless, it is almost cruel, to encourage women to become teachers," concludes the Calcutta University Commission after its prolonged survey.[8]

And the authors of an inquiry covering British India, one of whom is the Indian head of the Y.M.C.A., Mr. Kanakarayan T. Paul, report: [9]

The social difficulties which so militate against an adequate supply of women teachers are well known, and are immensely serious for the welfare of the country. All the primary school work in the villages is preëminently women's work, and yet the social conditions are such that no single woman can undertake it. . . . The lack of women teachers seems to be all but insuperable, except as the result of a great social change.

That a social stigma should attach to the woman who, under such circumstances, chooses to become a teacher, is perhaps inevitable. One long and closely familiar with Indian conditions writes: [10]

[7] Statement to the author, February, 1926.
[8] *Calcutta University Report,* Vol. II, Part I, p. 9.
[9] *Village Education in India, the Report of a Commission of Inquiry,* Oxford University Press, 1922, p. 98.
[10] *Census of India,* E. A. H. Blunt, C.I.E., O.B.E., I.C.S., 1911, Vol. XV, pp. 260-1.

It is said that there is a feeling that the calling cannot be pursued by modest women. *Prima facie*, it is difficult to see how such a feeling could arise, but the Indian argument to support it would take, probably, some such form as this: "The life's object of woman is marriage; if she is married her household duties prevent her teaching. If she teaches, she can have no household duties or else she neglects them. If she has no household duties she must be unmarried, and the only unmarried women are no better than they should be.[11] If she neglects her household duties, she is . . . no better than she should be.

This argument might seem to leave room for the deployment of a rescue contingent drafted from India's 26,800,000 widows, calling them out of their dismal cloister and into happy constructive work. The possibility of such a move is, indeed, discussed; some efforts are afoot in that direction, and a certain number of widows have been trained. Their usefulness, however, is almost prohibitively handicapped, in the great school-shy orthodox field, by the deep-seated religious conviction that bad luck and the evil eye are the widow's birthright. But, as writes an authority already quoted:[12]

A far more serious objection is the difficulty . . . to safe-

[11] *Census of India,* 1911, Vol. XV, p. 229. "It is safe to say that after the age of seventeen or eighteen no females are unmarried who are not prostitutes or persons suffering from some bodily affliction such as leprosy or blindness; the number of genuine spinsters over twenty is exceedingly small and an old maid is the rarest of phenomena." These age figures are set high in order to include the Muhammadan women and the small Christian and Brahmo Samaj element, all of whom marry later than the Hindu majority.

[12] *The Education of India,* Arthur Mayhew, p. 268.

guard these ladies who take up work outside the family circle. Their employment without offense or lapse seems possible only in mission settlements and schools under close and careful supervision. In a general campaign [widows] can play only an insignificant part.

In other words, the young widow school-teacher would meet in the villages the same temptations from within, the same pressure, exaction of complaisance, and obloquy from without, that await the single girl.

Thus is reached the almost complete ban which today brands teaching as socially degrading, and which, as an Indian writer puts it,[13] "condemns women to be economically dependent upon men, and makes it impossible for them to engage in any profession other than that of a housewife."

The rule has, however, its exceptions. In the year 1922, out of British India's 123,500,000 women, 4,391 were studying in teachers' training schools. But of that 4,391, nearly half—2,050—came from the Indian Christian community,[14] although this body forms but 1.5 per cent. of the total population. And exceedingly few of the few who are trained serve their country's greatest need.

Says a professional educator: [15]

It is notoriously difficult to induce Indian women of good position, other than Christians and Brahmos, to undergo train-

[13] *Reconstructing India,* Sir M. Visvesvaraya, London, P. S. King and Sons, 1920, p. 243.
[14] *Progress of Education in India,* 1917-22, Vol. II, pp. 14-15.
[15] *Quinquennial Review of Education in Eastern Assam and Bengal.*

ing for the teaching profession; and even of those who are trained . . . the majority refuse to go to places when they are wanted.

Now it chanced, in my own case, that I had seen a good deal of Indian village life before opportunity arose to visit the women's training schools. When that opportunity came, I met it, therefore, with rural conditions fresh in mind and with a strong sense of the overwhelming importance of rural needs in any scheme for serving the body politic.

"What are you training for?" I asked the students.

"To be teachers," they generally replied.

"Will you teach in the villages?"

"Oh, no!" as though the question were curiously unintelligent.

"Then who is to teach the village children?"

"Oh—Government must see to that."

"And can Government teach without teachers?"

"We cannot tell. Government should arrange."

They apparently felt neither duty nor impulse urging them to go out among their people. Such sentiments, indeed, would have no history in their mental inheritance; whereas the human instinct of self-protection would subconsciously bar the notion of an independent life from crossing their field of thought.

It would seem, then, taking the several elements of the case into consideration, that utterances such as Mr. Jinnah's and Lala Lajpat Rai's [16] must be classified, at

---

[16] See *ante,* p. 199.

best, as relating to the twig-tips, rather than to the root and trunk, of their "deadly upas tree."

Coming now to the villager himself—the cultivator or the *ryot*, as he is called—one finds him in general but slightly concerned with the village school. Whenever his boy can be useful to him—to watch the cattle, to do odd jobs—he unhesitatingly pulls him out of class, whereby is produced a complete uncertainty in the matter of attendance. Often the *ryot* is too poor to keep his little family alive without the help of the children's labor and of such wages as they can earn. Sickness, too, plays a large part in keeping school-going down—hookworm, malaria, congenital weakness. Or, often, the village astrologer, always a final authority, discovers in the child's horoscope periods inauspicious for school-going. And in any case, the Indian farmer, like the typical farmer of all countries, is skeptically inclined toward innovations. His fathers knew nothing of letters. He knows nothing of letters himself.[17] Therefore who is to tell him that letters are good? Will letters make the boy a better bargainer? A better hand at the plow?

"The school curriculum is not sufficiently practical," say many of the British working to better it. "Show the *ryot* that his boy will be worth more on the land after a good schooling, and he will find means somehow to send the boy to school." And such a writer as the Hindu Sir M. Visvesvaraya does not hesitate to

[17] Adult education, in connection with Government's rural coöperative credit movement, is now doing signal work among the peasant farmers of the Punjab.

accuse Government of deliberately making economic education unattractive in order to keep India dependent.[18] The report of Mr. Kanakarayan T. Paul's committee, based upon its India-wide inspection, gives, however, different testimony, saying: [19]

It is often assumed that the education given in the village school is despised because it is not practical enough. In many cases, however, the parent's objection is just the opposite. He has no desire to have his son taught agriculture, partly because he thinks he knows far more about that than the teacher, but still more because his ambition is that his boy should be a teacher or a clerk. If he finds that such a rise in the scale is improbable, his enthusiasm for education vanishes. Of the mental and spiritual value of education . . . he is ignorant.

"It is not change in the curriculum in this early stage," pursues the authority just quoted, "that is going to affect the efficiency of the school or the length of school attendance, *but the ability and skill of the teaching staff."*

[18] *Reconstructing India,* p. 258.
[19] *Village Education in India,* p. 20.

Chapter XVI

A COUNSEL OF PERFECTION

It was one of the most eminent of living Indians who gave me this elucidation of the attitude of a respected Hindu nobleman toward his own "home town."

"Disease, dirt and ignorance are the characteristics of my country," he said in his perfect English, sitting in his city-house library where his long rows of law-books stand marshaled along the walls. "Take my own village, where for centuries the head of my family has been chief. When I, who am now head, left it seventeen years ago, it contained some eighteen hundred inhabitants. When I revisited it, which I did for the first time a few weeks since, I found that the population had dwindled to fewer than six hundred persons. I was horrified.

"In the school were seventy or eighty boys apparently five or six years old. 'Why are you teaching these little children such advanced subjects?' I asked.

" 'But they are not as young as you think,' the school-teacher replied.

"They were stunted—that is all; stunted for lack of intelligent care, for lack of proper food, and from malaria, which, say what you like about mosquitoes, comes because people are hungry. Such children, such men and women, will be found all over western Bengal. They have no life, no energy.

"My question, therefore, is plain: *What have the British been doing in the last hundred years that my village should be like this?* It is true that they have turned the Punjab from a desert to a garden, that they have given food in abundance to millions there. But what satisfaction is that to me when they let my people sit in a corner and starve? The British say: 'We had to establish peace and order before we could take other matters up'; also, 'this is a vast country, we have to build bridges and roads and irrigation canals.' But surely, surely, they could have done more, and faster. And they let my people starve!"

Now this gentleman's village, whose decadence he so deplored, lies not over four hours by railroad from the city in which he lives. He is understood to be a man of large wealth, and himself informed me that his law practice was highly lucrative, naming an income that would be envied by an eminent lawyer in New York. Yet he, the one great man of his village, had left that village without help, advice, leadership, or even a friendly look-in, for seventeen years, though it lay but a comfortable afternoon's ride away from his home. And when at last he visited it and found its decay, he could see no one to blame but a Government that has 500,000 such villages to care for, and which can but work through human hands and human intelligence.

Also, he entirely neglected to mention, in accounting

for the present depopulation of his birthplace, that a large industrial plant lately erected near it had drawn away a heavy percentage of the villagers by its opportunities of gain.

It would be a graceless requital of courtesy to name the gentleman just quoted. But perhaps I may without offense name another, Sirdar Mohammed Nawaz Khan, lord of twenty-six villages in Attock District, northern Punjab.

This young Muslim went for his early education to the College for Punjab Chiefs, at Lahore, and thence to the Royal Military College at Sandhurst, to earn a commission in the Indian Army. During his stay in England, being from time to time a guest in English country houses, his attention was caught and fixed by the attitude of large English landlords toward their tenants.

Coming as a living illustration of the novel principles of landlord's duties laid down by the English headmaster of his college in Lahore, the thing struck root in his mind and soon possessed him. Dashing young soldier that he made, after eighteen months' service with a Hussar regiment, popular with officers and men, he resigned his commission and returned to his estates. "For I see where my place is now," he said.

There he spends his time, riding from village to village, working out better conditions, better farming methods, better sanitation, anything that will improve the status of his people. Twenty-seven years old and with an annual income of some four lakhs of rupees, he is an enthusiastic dynamo of citizenship, a living force for good, and the sworn ally of the equally enthusiastic and hard-working English Deputy Commissioner.

Curiously enough, he strongly objects to Government's new policy of rapid Indianization of the public services, takes no interest in Swaraj politics, and less than none in criticism of Government's efforts to clean up, educate, and enrich the people. His whole time goes to vigorous coöperation with Government betterment schemes, and to vigorous original effort.

If the good of the people is the object of government, then multiplication of the type of Sirdar Mohammed Nawaz Khan, rather than of the talkers, would produce the strongest argument for more rapid transfer of responsibility into Indian hands.

Meantime, of those who remain in the little towns and hamlets, "the upper classes and castes," says Olcott,[1] "are often not only indifferent to the education of the less fortunate villagers, but are actively opposed to it, since it is likely to interfere with the unquestioning obedience and service that has been offered by the lowest castes through the ages."

"There is in rural India very little public opinion in favour of the education of the common folk," says the Commission of Inquiry, and "the wealthy land-owner or even the well-to-do farmer has by no means discovered yet that it is to his interest to educate the agricultural labourer."[2]

[1] *Village Schools in India,* p. 93.
[2] *Village Education in India,* p. 26.

The village school-teacher is in general some dreary incompetent, be he old or young—a heavy wet blanket slopped down upon a helpless mass of little limp arms and legs and empty, born-tired child noddles. Consequently anything duller than the usual Indian village school this world will hardly produce. Fish-eyed listlessness sits upon its brow, and its veins run flat with boredom.

But I, personally, could find nothing to justify the belief that melancholy, as distinct from the viewpoint produced by the Hindu religion, is a necessary inborn trait of the Indian. The roots of joy certainly live within young and old. A smile, I found, brings forth a ready smile; a joke, a laugh; an object of novelty evokes interest from all ages, in any village gathering; and serious philosophical consideration crowned with ripe speech awaits new thoughts. The villagers are dignified, interesting, enlisting people, commanding affection and regard and well worthy the service that for the last sixty-odd years they have enjoyed—good men's best effort. Without their active and intelligent partnership, no native Government better than an oligarchy can ever exist in India.

But it is only to the Briton that the Indian villager of today can look for steady, sympathetic and practical interest and steady, reliable help in his multitudinous necessities. It is the British Deputy Commissioner, none other, who is "his father and his mother," and upon the mind of that Deputy Commissioner the villagers' troubles and the villagers' interests sit day and night.

In my own experience, it was an outstanding fact that in every one of the scores of villages I visited, from one end of India to the other, I got from the people a friendly, confiding, happy reception. King George and the young god Krishna, looking down from the walls of many a mud cottage, seemed to link the sources of benefit. All attempts to explain myself as an American proving futile, since a white face meant only England to them, an "American" nothing at all—I let it go at that, accepting the welcome that the work of generations had prepared.

Yet there are so few Britons in India—fewer than 200,000 counting every head, man, woman and child —and there are 500,000 British Indian villages!

"Would not your educated and brilliant young men of India," I once asked Mr. Gandhi, "be doing better service to India, if, instead of fighting for political advantage, social place and, in general, the limelight, they were to efface themselves, go to the villages, and give their lives to the people?"

"Ah, yes," Mr. Gandhi replied, "but that is a counsel of perfection."

To four interesting young Indian political leaders in Calcutta, men well considered in the city, I put the same question: "Would not you and all like you best serve your beloved Mother India by the sacrifice to her of your personal and political ambitions—by losing yourselves in your villages, to work there for the people, just as so many British, both men and women, are doing today? In twenty years' time, might not your accomplishment be so great that those political powers you now vainly and angrily demand would fall into your hands simply because you had proved yourselves their fit custodians?"

"Perhaps," said the three. "But talk, also, is work. Talk is now the only work. Nothing else can be done till we push the alien out of India."

"If I were running this country, I'd close every university tomorrow," said the chief executive of a great American business concern, himself an American long resident in India, deeply and sympathetically interested in the Indian. "It was a crime to teach them to be clerks and lawyers and politicians till they'd been taught to raise food."

"After twenty-odd years of experience in India," said an American educator at the head of a large college, "I have come to the conclusion that the whole system here is wrong. These people should have had two generations of primary schools all over the land, before ever they saw a grammar school; two generations of grammar schools before the creation of the first high school; and certainly not before the seventh or eighth generation should a single Indian university have opened its doors."

ALONG THE HIGHWAYS

Above: On the Grand Trunk Road. "Cotton for Japan" near Lahore. (*See* page 244.)

Below: The Deputy Commissioner of Attock objects to raw shoulders. (*See* page 66.)

Photo by M. Moyca Newell

DR. J. F. KENDRICK, OF THE INTERNATIONAL HEALTH
BOARD OF THE ROCKEFELLER FOUNDATION, A MADRAS CITY
MILK-MAN, AND HIS STUFFED CALF.

(*See* page 245.)

PART IV

Interlude

MR. GANDHI

A small stone house, such as would pass unremarked in any small town in America. A wicket gate, a sunbaked garden, a bare and clean room flooded with light from a broadside of windows. In the room, sitting on a floor cushion with his back to a blank wall, a man. To his right two younger men, near a slant-topped desk perhaps eighteen inches high. To his left, a backless wooden bench for the use of western visitors. If there are other objects in the room, one does not see them for interest in the man with his back to the wall.

His head is close-shaven, and such hair as he has is turning gray. His eyes, small and dark, have a look of weariness, almost of renunciation, as of one who, having vainly striven, now withdraws from striving, unconvinced. Yet from time to time, as he talks, his eyes flash. His ears are large and conspicuously protruding. His costume, being merely a loin-cloth, exposes his hairy body, his thin, wiry arms, and his bare, thin, interlaced legs, upon which he sits like Buddha with the soles of his feet turned up. His hands are busy with a little wooden spinning-wheel planted on the ground before him. The right hand twirls the wheel while the left evolves a cotton thread.

" 'What is my message to America?' " he repeated.

in his light, dispassionate, even voice. "My message to America is the hum of this spinning-wheel."

Then he speaks at length, slowly, with pauses. And as he speaks the two young men, his secretaries, lying over their slant-topped desk, write down every word he says.

The wheel hums steadily on. And the thread it spins for America appears and reappears in the pages of this book.

Chapter XVII

THE SIN OF THE SALVATION ARMY

"Why, after so many years of British rule, is India still so poor?" the Indian agitator tirelessly repeats.

If he could but take his eyes from the far horizon and direct them to things under his feet, he would find an answer on every side, crying aloud for honest thought and labor.

For example, the cattle question, by itself alone, might determine India's poverty.

India is being eaten up by its own cattle. And even at that the cattle are starving.

The Live-Stock Census taken over British India in 1919-20 showed a total of 146,055,859 head of bovine cattle. Of these, 50 per cent., at a flattering estimate, are reckoned unprofitable. Because of their uneconomic value, the food they consume, little as it is, is estimated to represent an annual loss to the country of $588,000,000, or over four times more than the total land revenue of British India.[1]

The early Hindu leaders, it is surmised, seeing the importance of the cow to the country, adopted the expedient of deifying her, to save her from and for the people. Accordingly, Hindu India today venerates

[1] See *Proceedings of Board of Agriculture of India, at Bangalore*, Jan. 21, 1924, and following days. Also see *Round Table*, No. 59, June, 1925

the cow as holy. In the Legislative Assembly of 1921, a learned Hindu member phrased the point in a way that, probably, no Hindu would dispute:[2]

Call it prejudice, call it passion, call it the height of re-- ligion, but this is an undoubted fact, that in the Hindu mind nothing is so deep-rooted as the sanctity of the cow.

To kill a cow is one of the worst of sins—a deicide. His Highness, the late Maharaja Scindia of Gwalior, once had the misfortune to commit that sin. He was driving a locomotive engine on the opening run over a railway that he had just built. The cow leaped upon the track. The engine ran her down before the horrified Prince could forestall his fate. "I think," he told a friend, years after, "that I shall never finish paying for that disaster, in penances and purifications, and in gifts to the Brahmans."

Prince or peasant, the cow is his holy mother. She should be present when he dies, that he may hold her tail as he breathes his last. Were it only for this reason, she is often kept inside the house, to be in readiness. When the late Maharaja of Kashmir was close upon his end, the appointed cow, it is said, refused all inducements to mount to his chamber; wherefore it became necessary to carry the Prince to the cow, and with a swiftness that considered the comfort of his soul only.

[2] *Legislative Assembly Debates,* 1921, Rai Bahadur Pandit J. L. Bhargava, Vol. I, Part I, p. 530. See also *Commentaries of the Great Afonso Dalboquerque,* translation of Walter de Gray, London, Hakluyt Society, 1877. Vol. II, p. 78.

Also, the five substances of the cow—milk, clarified butter (*ghee*), curds, dung, and urine, duly set in a row in five little pots, petitioned in prayer for forgiveness and assoilment and then mixed together and swallowed, surpass in potency all other means of purifying soul and body. This combination, known as *panchagavia*, is of grace sufficient to wipe out even the guilt of sin intentionally committed. Says the Abbé Dubois: [3]

Urine is looked upon as the most efficacious for purifying any kind of uncleanness. I have often seen . . . Hindus following the cows to pasture, waiting for the moment when they could collect the precious liquid in vessels of brass, and carrying it away while still warm to their houses. I have also seen them waiting to catch it in the hollow of their hands, drinking some of it and rubbing their faces and heads with the rest. Rubbing it in this way is supposed to wash away all external uncleanness, and drinking it, to cleanse all internal impurity.

Very holy men, adds the Abbé, drink it daily. And orthodox India, in these fundamentals, has changed not a whit since the Abbé's time.

We of the West may reflect at our leisure that to this eventual expedient are we driving our orthodox Hindu acquaintances when, whether in India or in America, we, cow-eaters, insist on taking them in greeting by the hand. One orthodox Prince, at least, observes the precaution, when going into European society, always to wear gloves. But it is told of him that,

[3] *Hindu Manners, Customs and Ceremonies,* p. 43. See also pp. 152, 195 and 529.

at a certain London dinner party, when he had removed his gloves, the lady beside him chanced to observe a ring that he wore.

"What a beautiful stone, your Highness!" she remarked. "May I look at it?"

"Certainly," said he, and, removing the ring from
his finger, laid it by her plate.

The lady, a person of rank, turned the jewel this
way and that, held it up to the light, admired it as it
deserved, and, with thanks, laid it beside the plate of
the owner. The latter then, by a sidewise glance, indicated the ring to his own attendant who stood behind
his chair.

"Wash it," ordered the Prince, and, undisturbed,
resumed his conversation.

This seeming digression from the chapter's original
text may help to make clear the nature of the cow's
hold upon India. And, as you see them of mid-morn-
ings, trooping in hundreds out from the cities and villages on their slow, docile way to jungle pasturage,
you might well fancy they know and are glad of their
place in the people's mind. Bright strings of beads—
blue, coral, red—adorn their necks. And in their eyes
and the eyes of the bullocks, their sons, lies a look of
slumbrous tranquillity.

That tranquil, far-off gaze is, indeed, often remarked and acclaimed by the passing traveler as an outward sign of an inner sense of surrounding love. In
Holland, in England, you may observe an extraordinary tranquillity, peacefulness, friendliness, even in

pastured bulls, which may reasonably be attributed to the gentle handling to which they are accustomed, to good food and much grooming, and to the freedom they enjoy. But in India, after examining facts, one is driven to conclude that the expression in the eyes of the cows is due partly to low vitality, partly to the close quarters with humanity in which they live, and for the rest, simply to the curious cut of the outer corner of the lid, subtly beautiful like an Aubrey Beardsley woman's.

Fifty years ago, the political Indians say, India had pasturage enough for all her cattle. However that may have been, judged by a western definition of "enough," the facts today are otherwise. One of Mr. Gandhi's Indian writers, Mr. Desai, sees the matter in this way: [4]

In ancient times and even during the Musalman period, cattle enjoyed the benefit of common pastures and had also the free run of the forests. The maintenance of the cattle cost their owners practically nothing. But the British Government cast a greedy eye upon this time-honoured property of the cattle, which could not speak for themselves and which had none else to speak on their behalf, and confiscated it, sometimes with an increase in the land-revenue in view, and at other times in order to oblige their friends, such as the missionaries.

This writer then supports his last-quoted phrase by the statement that the Salvation Army was once allowed by Government to take up 560 acres of public

[4] *Young India*, June 3, 1926, V. G. Desai, p. 200.

grazing-ground in Gujarat for farm purposes. He continues:

> The result of this encroachment upon grazing areas has been that at the present day in India the proportion of grazing grounds to the total area is the smallest of all countries. . . . It is not therefore a matter for surprise that our cattle should have rapidly deteriorated under British rule.

And he cites figures for the United States as leading the list of happier peoples whose grazing areas are large.

But unfortunately, in choosing his American statistics, Mr. Desai omits those which carry most value for needy India. We have, it is true, great grazing areas— but we rotate them and protect them from over-grazing—a matter unconceived by the Indian. And even in the section where this area is widest, our semi-arid and arid western range country, we devote three-fifths of our total cultivated ground to raising feed for our cattle. Our cotton belt gives 53 per cent. of its crop area to live-stock feed, as corn, cow-peas, beans, peanuts, against 10 per cent. used to grow food for man; our corn and winter wheat belt uses 75 per cent. of its cultivated land to grow similar forage for its cattle; our corn belt gives 84 per cent. of its crop-land to forage-growing, and only 16 per cent. to man's food; and the North and East devote about 70 per cent. of their crops to fodder. Seven-tenths of our total crop area is devoted to harvested forage. We have 257,000,000 acres in crops for cattle's feed, against 76,000,000 acres in crops for human food, and we have one milking cow to every family of 5.[5]

These are figures that should concern the Indian sincerely interested in the welfare of his great agricultural country, and I confess to placing them here at such length in the hope that they may challenge his eye.

Still pursuing the question of India's cattle, Mr. Gandhi invoked the counsel of an Italian-trained specialist, domiciled in India. From him came the impatient reply of the practical man who sees small beauty in the spared rod where childish folly is wasting precious substance. If the Indian were not so callous, and so unintelligent as to the needs of his cattle—if he were only compelled to rotate crops and to grow fodder as Italians do in circumstances no better than the Indians', his troubles were done, says this witness, continuing: [6]

Rotated crops require no more expenditure of money than stable crops. In Java the Dutch forced paddy rotation on the people a century ago, by the *sjambok* [rhinoceros-hide whip]. The population of Java has increased from 2 million to 30 million during their rule, and the yield of the rice and sugar fields has increased proportionately. The change was brought about not by capital expenditure but by an intelligent government using force. In India there is no question of using the *sjambok*. We wish to convince, not to compel.

[5] *U. S. Department of Agriculture Bulletin No. 895,* "Our Forage Resources," Government Printing Office, 1923, pp. 312-26.
[6] *Young India,* May 13, 1926, Mr. Galletti-di-Cadilhac, "The Cattle Problem," p. 177.

The writer continues: [7]

Where the cow is a valuable possession [as in Italy], she is
tended with care and love, and crops are grown for her and
palaces are built for her. Here [where] she is merely an object
of veneration, she is left to stand and starve in the public
standing- and starving-grounds, which are miscalled grazing-
grounds in India. India should abolish these places of torture
and breeding-grounds of disease and abortion, and every Indian should devote three-fifths or two-thirds of his land to
growing grass and fodder for his cattle.

No one who has seen the public pasturage will be
likely to dispute the accuracy of the last-quoted witness. "Public standing- and starving-grounds" they are,
nor is there the faintest reason, despite the celebrants of
the past, for supposing that they were ever materially
better. Bernier, the French traveler of the Mussalman
period, testifies: [8]

Owing to the great deficiency of pasture land in the Indies,
it is impossible to maintain large numbers of cattle. . . . The
heat is so intense, and the ground so parched, during eight
months of the year, that the beasts of the field, ready to die
of hunger, feed on every kind of filth, like so many swine.

And one's own eyes and common sense, together with
the history of men and forests, are enough to satisfy
one's mind.

Further, the general conditions under which Indian

[7] *Young India*, p. 109.
[8] *Travels in the Mogul Empire*, p. 326.

[230]

animals have lived and propagated might have been specially devised for breeding down to the worst possible type.

Cattle experts know that if a hundred and twenty cows are put without other food on pasturage that will keep alive only one hundred, the twenty that perish will be the twenty best milkers; for the reason that a good milch cow throws her strength to her milk production, leaving herself a diminished maintenance reserve. The Indian practice of selection by starvation, therefore, works the breed downhill, through the survival of the least useful strain. Again, in India the bull runs with the herds, which may number three hundred cows. Though he were of the best, such extravagance must exhaust him. But, on the consistent contrary, he is so far from the best as to be deliberately of the worst that can be found.

When a man needs specially to placate the gods, as upon the death of his father, he may vow a bull to the temple. And, since one bull will do as well as another, he naturally chooses his feeblest, his most misshapen. Or, if he buys the offering, he buys the cheapest and therefore the poorest to be had. The priests accept the animal, which, receiving the temple brand, thereupon becomes holy, goes where he pleases, and serves as sire to a neighborhood herd. Straying together, starving together, young and old, better and worse, the poor creatures mingle and transmit to each other and to their young their manifold flaws and diseases. Half of In-

dia's cattle,[9] if given the food consumed by the worse
half, would produce, it is affirmed, more than India's
present total milk supply.

In eastern Bengal, one of the most fertile countries
of the world, pasturage scarcely exists, the country
being entirely taken up with rice-paddy and jute. They
grow no fodder crops for their cattle and feed a bit of
chopped rice-straw or nothing. In western Bengal,
some districts report the loss of 25 per cent. of the
cultivated crops by depredations of hungry stock. The
country being everywhere without fences or hedges, a
man may easily turn his cows into his sleeping neighbors' crops. The sin is small—the cows are holy as well
as hungry, and the neighbor's distress is both his illu-
sion and his fate.

I have seen the cow driven by starvation so far from
her natural niceness as to become a scavenger of human
excrement. The sight is common.

In certain districts some green fodder is grown, to be
sure, and during the rains and the earlier cold weather
a poor sort of grass exists on the grazing-grounds of all
but the most desert sections. By January, however, the
gray cracked earth is eaten bare, so to remain until the
late spring rains set in—and starvation begins in
earnest.

Mr. Gandhi's correspondent has shown us in the
cow's hunger one of the evil effects of British rule.

[9] Samuel Higginbottom, Director of the Allahabad Agricultural Institute, testimony before the Indian Taxation Enquiry Committee,
1924-25.

And British rule is indeed largely responsible for the present disastrous condition.

Up to the advent of the British in India, raids great and small, thieving, banditry and endless internal broils and warfares kept the country in chronic distress; and a sure butt of every such activity was the cattle of the attacked. Consequently, with a spasmodic regularity whose beneficent effect is more easily appreciated today than can well have been possible at the time, the cattle of any given area were killed off or driven away, the grazing-grounds of that area, such as they were, got an interval of rest, and, for the moment, inbreeding stopped. For new animals had to be slowly accumulated.

Upon this order broke the British with their self-elected commitment, first of all, to stop banditry, warfare and destruction and to establish peace. The task was precisely the same that America set for herself in the Philippines. As we achieved it in the Philippines, so did the British achieve it in India—in a greater interval of time commensurate with the greater area and population to be pacified. About fifty years ago Britain's work in this respect, until then all-absorbing, stood at last almost accomplished. Life and property under her controlling hand had now become as nearly safe as is, perhaps, possible. Epidemics, also, were checked and famine largely forestalled. So that, shielded from enemies that had before kept down their numbers, men and cattle alike multiplied. And men must be fed. Therefore Government leased them

[233]

land [10] in quantity according to their necessities, that they might raise food for themselves and not die.

They have raised food for themselves, but they will not raise food for their mother the cow. So the cow starves. And the fault—is the greed of Britain or of the Salvation Army. [11]

[10] By ancient law all land ownership is vested in Government.

[11] Government has largely entrusted to the Salvation Army, because of its conspicuous success therewith, the reformation of the criminal tribes, nomads, whose first need is domestication in a fixed habitat where they may be trained to earn an honest and sufficient livelihood by agriculture, cattle-raising, and handiwork. For this purpose and to further its excellent work for the Untouchables in general, the Salvation Army has received from Government the use of certain small and scattered tracts of uncultivated land in Gujerat and elsewhere. It is to this step that Mr. Gandhi's organ objects. See *ante, p. 227.* See, further, *Muktifauj,* by Commissioner Booth-Tucker, Salvationist Publishing and Supplies, London.

VILLAGE IN LYALLPUR, PUNJAB

MALAVALI WOODCUTTERS IN THE NILGARI MOUNTAINS

MYSORE

Above: Draught Bullocks of His Highness the Maharajah. The famous *Amritmahal* breed, capable of traveling ten miles an hour.

Below: Nandi, the Great Stone Bull of Siva, on Chamundi Hill.

Chapter XVIII

THE SACRED COW

Turning from the people and the cattle within their gates to Government's experimental work on Government farms, we find one world-contribution. They have solved a main domestic problem of low latitudes—how to get milk for the babies.

Only those who have lived in the tropics are likely to appreciate what this means, in terms of family security, health and happiness. In the Philippines our own hopeful work was nipped in the bud by the Filipinization of the Agricultural Department. From that day, cattle-breeding became a farce, played out in office chairs by vague young men spinning webs of words learned by rote in one or another American college, while a few rough and neglected animals wearied out a beggar's existence in the corral. And so, as far as colonial America is concerned, the old notion still reigned—that the cow can neither be bred nor led to give real milk, in real quantity, in the tropics.

In other words, our work in that field is yet to do.

But the British in India have given us a tremendous lift and encouragement to effort. On the Imperial Dairy Farm at Bangalore their breeding experiments have conclusively proved that, with skill, care and per-

[235]

sistence, a cow can be developed that will stand up against the tropical climate for fifteen lactations and still produce well, doing her duty as a human life-saver. In the Government Military Dairy Farm at Lucknow, I saw "Mongia," a half-bred cow sired by an imported American Friesian on a native dam of the Punjab Hariana stock. Mongia, with her eighth calf, had given 16,000 pounds [1] of milk in a lactation period of 305 days. With her seventh calf she gave 14,800 pounds. "Edna," another of the herd, had reached a production of 15,324 in 305 days. Butter-fat, with these sturdy half-breeds, runs from 4.05 per cent. in full lactation to about 5.05 per cent. during hottest weather, which is beyond even our American home requirements.

Again, these cows' milk production drops scarcely at all in hot weather. Edna began her 1925 lactation in August, starting off at a steady seventy-pound daily yield. Edna and Mongia are, to be sure, admittedly stars; but the average daily production of the Lucknow herd of 105 milking cows of Indo-western crosses was twenty-one pounds per capita, and the work is yet young.

The best milch breed native to India is the Saniwal, of the Punjab, which averages only 3,000 pounds a lactation period, and is too small to be usefully cross-bred with our big western milch stock. But Government within the last ten years have developed on their farm in Pusa a cross-breed of Saniwal with Mont-

[1] 2.15 pounds of milk make a quart.

[236]

gomery, a second Punjabi strain, that has more than doubled the previous Saniwal record, while further interesting experiments, as of crossing native Sindi stock with imported Ayrshires, are in course of development at other Government breeding stations.

The significance of all this may be measured in part by the fact that over 90 per cent. of the cows in India give less than 600 pounds of milk a year, or less than a quart a day.[2]

Government began experiments in the year 1912. Then came the Great War, preventing the bringing of animals from abroad. Directly the war was over, Government imported from America, for the Lucknow farm, two more Friesian bulls, "Segis" and "Elmer." Other experimental stations were similarly supplied, and the work went on.

Enough has now been accomplished to prove that stamina goes with the half-breed, and that, beyond the fifty-fifty point, imported blood weakens the result, creating extra-susceptibility to the many diseases of the country. Every cow over half-blood, therefore, is now bred back to a native bull.

Thus, by selective breeding, by crossing, and by better feeding and housing, slowly and steadily the results of centuries of inbreeding, starvation, infection, and of breeding from the worst are being conquered; definite pedigree types are being fixed; and the foundations of distinct breeds are building.

[2] *The Gospel and the Plow*, London, 1921. Samuel Higginbottom, p. 60.

The trail is opened, the possibilities revealed. When the people of India are ready to accept it, their profit is ready to their hand.

Cattle-lovers, at this point, will be interested in the fact that India demands a dual-purpose cow, but that "dual purpose," in India, signifies, not the combination upon which some of us in America look askance—milk and beef, but—milk and muscle!

The sale of cattle as beef is small; the price of beef in Lucknow in 1926 was two cents a pound. The Indians' use for a cow, aside from her religious contribution earlier described, is to produce, first, milk and butter; second, dung to be used as fuel or to coat the floors and walls of their dwellings; and, third, to produce draft animals for the cart and plow. To breed for milk and for draft might seem a self-canceling proposition. But such is the demand of the country, and the concern of Government is to get on with the job and strike the best possible compromise.

On the Government farms, foreign fodder crops, such as Egyptian clover, have also been introduced; much emphasis is laid on fodder developments; and the use of silage, economically stored in pits, is demonstrated. Men are sent out to deliver illustrated lectures and to install silage pits in the villages. And young pedigreed herd bulls, whether as loans, or as gifts, or to purchase, are offered to the people.

All the fine animals produced at Lucknow, Pusa, Bangalore and the other Government plants, are conscientiously watched over by British breeders. In point of general competence, of cleanliness and order, and of simple practicality, the plants stand inspection. But all such matters are utterly foreign to the minds of the Indian peasant, and for those who might best and quickest teach the peasant—the Indian aristocrat, the Indian intelligentsia—rarely do peasant or cattle carry any appeal.

With the exception of certain princes of Indian states who have learned from England to take pride in their herds, and again with the exception of a mere handful of estate-holders scattered over the country, cattle-breeding is left entirely to a generally illiterate class known as *gvalas,* who lack enterprise, capital and intelligence to carry on the work.

I saw little, anywhere, to suggest a real appreciation of the importance of change and much of opposite import, such, for example, as the spectacle of a fine pedigreed herd bull, lent by Government for the improvement of the cattle of a village and returned a wreck from ill-usage. He was brought into a Government Veterinary Hospital during my visit in the place, and it needed no testimony other than one's eyes to see that he had been starved, cruelly beaten and crippled, while the wounds on one leg, obviously inflicted by blows, were so badly infected that healing seemed scarcely possible.

"What will you do?" I asked the British official in charge.

"Fine the head man of the village, probably. But it does little good. It is a human trait not to appreciate

what one doesn't pay for. And they won't pay for bet
tering their cattle."

Further, to take at random another point, it is difficult to get intelligent selective breeding work out of a
people who, for example, refuse to keep record of the
milk-yield of a cow on the ground that to weigh or to
measure the gift of God is impious. "We will not do
it!" the milkers of the Punjab declare. "If we did,
our children would die."

Meantime, aside from the selection of the worst, by
starvation and by breeding from the worst through
sacred runt bulls, a third force works to remove the
best milch cows from a land whose supply of milk is
already tragically short. Government, at Karnal, has
amply demonstrated the feasibility of producing milk
in the country and transporting it to the city in bulk,
even as far as a thousand miles. And the Calcutta co-
operative dairies have shown the possibilities of local
service from suburb to town. But the Indian milk pur-
veyor in general sees naught in that. His practice is to
buy the best up-country young milch cows he can find,
bring them to the city in calf, keep them during their
current lactation, to prolong which he often removes
their ovaries, and then to sell them to the butcher. This
happens on the grand scale, kills off the best cows, and
thereby constitutes a steady drain on the vital resources
of the country.

The Indian holds that he cannot afford to maintain
an animal in the city during her dry season, and he has
no plan for keeping her elsewhere. Therefore he ex-

terminates her after her lactation; most of the cost of her raising goes to waste, and her virtues die with her.[3]

Government, all over India, have learned to prepare for trouble on the annual Muhammadan feast one of the features of which is the sacrificial killing of cows. Hindu feeling, at that period, rises to the danger pitch, and riots, bloodshed and destruction are always the likely outcome. For is not the embodied Sacrosanctity that lies at the root of Hinduism being done to death by the infidel in the very arms of her adorers?

Given this preliminary reminder, nothing is more characteristic of the Indian mentality than the balancing facts pointed out in Mr. Gandhi's *Young India* of November 5, 1925:

> We forget that a hundred times the number of cows killed for *Kurbani*[4] by the Musalmans are killed for purposes of trade. . . . The cows are almost all owned by Hindus, and the butchers would find their trade gone if the Hindus refused to sell the cows.

Four weeks after the publication of the leading article above quoted, Mr. Gandhi returns to the subject, citing what he describes as "illuminative extracts" from a report of the Indian Industrial Committee sitting in Bengal and the Central Provinces.[5] The hearing is on the commercial slaughter of cows for beef and hides. The investigating committee asks, concern-

---

[3] W. Smith, Imperial Dairy Expert, in *Agricultural Journal of India*, Vol. XVII, Part I, January, 1922.
[4] The annual Muhammadan feast above mentioned.
[5] *Young India*, Nov. 26, 1925, p. 416.

ing the attitude of the surrounding Hindu populace
toward the industry:

> Have these slaughterhouses aroused any local feeling in the
> matter?

The witness replies:

> They have aroused local feelings of greed and not of indig-
> ration. I think you will find that many of the municipal
> members are shareholders in these yards. Brahmans and Hin-
> dus are also found to be shareholders.

"If there is any such thing as a moral government in
the universe, we must answer for it some day," Mr.
Gandhi's commentor helplessly laments.

This example of the selling of the cow by the Hindu
for slaughter—he who will rise in murdering riot if a
Muhammadan, possibly not too averse to the result,
kills a cow outside a Hindu temple door—opens a topic
that should perhaps be examined for other than its face
value.

We of the West are continually in danger of mis-
understanding the Indian through supposing that the
mental picture produced by a given word or idea is the
same in weight and significance to him and to us. His
facility in English helps us to this error. We assume
that his thought is like his tongue. He says, for example, that he venerates all life and is filled with ten-
derness for all animals. Lecturing in America, he speaks
of the Hindu's sensitive refinement in this direction
and of his shrinking from our gross unspirituality, our

Photo by M. Moyca Newell

MOPLAHS

(*See* page 329.)

Photo by M. Moyca Newell

JUNGLE BOYS

In the Wynaad Hills, Madras

incomprehension of the sacred unity of the vital spark.

But if you suppose, from these seemingly plain words, that the average Hindu in India shows what we would call common humaneness toward animal life, you go far astray.

To the highly intelligent Brahman foreman of the Goverment farm at Bangalore, I one day said: "I regret that all over India you torture most bullocks and some cows by the disjointing of their tails. Look at the draft bullocks in that cart over there. Every vertebra in their tails is dislocated. As you are aware, it causes exquisite pain. Often the tail is broken short off."

"Ah, yes," replied the young Brahman, indifferently, "it is perfectly true that we do it. But that, you see, is necessary. The animals would not travel fast enough unless their tail-nerves are wrenched."

You may stand for hours on the busy Howrah Bridge in Calcutta, watching the bullock carts pass, without discovering a dozen animals whose tails are not a zig-zag string of breaks. It is easier, you see, for the driver to walk with the animal's tail in his hand, twisting its joints from time to time, than it is to beat the creature with his stick. If you ride in the bullock cart, however, with the driver riding before you, you will discover that, from this position, he has another way of speeding the gait. With his stick or his long hard toe-nails he periodically prods his animals' genital glands.

And only the alien in the land will protest.

It is one of the puzzles of India that a man whose bullock is his best asset will deliberately overload his

[243]

animal, and then, half starved as it is, will drive it till it drops dead. The steep hillsides of Madras are a Calvary of draft bullocks. One sees them, branded from head to tail, almost raw from brands and blows, forced up-hill until they fall and die. If a British official sees this or any other deed of cruelty, he acts. But the British are few in the land. Yet far fewer are the Indians whose sensibilities are touched by the sufferings of dumb beasts, or whose wrath is aroused by pain and abuse inflicted upon defenseless creatures.

The practice of *phúká* is common in most parts of India. Its object is to increase and prolong the milk production of cows. It is committed in several ways, but usually consists in thrusting a stick on which is bound a bundle of rough straw into the vagina of the cow and twisting it about, to produce irritation. The thing gives intense pain to the cow, and also produces sterility— a matter of indifference to the dairyman, since he will in any case sell her for slaughter when she dries. Mr. Gandhi cites authority [6] that out of ten thousand cows in Calcutta dairy sheds, five thousand are daily subjected to this process.

Mr. Gandhi quotes another authority on the manufacture of a dye esteemed by Indians and known as *peuri*: [7]

By feeding the cow only on mango leaves, with no other form of feed nor even water to drink, the animal passes in the form of urine a dye which is sold at high rates in the

[6] *Young India*, May 6, 1926, pp. 166-7.
[7] *Ibid.*, p. 167.

bazaar. The animal so treated does not last long and dies in agony.

The young milch cow is usually carrying her calf when she is brought to the city. The Hindu dairyman does not want the calf, and his religion forbids him to kill it. So he finds other means to avoid both sin and the costs of keeping. In some sections of the country he will allow it a daily quarter- to half-cup of its mother's milk, because of a religious teaching that he who keeps the calf from the cow will himself suffer in the next life. But the allowance that saves the owner's soul is too small to save the calf who staggers about after its mother on the door-to-door milk route as long as its trembling legs will carry it. When the end comes, the owner skins the little creature, sews the skin together, stuffs it crudely with straw, shoves four sticks up the legs, and, when he goes forth on the morrow driving his cow, carries his handiwork over his shoulder. Then, when he stops at a customer's door to milk, he will plant before the mother the thing that was her calf, to induce her to milk more freely. Or again, in large plants, the new-born calves may be simply tossed upon the morning garbage carts, at the dairy door, and carried away to the dumps where they breathe their last among other broken rubbish.

The water buffalo—the carabao of the Philippines— is in India an immensely useful creature. The best of the Delhi blood give yearly from six to ten thousand pounds of milk carrying from 7.5 to 9 per cent. butter-

fat. The buffalo bull makes a powerful draft animal
for cart and plow. But the species is large, and expen-
sive to raise. Therefore it is usual for milk dealers to
starve their buffalo calves outright. *Young India* [8]
quotes testimonies showing various phases of this practice. One of these draws attention to

> . . . the number of buffalo calves . . . being abandoned to
> die of starvation in public streets, and often when they fall
> down through sheer exhaustion, being mutilated by trams,
> motor-cars and carriages. These animals are generally driven
> out from the cattle stables at night . . . simply to save all
> the milk the mother has, for sale.

Otherwise, the calf is tied to a stake anywhere about
the place and left without food or water till it dies.

The water buffalo, having no sweat-glands, suffers
severely in the hot sun and should never be compelled
to endure it unprotected. Therefore, says another of
Young India's authorities, "one finds that [the starving
buffalo calves] are usually tied in the sunniest part of
the yard. The dairymen appear systematically to use
these methods to kill off the young stock."

And then, turning from city dairymen to country
owners and country regions, Mr. Gandhi gives us this
picture: [9]

> In Gujarat [northern Bombay Presidency], the he-calf is
> simply starved off by withholding milk from him. In other
> parts he is driven away to the forests to become the prey of

---

[8] May 6, 1926, p. 167.
[9] *Young India*, May 6, 1926, p. 167.

wild beasts. In Bengal he is often tied up in the forest and left without food, either to starve or be devoured. And yet the people who do this are those who would not allow an animal to be killed outright even if it were in extreme suffering!

In this, one is reminded of the fate of the villagers' cows, which, when they are too diseased or too old to give further service, are turned out of the village, to stand and starve till they are too weak to defend themselves with heel or horn and then are pulled down and devoured by the starving village dogs.

Surely no Westerner, even the most meteoric tourist, has passed through India without observing those dogs. They haunt every railway platform, skulking along under the car windows. Bad dreams out of purgatory they look, all bones and sores and grisly hollows, their great, undoglike eyes full of terror and furtive cunning, of misery and of hatred. All over the land they exist in hosts, forever multiplying. In the towns they dispute with the cows and goats for a scavenger's living among the stalls and gutters of the bazaars. Devoured with disease and vermin, they often go mad from bites received from mad jackals of the packs that roam even city parts by night.

And, according to the Hindu creed, nothing can be done for them. Their breeding may not be stopped, their number may not be reduced, and since a dog's touch defiles, their wounds and sores and broken bones may not be attended.

In this connection an interesting discussion has recently developed in the pages of *Young India*.[10] The incident that gave it birth was the destruction of sixty mad dogs, collected on the premises of an Ahmedabad mill-owner. The mill-owner himself, though a Hindu, had ordered their killing. This act aroused much ill feeling in the town, and the Hindu Humanitarian League referred the question to Mr. Gandhi, as a religious authority, asking:

> When Hinduism forbids the taking of the life of any living being, . . . do you think it right to kill rabid dogs? . . . Are not the man who actually destroys the dogs, as also the man at whose instance he does so, both sinners? . . . The Ahmedabad Municipality . . . is soon going to have before it a resolution for the castration of stray dogs. Does religion sanction the castration of an animal?

Mr. Gandhi's reply is full of light on Hindu thinking:

> There can be no two opinions on the fact that Hinduism regards killing a living being as sinful. . . . Hinduism has laid down that killing for sacrifice is no *himsa* [violence]. This is only a half-truth. . . . But what is inevitable is not *regarded* as a sin, so much so that the science of daily practice has not only declared the inevitable violence involved in killing for sacrifice as permissible but even regarded it as meritorious. . . . [But the man] who is responsible for the protection of lives under his care and who does not possess the virtues of the recluse [to heal by spirit], but is capable of

[10] October and November, 1926. The issue of November 11, 1926, gives the following figures for cases of hydrophobia treated in the Civil Hospital of the town of Ahmedabad: Jan. to Dec., 1925, 1117; Jan. to Sept., 1926, 990.

destroying a rabid dog, is faced with a conflict of duties. If he kills the dog he commits a sin. If he does not kill it, he commits a graver sin. So he prefers to commit the lesser one. . . . It is therefore a thousand pities that the question of stray dogs, etc., assumes such a monstrous proportion in this sacred land of *ahimsa* [non-violence]. It may be a sin to destroy rabid dogs and such others as are liable to catch rabies. . . . It is a sin, it should be a sin, to feed stray dogs.

In the land of *ahimsa*, the rarest of sins is that of allowing a crumb of food to a starving dog, or, equally, of putting him out of his misery. Mr. Gandhi's approval of the latter step, even as to animals gone mad, has brought down upon him such an avalanche of Hindu protest that he sighs aloud under its burden upon his time.

And since the only remaining resource, castration, lies under religious ban because it interrupts the ordained stages of life, the miseries of the dog, like many another misery of India, revolves in a circle.

Chapter XIX

THE QUALITY OF MERCY

"We will pose as protectors of the cow, and quarrel with Mussalmans in her sacred name, the net result being that her last condition is worse than the first," [1] laments the faithful accuser on Mr. Gandhi's staff, and again:

"In spite of our boasted spirituality, we are still sadly backward in point of humanity and kindness to the lower animals." [2]

Legislation for the prevention of cruelty to animals was enacted in the early years of Crown rule in India. But such legislation, anywhere, must rest for effectiveness on public opinion, and the opinion of Mr. Gandhi's paper is, in this matter, as a voice crying in the wilderness, awakening but the faintest of echoes. If the people feel no compassion; if the police, themselves drawn from the people, privately consider the law a silly, perhaps an irreligious law, whose greatest virtue lies in the chance it gives them to fill their pockets; and if little or no leaven of another sentiment exists in the higher classes, Government's purpose, as far as it means immediate relief, is handicapped indeed.

[1] *Young India,* May 6, 1926, V. G. Desai, p. 167.
[2] *Ibid.,* August 26, 1926, p. 303.

Laws in India for the prevention of cruelty to animals have uniformly originated as Government bills. Whether of the Central or of the Provincial Administrations, measures for the protection of animals from cruelty have been passed over the indifference, if not over the pronounced hostility, of the Indian representation.

Thus, a bill to limit the driving of water buffaloes, heavily laden, through the hottest hours of the day in the midst of the hottest season of the year, was introduced in the Bengal Legislative Council by Government, on March 16, 1926. In the streets of Calcutta the sufferings of buffaloes so driven had long been, to Western susceptibilities, a public scandal. But this proposal for the animals' relief was finally enacted into law despite the resistance of the leading Indian merchants, who saw in it merely a sentimentality inconvenient to their trade.

The practice of *phúká*, the deliberate daily torture of the cow in order that the worth of a few more pennies may be wrung from her pain, has been forbidden and heavily penalized by the Governor-General-in-Council and by successive provincial laws. Mr. Gandhi finds room, in the columns of *Young India*,[3] to print an Englishman's protest against *phúká*. But if any mass of Hindu feeling exists against it, the vitality of that feeling is insufficient to bring it forth into deeds.

In 1926, the Government of Bombay Presidency introduced in the Bombay Legislative Council a meas-

[3] May 13, 1926, p. 174.

ure [4] amending the Police Act of the City of Bombay so that police officers should have power to kill any animal found in such a condition, whether from hurt or from disease, that it would be sheer cruelty to attempt to remove it to a dispensary. In order to safeguard the owner's interests in the matter, the amendment further provided that, if the owner is absent, or if he refuses to consent to the destruction of the suffering animal, the police officer must secure, before he can proceed under the law, a certificate from one of several veterinarians whom the Governor-in-Council should appoint.

No small part of the necessity for a law such as this would arise from the Indians' habit, already described, of turning diseased and dying cows, and calves that he is in process of starving to death, into the streets to wander until they die what he calls "a natural death." As their strength fails, they become less and less able to guide their movements, and, in the end, are often caught and crushed by some vehicle against whose wheels they fall.

The debates evoked by the Bombay Government's proposal of relief throw so much general light on Indian modes of thought that their quotations at some length may be justified. On the introduction of the measure, a Hindu member, Mr. S. S. Dev, came at once to his feet with: [5]

[4] *Bill No. V of 1926,* "A Bill Further to Amend the City of Bombay Police Act, 1902."
[5] *Bombay Legislative Council Debates,* Official Report, 1926, Vol. XVII, Part VII, pp. 579-80.

The principle of the bill is revolting to an Indian mind. . . . If you will not shoot a man in similar circumstances, how can you shoot an animal, in the name of preventing cruelty to animals? . . . Further, the bill, if it becomes law, may in actual operation give rise to fracas in public streets.

Then follows Mr. Pahalajani, of Western Sind. Says he:[6]

This section makes no exception whatever whether the animal is a cow or a horse or a dog. The policeman with the certificate of the veterinary practitioner can destroy any animal. The official [British] members of the Council ought to know —some of them have remained here for over 30 years—that no Hindu would allow a cow to be destroyed in whatsoever condition it is. There are *pinjrapoles* [7] in which the worst diseased animals are nursed and fed. . . . [This measure] proceeds on the assumption that animals have no soul, and they deserve to be shot if they are not in a condition to live. The Hindu idea of soul is quite different from that held by Westerners. . . . A measure of this kind would wound the religious susceptibilities of Hindus.

To this declaration Mr. Montgomerie, Secretary to Government, responds, with a picture from the daily life of the city:[8]

I can hardly think that the honourable member means what he says. Is it a decent sight to see some poor animal disembowelled, legs broken and bleeding, in the streets of Bombay? The only humane thing . . . is to put the beast out of mis-

6 *Ibid.*, 580.
7 Animal asylums, later to be described.
8 *Bombay Legislative Council Debates*, p. 581.

ery. It is inhumanity to allow this animal to suffer and remove it with the probability that it may break to pieces while
being so moved.

But Hindu after Hindu decries the measure, and **on**
grounds of offended sentiment alone, save that one of
their number, Mr. Soman, takes thought that a question of expense is involved. For the bill empowers
Government to appoint a few area veterinarians, to be
locally handy to the police. This charge upon public
funds, Mr. Soman feels, goes beyond any suffering animal's proper claim. As he puts it: [9]

If any generous minded practitioners come forward to help
the police officers, so much the better. But if any new posts
are to be created, which are to be maintained at public expense,
I would like certainly to oppose the bill.

And the debate, for the day, closes on the note of
fate. Says Rao Sahib D. P. Desai, member from
Kaira. [10]

All the trouble arises from having two conflicting ideals of
mercy. The framers of the bill think that shooting an animal
which is diseased and which could not be cured is much better.
We on the other hand think that God himself has ordained
what is to come about.

On the resumption of the reading of the bill, over
three months later,[11] the Honorable Mr. Hotson, Chief

[9] *Bombay Legislative Council Debates,* March 2, 1926, p. 583.
[10] *Ibid.,* p. 585.
[11] July 26, 1926.

Secretary to Government, assumes the labor of trying to win Indian support. He pleads: [12]

The one object of this bill is to make it possible to deal with injured animals which are lying in the street or in any other public place in a state of suffering and pain, for which there is no relief for them. It is open to the owners of such animals to remove them, [or] to have them taken away by other charitable persons to a *pinjrapole* or to any other place where animals are received and cared for. It is only in cases where the animal is neglected in its misery, where, as things are now, the animal has to lie in the public streets of Bombay for many hours, perhaps until death brings relief, that the power . . . will be exercised. That such an animal should be in such a condition in a public place where there are many passers-by in a great city like Bombay . . . causes pain to observers of all classes and it is desirable not only that the animal should be relieved . . . but that the feelings of the passers-by should be saved from the extreme discomfort caused by such sights. That is all that this bill seeks to attain.

But the Hindu position remains unshaken. The old arguments [13] come forward until, presently, they arouse the Honorable Ali Mahomed Khan Dehlavi, Muhammadan, Minister of Agriculture in the Bombay Government. Says he, expressing himself as "rather anxious in the interests of agriculturists": [14]

It was argued at the last session that every animal having a soul should not be destroyed. I have been tackled severely

[12] *Bombay Legislative Council Debates,* Vol. XVIII, Part I, pp. 70-1.
[13] *Ibid.,* pp. 72-3.
[14] *Ibid.,* p. 73.

in this House by honourable members on the opposite benches for not taking sufficient precaution and for not spending sufficient money to kill elephants, [wild] pigs and rats in the interests of agriculturists. And if this is a question of killing a soul, I think an elephant has a bigger soul than a pig, and the latter a bigger soul than a rat. If that principle were applied to the agricultural department, I shall be asked to stop killing the animals I have mentioned. The result will be that the agriculturists in the country will suffer very much. I say, Sir, there is absolutely no difference at all between the case of an animal in the streets of cities like Bombay, or in the jungles or fields in the country outside.

The concern of the Minister of Agriculture for the cultivators, his special charges, again uncovers the usual attitude of the Indian politician toward that body of humanity which constitutes over 72 per cent. of the people of India. Says Rao Sahib D. P. Desai, frankly tossing off their case: [15]

The agriculturists should not be taken as the whole of Indian society. . . . But even if the agriculturist thinks that it is desirable that any animals that are dangerous to agriculture should be destroyed, it should not be taken that the whole Hindu society agrees with that view of the agriculturists, and I think that no weight should be given such views in this House.

Out of the remainder of the day's debate emerge much sterile criticism and accusation of Government's effort and no fresh thought excepting that of the old

[15] *Bombay Legislative Council Debates*, p. 76.

[256]

Muhammadan member from the Central Division, Moulvi Rafiuddin Ahmad, who counsels, Nestor-wise: [16]

It is not the intention in the remotest degree of the Government to injure the susceptibilities of any classes of His Majesty's subjects in India. . . . If [anything] can be done by any other means than by the provisions of this bill, I think Government will be only too pleased to adopt them, and as far as I know—and I have been in this house long enough—there has never been any question of sentiment which Government have not taken into consideration, and I do admire them for that. . . . In this House Hindus and Muhammadans have joined to oppose Government if in any remote degree they thought that Government were mistaken and on many occasions Government have conceded. . . . It is no use coming here with empty heads, there must be some suggestions offered, it is easy to criticise, but it is at the same time our duty also to suggest better measures. I appeal to all those persons that have .aised objections. . . . Government is quite open to reason.

"Are you authorized to speak on behalf of Government?" a Hindu hotly interrupts.

"I am authorized to speak on behalf of every person with whom this Council is concerned. I do say this, this objection is altogether unreasonable," the other returns.

But his appeal wins no response. On the contrary, a Hindu member grimly suggests that if by chance a Muhammadan were to be appointed veterinary and

[16] *Ibid.*, pp. 77-8.

were to approve the killing of a sick cow, the peace of the city as between Hindus and Muhammadans would go up in smoke.

And the discussion ends by the referring of the bill to a select committee of the House, composed of nine Indians—Hindu, Muhammadan, and Parsi, and of two Britons.

In the second reading of this bill,[17] we find the Chief Secretary of Government, Mr. Hotson, presenting the select committee's report with the comment that the committee "has gone so far in the desire to avoid giving offense to any of our brethren" that the usefulness of the bill has been impaired—a mild and diplomatic phrasing of the emasculation that has taken place.

Cows and bulls are now excepted from the proposed law, and temple precincts are put beyond its reach; anything may happen there. Yet, without a single constructive proposal of any sort, the Hindu opposition keeps up. Members urge that legislation be delayed if not abandoned, that Government are indiscreet in urging any action; that "the agonies of the animals" are not so great that sympathy need pass the point of theory; that, in any event, Hindu policemen should be exempt from the duty of shooting animals, since to do so is contrary to their religion; that to avoid invidious distinctions Muhammadan officers may likewise claim exemption; that, because Indian officers bungle with firearms, British police sergeants "whose marksmanship is

[17] August 5, 1926.

perfect" be charged with the duty. Says Mr. Surve, Hindu member from Bombay City, advocating the last suggestion:

"To kill a disabled animal which is just about to die, that kind of butchery we are incapable of . . . that is not our chivalry." [18]

So failed, for this time at least, Government's attempt to defend the cow from her worshipers. With its intended chief beneficiary left out, the bill passed. Yet, Government's argument, so patiently and courteously pursued, did, as it continued, educe a certain amount of Indian support. And in view of the fact that the principle involved is a complete exotic in minds committed to the expiatory journey of the soul, each bit of ground so gained speaks of reward, however distant.

It was in 1890 that the Governor-General-in-Council passed the Act for the Prevention of Cruelty to Animals, of which Act the fifth section prohibited the killing of any animal in an unnecessarily cruel manner. In 1917 it was found necessary to clarify the intentions of Section V, expressly directing it upon persons cruelly killing a goat, or having in their possession the skin of a goat so killed. Provincial Governments have enacted the same laws. And yet the offense against which these measures are aimed continues in the land.

It is the skinning of goats alive.

The skin stripped from a living goat can be stretched

[18] *Bombay Legislative Council Debates,* August 5, 1926, p. 716.

a little larger, and therefore brings a little higher price, than one removed after killing.

It will scarcely be necessary to amplify this point. In the Province of Behar and Orissa in the year 1925, thirty-four cases of the flaying alive of goats were brought to court by the police. But light fines, meted out by Indian judges whose sentiment is not shocked, are soon worked off in the extra price fetched by the next batch of flayed-alive skins. The risk of prosecution is small; and "there is every reason," concludes the Provincial Police Administration report, "to suppose that the number of reported cases is no criterion of the prevalence of this outrage." Many skins so stripped have been shipped to America.

Britain, by example and by teaching, has been working for nearly three-quarters of a century to implant her own ideas of mercy on an alien soil. In this and in uncounted other directions she might perhaps have produced more visible results, in her areas of direct contact, by the use of force. But her administrative theory has been that small constructive value lies in the use of force to bring about surface compliance where the underlying principle is not yet grasped. And, given a people still barbarian in their handling of their own women, it is scarcely to be expected that they should yet have taken on a mentality responsive to the appeal of dumb creatures.

Unhappily for the helpless animal world, Prevention of Cruelty to Animals is, under the current Indianization movement, a "transferred subject" of Government. That is to say: in each province working the "Reforms" the administration of this branch has been transferred by the British Parliament into the hands of an Indian minister. Dumb creation pays with its body the costs of the experiment.

Chapter XX

IN THE HOUSE OF HER FRIENDS

"This country is the cruelest in the world, to animals," said an old veterinarian, long practicing in India. It would perhaps be fairer to repeat that the people of India follow their religions, which, save with the small sect called Jains, produce no mercy either to man or to beast, in the sense that we of the West know mercy.

Mr. Gandhi himself writes: [1]

In a country where the cow is an object of worship there should be no cattle problems at all. But our cow-worship has resolved itself into an ignorant fanaticism. The fact that we have more cattle than we can support is a matter for urgent treatment. I have already suggested the taking over of the question by cow protection societies.

Cow Protection Societies maintain *gaushalas*, or cow asylums. These asylums, like the *pinjrapoles*, or asylums for all animals, are maintained by gifts, and have access, through rich Hindu merchants, to almost unlimited funds. "Let Government of India promise to stop the killing of cows in India and they can have all the money they can use—plus a war with the Muham-

[1] *Young India*, Feb. 26, 1925.

madan," an experienced old Hindu official once told me.

A strong claim to the bounty of the gods is believed to be established through saving the life of a cow. Yet as a Hindu, you are not disturbed in conscience by selling your good cow to a butcher, because it is he, not you, who will kill the cow. Then, taking the money he gives you, you may buy of him, for a fraction of that sum, the worst cow in his shambles, turn her over to the *gaushala* to care for, and thereby acquire religious merit, profiting your soul and your purse in one transaction.

Having personally visited a number of *gaushalas* and *pinjrapoles*, I cannot but wonder whether those who support them so lavishly, those who commit animals to their care, and those who, like Mr. Gandhi, so strongly advocate their maintenance and increase, ever look inside their gates. I first heard of them through a western animal lover long domiciled in India. He said:

"The Hindu who, as an act of piety, buys a cow of the butcher and places her in the *gaushala*, always buys a poor diseased animal because he gets her cheap. When he places her in the *gaushala* he does not give money with her, or, at best, not money enough for her decent keep. And even if he did, the keeper would pocket most of it. The suffering in these places is terrible. In one of them I recently saw an old cow lying helpless, being consumed by maggots which had begun at her hind quarters. It would take them ten days to eat up to her heart and kill her. Till then she must lie as she lay.

[263]

" 'Can't you do something for her?' I asked the keeper.

" 'Why?' he replied, honestly enough. 'Why should I? What for?' "

My second informant was an American cattle specialist living in India, a highly-qualified practical man. He said:

"I was asked to visit some of these *gaushalas* and give advice. And because the political unrest since the War has inclined many of these people to shut their minds to the council of British officials, I hoped that, as an American and an outsider, I could be of use. But I found in every place that I visited either intentional dishonesty or gross mismanagement. In all cases the animals imprisoned there were the least of anybody's concern. My advice was not welcome. When they found I would not give them a rubber-stamp approval, they had no use for me at all."

I next consulted a notable religious leader, the *Guru* [2] of Dial Bagh. His words were:

"I have visited two of these places, both times taking them by surprise. The sights that I saw there were so horrible that for two days afterward I could not take food."

Finally, I recorded the testimony of an Indian trained in the western school of cattle-breeding and dairying and now occupying a position of considerable responsibility in that line. Describing the *pinjrapole* as "a lane or square full of animal's pens," he went on:

[2] Religious master.

"Religious sentiment puts the creatures there, but there it stops. They are much neglected and suffer torments through neglect. Rich merchants and bankers subscribe annually tons of money for their care, but the money all goes to graft and waste. The creatures in most of the asylums are far worse off than they were when they scavenged in the gutters for a living, with a happy chance of getting killed by passing cars. They are miserable, dying skeletons. The caretakers have no knowledge of the care of animals and no previous training or experience. The money spent in such big sums is not spent on them! There *are* good animal asylums in India, but they are few!"

The first *gaushala* that I saw for myself was in the suburbs of a central Indian city. Over the entrance gate was a charming painting of the blue god Krishna in the forest, piping to white cows.

Inside the high walls at a distance lay a large pleasant garden of fruit-trees and vegetable beds encircling a pleasant bungalow—the keeper's house. On the hither side of the garden was the place of the cows. This was a treeless, shrubless, shelterless yard of hard-trodden, cracked, bare clay, which, in the rains, would be a wallow of foul mud, inhabited by animals whose bones, in some cases, were literally cutting through their skins. Some lay gasping, too weak to stand. Some had great open sores at which the birds, perched on their hipbones or their staring ribs, picked and tore. Some had broken legs that dangled and flopped as they

[265]

stirred. Many were diseased. All were obviously starved.

Bulls as wretched as the cows stood among them, and in a little pen at the side were packed some 250 small calves. From these last arose a pitiful outcry, at the sound of approaching steps; and as I looked down over the pen-wall at their great brown eyes, their hollow sides and their shaking legs, it occurred to me to ask what they were fed. The answer, frankly given by the *gaushala* attendant, was that each calf gets the equivalent of one small tea-cupful of milk a day, until it dies—which as a rule, and happily, it shortly does—the rest of the milk being sold in the bazaar by the keeper of the *gaushala*.

Asking next to see the daily ration of a cow, I was shown the granary—a bin measuring perhaps five by three by two feet, containing small seeds heavily mixed with husks. Of this each full-grown animal got one half-pound daily. Nothing else whatever was fed, excepting a little dry chopped straw. Straw contains no food values, but would serve for a time to keep the creatures' two sides from touching. No paddock was provided, and no grazing of any sort. The animals merely stood or lay as I saw them until the relief of death.

One cow had but three legs, the hind leg having been amputated below the knee, "because she kicked when they milked her."

In other *gaushalas* I saw cripples who had been made so in the process of creating monsters. For this purpose they cut a leg from one calf and graft it anywhere on the body of another, to exhibit the result for money as a natural portent. The maimed calf, if it does not bleed or starve or rot to death, may be bought for a song and sent to a *gaushala*. No dissatisfaction seemed to be felt as to this history.

In the heart of the city of Ahmedabad, within a few miles of Mr. Gandhi's pleasant and comfortable home in which he writes his earnest pleas for the support of cow shelters and *pinjrapoles*, I visited a large *pinjrapole* whose description, after what has already been said, need not be inflicted upon the reader's sensibilities. I hope that every animal that I saw in it is safely dead.

But from such memories it is a pleasure to turn to the one exception that my personal experience revealed, an establishment maintained by "The Association for Saving Milch Cattle from Going to the Bombay Slaughter House."

This society is composed practically entirely of rich Indian merchants and merchants' associations. Its latest report [3] affords some interesting reading. It begins with a statement incorporating the estimate that, during the five years from April 1, 1919, to March 31, 1924, 229,257 cows were slaughtered in Bombay City, and that 97,583 calves and young buffaloes were "tortured to death in the stables."

The report proceeds with an appeal against all

[3] *An Appeal by Shree Ghatkopar Sarvajanika Jivadaya Khata,* 75 Mahabir Building, Bombay.

slaughter, even of bullocks, sheep and goats, for which
the figures are also given. Then it concerns itself with
the question of the shortage of milk:

We Hindus claim to protect the cow. If this claim were
just, India should be a land flowing with milk. But as a
matter of fact this is not the case. Milk in cow-protecting
Bombay, for instance, is nearly as dear as in cow-killing London or New York. Good milk cannot be had for love or
money and the direct consequence of this state of things is a
really terrible mortality among infants and a heavy death rate
among adults. . . .

The "dairy" plant that the Association itself maintains in the country on the outskirts of Bombay consists
of a decent set of cowsheds, substantially and practically built for shelter, air and sanitation, and reasonably clean. The superintendent said he was feeding fifteen pounds of hay, with eight pounds of grain and
oil cake, per head, daily. And the cattle, such as they
were, did not look hungry. The herd consisted of 277
head, whose aggregate milking came to about 130
quarts a day, which, sold to some 130 families, gave a
daily income of about $22.50 to the establishment.
Fresh cows were sold out of the plant on condition that
the purchaser should never sell them to be killed.

The staff, entirely Indian, impressed me as being
eager and interested as to their work. Said the chief:

"If this place were merely commercial there would
not be so many non-commercial cattle here. We have
to buy out of the slaughter house; but where once we

[268]

bought the poorest and cheapest, now we have learned to buy the best. And besides, the idea of any sort of commercial element, in a *gaushala,* is new to India. Up to the present we have not put any private milk-men out of business, or appreciably reduced the city's slaughter. But we hope to do so, in the long run. On my staff here I have two or three Bachelors of Agriculture—young men trained on the Government Breeding and Dairy farms to understand cattle. And that you will never find in any other *gaushala* or *pinjrapole* in all India. We, here, believe in scientific care."

Looked at from the point of view of an American farmer, the whole thing was too primitive to discuss. Looked at from the Indian background, it was a shining light, and one felt almost guilty in noticing that all the staff were cousins, nephews, or close relatives of the superintendent.

But, it was a British-trained Indian in Government employ under the direction of a British chief, who rescued this *gaushala* from a bad start, devised the present advanced scheme and pursuaded the Association to adopt it.

Meantime, the Indian politicians, at home and abroad, curse "the criminal negligence of the Government," [4] beat the air with words, spurn agriculture and the agriculturalist, and, when publicity dictates, send small contributions to the other kind of *gaushala.*

[4] *Young India,* May 13, 1926, p. 174.

Chapter XXI

HOME OF STARK WANT

One hears a great deal from the new Indian intelligentsia about the glories of the "Golden Age"—a period in the shadowy past when the land smiled with health and plenty, wisdom, beauty and peace and when all went well with India. This happy natural condition was done to death, one is given to understand, by the mephitic influence of the present Government.

The argument for the Golden Age is wont to take typical forms, such as this:

"You admit that the Emperor Chandragupta lived? And that he was the man who fought Seleucus, who fought Alexander? Very well: In Chandragupta's day a girl of fourteen, beautiful and loaded with jewels, could walk abroad in perfect safety. And there was perfect peace, no poverty, no famine, no plague. But Britain ruined our Golden Age."

Or again, the accuser first paints a picture of an idyllic land, distinguished by science, philosophy and pastoral grace, then suddenly confronts his hearer with the challenge: "Can you show me, in all India, any remnant of that life? No? Exactly. Then, if it exists nowhere, does it not follow that Britain must have destroyed it?"

But the period of Chandragupta, whatever its quality, was removed from that of England's first acquisition of foothold in India by over nineteen hundred years.[1] Chandragupta's dynasty having disappeared into mists of legend out of which the one great figure of Asoka dimly looms, the Scythians and the Turks rode through the northern mountain passes, helped themselves to northern India and set up their kingdoms there. And the native Hindu mass, as years rolled by, merged its conquerors, both Scythian and Turk, into its own body.

The fourth and fifth centuries, A.D., comprised the great period of Hindu art and history—the age of the Gupta Kings. Then again the hand grew lax that held the northern passes; and again down out of Central Asia poured wave after wave of wild humanity, this time the terrible nomad White Huns, brothers to the forces of Attila. Ravenous for the wealth of the land, they had watched the frontier for their hour. When it struck, leaping through like a loosened torrent, they swept the country bare of all that had been its social fabric.

By the beginning of the sixth century the northern half of the territory we call India had become one of the provinces of the Huns. And the impact of successive Hun hordes, striking down through the mountain barrier, had again so thoroughly wiped out the past that no authentic family or clan tradition of today can go behind that point.

The Huns, like the Scythians and the Turks before

[1] Chandragupta reigned B.C. 322-298.

them, were gradually absorbed in the native stock. Hinduism, for a time disputed by Buddhism, regained possession of the land. Its disintegrating tenets and its cumulative millions of terrifying gods did their work. Henceforth, save during a few years in the seventh century, no successful attempt was made, north or south, to establish political unity or a permanent state, while forces of disunion multiplied and grew strong.

The history of northern India from the middle of the seventh century through the next five hundred years is a tangled web of the warfare of little clans and states, constantly changing in size and in number with the changing fortunes of battle and intrigue. Small chiefs march and countermarch, raid, seize, annex, destroy, slay and are slain, each jealous of each, each for himself alone, embroiling the entire northern and central part of the country in their constant feuds.

Meantime, peninsular India remained always a place apart, untouched by the currents of the north and defended therefrom by the buttress of her hills and jungles. Here lived the dark-skinned aboriginals, Tamils, without infusion of Aryan blood, fighting their own fights and worshiping the demons of their faith. And when at last Hindu missionaries sallied south along the coast, these recommended their creed, it would seem, by the familiar process of adding the local demons to the number of their own gods.

The Tamils had developed a rich native art; and in one at least of their many and ever-changing little kingdoms they had brought forth an elaborate and in-

teresting system of village government. By the end of
the twelfth century, however, this feature had utterly
perished, crushed out. And it is well to observe that,
north or south, a history made up of endless wars and
changes of dynasty developed no municipal institutions,
no free cities, no republics, no political consciousness
in the people. Each region lay forever prostrate, su-
pine, under the heel of a despot who in his brief hour
did as he pleased with his human herds until some
other despot pulled him down to destruction.

For a rapid survey of the next era in India's history
one cannot do better than turn to Sir T. W. Holderness's *Peoples and Problems of India:* [2]

The first comers were Arabs, who founded dynasties in
Sind and Multan as early as [A.D.] 800. . . . About [the
year] 1000 the terror came. By that time the Tartar races
had been brought into the fold of Islam, and the Turks, the
most capable of these races, had started on the career which
in the West ended in their establishment at Constantinople.
. . . In 997, Mahmud [a Turkish chieftain] descended upon
India. His title, "the Idol-breaker," describes the man. Year
by year he swept over the plains of India, capturing cities
and castles, throwing down idols and temples, slaughtering
the heathen and proclaiming the faith of Muhammad. Each
year he returned with vast spoils [to his home in Afghanistan].

For five hundred years, reckoning from A.D. 1000, successive hosts of fierce and greedy Turks, Afghans and Mon-
gols trod upon one another's heels and fought for mastery in
India. At the end of that time, Babar the Turk founded in

[2] Williams & Norgate, London, 1920, pp. 48-50.

1526 the Mughal Empire; thenceforward for two hundred years the passes into India were closed and in the keeping of his capable successors.

Says Holderness on another page: [3]

The Mughal Empire . . . was of the ordinary type of Asiatic despotisms. It was irresponsible personal government. For India it meant the substitution of a new set of conquerors for those already in occupation. But the new comers brought with them the vigour of the north—they came from the plains of the Oxus beyond the Kabul hills—and they drew an unlimited supply of recruits from the finest fighting races of Asia. In physical strength and hardihood they were like the Norsemen and Normans of Europe.

To check the Islamic tide in its flood toward the south, a Hindu power, known as the Empire of Vijayanagar, sprang up among the Tamils. Its rulers built a gorgeous city and lived in unbounded luxury. But here, as elsewhere all over India, the common people's misery provided the kings' and nobles' wealth, and only their abject submission made possible the existence of the state. Yet the glories of the Hindu stronghold soon eclipsed. In the year 1565 one blow of Muslim arms, delivered by the sultans of small surrounding states, slaughtered its people and reduced the splendid city to a heap of carven stones.

Yet the earlier of the great Mughal Emperors tolerated the old religion. Their chief exponent, Akbar, even married a native lady, and admitted Rajput chiefs

[3] *Peoples and Problems of India,* p. 53.

TRIBESMEN OF THE NORTH

"Hawk-nosed men in big sheep-skin coats." (*See* page 322.)
"Superb fighters." (*See* page 346.)

Photos by M. Moyca Newell

IN THE KHYBER PASS

Right: A fighting tower of the Zakha-khel Afridis.

Left: A Zakha-khel Rifleman, photographed on its uppermost level.
'In all the world are no better fighters."

and Brahman scholars to place and posts. But the Mughals administered always as conqueror strangers; and though they made use of the talents or learning of individuals among the Hindus, they took care constantly to strengthen the Muslim hand from their own transmontane source.

Then, in 1659, the Emperor Aurangzeb again brought to the Mughal throne an Islamism that would not countenance the idolatry of the Hindu mass. His heavy hand, destroying temples and images, broke the Rajput's fealty and roused the Hindu low-caste peasantry of the Deccan—the Mahrattas—in common wrath. So that when Aurangzeb, in his ambition for more power, more wealth, attacked even the little Muhammadan kings of the Deccan, the Mahrattas rose up as guerilla bands, and, under cover of the general embroilment, robbed, slew and destroyed on their own account, wasting the land. A half-century of Aurangzeb's disjointing rule so weakened the Mughal Empire that, at his death, it fell asunder, leaving the Mahratta hordes, now trained in raids and killings under their bandit chiefs, to play a brief rôle as the strong hand in India.

Then again happened the historic inevitable, as happen it will whenever the guard of the north is down. The Mughal Empire fallen, the door open to Central Asia, Central Asia poured in. First came the Persian, then the fierce Afghan, who, in a final battle delivered in 1761, drove the Mahrattas with wholesale slaughter back to their Deccan hills.

Now, in the scanty official records of all these troubled centuries, little indeed is said of the common people. The histories are histories of little kings and tribal chiefs, their personal lives, ambitions, riches, intrigues, fights and downfalls. Such glimpses as appear, however, show the populace generally as the unconsidered victims of their master's greed, be that master Hindu or Muhammadan. Hungry, naked, poverty-stricken, constantly overridden by undisciplined mobs of soldiers, bled of their scanty produce, swept by exterminating famines and epidemics, our clearest knowledge of them comes from the chronicles of strangers who from time to time visited the country.

Many western travelers—French, Dutch, Portuguese, Spanish—have left records of the country, north and south, as it was during and after Akbar's day. All agree in the main points.

The poor, they say, were everywhere desperately poor, the rich forever insecure in their riches. Between common robbers and the levies of the throne, no man dared count on the morrow. The Hindu peoples constituted the prostrate masses. The nobles and governing officials, few in numbers, were almost all foreigners, whether Turks or Persians. Their luxury and ostentation arose, on the one hand, from an insatiable hunger for sensual pleasure, and, on the other, from the necessity not to be outshone at court. All places and favors were bought by costly bribes, and the extravagance of life was increased by the fact that, in northern India at least, whatever a rich man possessed at the time of his death reverted to the royal treasury.

To acquire means to keep up their gorgeous state the officials, from the pro-consuls down, had but one method—to squeeze the peasantry. They squeezed.

In Madras, wrote van Linschoten, who saw the country in the decade between 1580 to 1590, the peasants [4]

. . . are so miserable that for a penny they would endure to be whipped, and they eat so little that it seemeth they live by the air; they are likewise most of them small and weak of limbs.

When the rains failed, they fell into still deeper distress, wandered like wild animals in vain search of food and sold their children for "less than a rupee apiece," while the slave-market was abundantly recruited from those who sold their own bodies to escape starvation, of which cannibalism, an ordinary feature of famine, was the alternative.

The Bádsháh Námah of 'Abd Al Hamíd Láhawrí bears witness that in the Deccan during the famine of 1631, "pounded bones of the dead were mixed with flour and sold. . . . Destitution at length reached such a pitch that men began to devour each other and the flesh of a son was preferred to his love. The number of the dying caused obstruction in the roads." The Dutch East India Company's representative, in the same year, recorded that in Surat the dearth was so

[4] *The Voyage of John Huyghen van Linschoten to the East Indies,* edited for the Hakluyt Society, 1884.

⌈277⌉

great that "menschen en vee van honger sturven . . .
moeders tegen natuer haere kinderkens wt hongers-
noot op gegeten hebben." Two years later Christopher Read reported to the British East India Company
that Mesulapatam and Armagon were "sorely oppressed with famine, the liveinge eating up the dead
and men durst scarcely travel in the country for feare
they should be kild and eaten." And Peter Mundy
wrote from Gujerat during the same period that "the
famine it selfe swept away more than a million of the
Comon or poorer Sort. After which, the mortallitie
succeeding did as much more among rich and poore.
Weomen were seene to rost their Children. . . . A
man or woman noe sooner dead but they were Cutt in
pieces to be eaten." These testimonies will be found,
and at greater length, in the text and Appendix of the
Hakluyt Society's edition of the *Travels of Peter
Mundy*. Other old chronicles corroborate them.

Slaves cost practically nothing to keep and were
therefore numerous in each noble's household, where
their little value insured their wretched state. The elephants of the nobles wore trappings of silver and gold,
while "the people," says the contemporaneous observer,
de Laet,[5] "have not sufficient covering to keep warm
in winter."

Merchants, if prosperous, dared not live comfort-
ably, dared not eat good food, and buried their silver
deep under ground; for the smallest show of means

[5] *De Imperio Magni Mogolis*, J. de Laet, Leyden, 1631.

brought the torturers to wring from them the hiding place of their wealth.

The village masses constituted practically the only productive element in the land. All their production, save their bare subsistence, was absorbed by the State. As to its redistribution, that took a single route, into the pockets of the extremely small body of foreigners constituting the ruling class. None of it returned to the people. No communal benefits existed.

A very few bridges and such roads as are made by the plodding of bullocks' feet through dust and mud comprised the communication lines of the land. No system of popular education or of medical relief was worked, and none of legal defense. Fine schemes were sometimes set on paper by rulers and their ministers, but practically nothing was actually done toward the economic development of the country; for if any one ruler began a work, his successor destroyed it or let it decay.[6]

Fifteen years after the death of Akbar, or in the year 1620, the Hollander, Francisco Pelsaert, began that seven years' residence in India of which he left so valuable and so curious a record. In the course of his narrative Pelsaert writes:[7]

The land would give a plentiful, or even an extraordinary

---

[6] *India at the Death of Akbar,* by W. H. Moreland, Macmillan & Co., London, 1920, gives an elaborate and heavily documented digest of contemporaneous authority on this general subject.

[7] *The Remonstrantie of Francisco Pelsaert,* translated from the Dutch by W. H. Moreland and P. Geyl Heffers, Cambridge, 1925, pp. 47-59.

yield, if the peasants were not so cruelly and pitilessly oppressed; for villages which, owing to some small shortage of
produce, are unable to pay the full amount of the revenue-
farm, are made prize, so to speak, by their masters or governors, and wives and children sold, on pretext of a charge of
rebellion. Some peasants abscond to escape their tyranny . . .
and consequently the fields lie empty and unsown and grow
into wildernesses.

. . . As regards the laws, they are scarcely observed at all,
for the administration is absolutely autocratic. . . . Their
laws contain such provisions as hand for hand, eye for eye,
tooth for tooth; but who will ex-communicate the Pope? And
who would dare to ask a Governor "Why do you rule us this
way or that? Our Law orders thus." . . . In every city
there is a . . . royal court of Justice . . . [but] one must
indeed be sorry for the man who has to come to judgment
before these godless "un-judges"; their eyes are bleared with
greed, their mouths gape like wolves for covetousness, and
their bellies hunger for the bread of the poor; every one stands
with hands open to receive, for no mercy or compassion can
be had except on payment of cash. This fault should not be
attributed to judges or officers alone, for the evil is a universal plague; from the least to the greatest, right up to the
King himself, every one is infected with insatiable greed.

. . . It is important to recognise that [the King, Jahangir]
is to be regarded as king of the plains or the open roads only;
for in many places you can travel only with a strong body
of men, or on payment of heavy tolls to rebels . . . [and]
there are nearly as many rebels as subjects. Taking the chief
cities, for example, at Surat the forces of Raja Piepel come
pillaging up to, or inside the city, murdering the people and
burning the villages, and in the same way, near Ahmedabad,

[280]

Burhanpur, Agra, Delhi, Lahore, and many other cities, thieves and robbers come in force by night or day like open enemies. The Governors are usually bribed by the thieves to remain inactive, for avarice dominates manly honour, and, instead of maintaining troops, they fill and adorn their *mahals* with beautiful women, and seem to have the pleasure-house of the whole world within their walls.

The observant Dutchman [8] repeatedly dwells on the disastrous contrast between

the manner of life of the rich in their great superfluity and absolute power, and the utter subjection and poverty of the common people—poverty so great and miserable that the life of the people can be depicted . . . only as the home of stark want and the dwelling-place of bitter woe.

Nevertheless, he says, having discovered the numbing influence of the doctrines of fate and caste: [9]

The people endure patiently, professing that they do not deserve anything better; and scarcely any one will make an effort, for a ladder by which to climb higher is hard to find, because a workman's children can follow no occupation other than that of their father, nor can they inter-marry with other castes. . . . For the workman there are two scourges, the first of which is low wages. . . . The second is [the oppression by] the Governor, the nobles, the Diwan . . . and other royal officers. If any of these wants a workman, the man is not asked if he is willing to come, but is seized in the house or in the street, well beaten if he should dare to raise any

[8] *The Remonstrantie of Francisco Pelsaert*, p. 60.
[9] *Ibid*.

objection, and in the evening paid half his wages or nothing at all.

Forty years after Pelsaert's departure from India came a French traveler, François Bernier. His stay covered the period from 1656 to 1668. His chronicle perfectly agrees with that of other foreign visitors, and gives a vivid picture of men, women and things as he found them in the reigns of Shahjahan and Aurangzeb —the climax of the Mughal Empire. Speaking on the subject of land-tenure and taxation, this observer writes: [10]

The King, as proprietor of the land, makes over a certain quantity to military men, as an equivalent for their pay. . . . Similar grants are made to governors, in lieu of their salary, and also for the support of their troops, on condition that they pay a certain sum annually to the King. . . . The lands not so granted are retained by the King as the peculiar domains of his house . . . and upon these domains he keeps contractors, who are also bound to pay him an annual rent.

Bengal, he thinks probably "the finest and most fruitful country in the world." But of the other regions he writes: [11]

As the ground is seldom tilled otherwise than by compulsion, and as no person is found willing and able to repair the ditches and canals for the conveyance of water, it happens that the whole country is badly cultivated, and a great

[10] *Travels in the Mogul Empire,* François Bernier, Oxford University Press, 1916, p. 224.
[11] *Ibid.,* pp. 226-7, 230.

part rendered unproductive from the want of irrigation. . . .
The peasant cannot avoid asking himself this question: "Why
should I toil for a tyrant who may come tomorrow and lay
his rapacious hands upon all I possess and value?" . . . The
Governors and revenue contractors, on their part reason in this
manner: "Why should the neglected state of this land create
uneasiness in our minds? and why should we expend our own
money and time to render it fruitful? We may be deprived
of it in a single moment and our exertion would benefit
neither ourselves nor our children. Let us draw from the soil
all the money we can, though the peasant should starve or
abscond, and we should leave it, when commanded to quit, a
dreary wilderness." . . . It is owing to this miserable system
of government . . . that there is no city or town which, if
it be not already ruined and deserted, does not bear evident
marks of approaching decay.

The country is ruined by the necessity of defraying the
enormous charges required to maintain the splendour of a
numerous court, and to pay a large army maintained for the
purpose of keeping the people in subjection.

Now, to touch as briefly as possible on the history of
European powers in India: At the time of Akbar's ac-
cession—1556—the Portuguese were already rooted
and fortified on the western coast of the Peninsula, at
Goa, which, with its environing territory, they had
taken from the Muhammadan kinglets of the Deccan.
Thence they controlled the merchant traffic of the
Arabian Sea and the Persian Gulf. No other European
power had yet secured a base in the land, and no Englishman had yet set foot on the soil of India. [12]

[12] *Oxford History of India*, p. 348.

The Portuguese hand in India soon weakened, on lines of debauchery and cruelty. Thus came the decay that, in the early sixteen hundreds, let fall all the Portuguese settlements, save only Goa itself, into the hands of the Dutch.

Dutch and English merchants, at that period, were equally keen for the trade of the East. The Dutchmen's main interest, however, lying with Java and the Spice Islands, their English rivals soon stood in India practically alone.

British merchant adventurers, by charter and concessions granted by Queen Elizabeth and by the Mughal Emperor, now from time to time established trading stations along the West coast. Their post in the Bay of Bengal antedated by five years the settlement of Boston by the Puritans. Nine years later the first English proprietary holding in India was secured, by agreement between the local Hindu ruler and the "Governor and Company of Merchants of London, Trading with the East Indies." By this treaty the latter were allowed to rent and fortify as a trading post a bit of rough shoreland now the site of the city of Madras. Here, presently, was to come Elihu Yale, once of Boston in Massachusetts, as Governor in the Company's behalf. Here was earned the means to benefit the Connecticut University that bears his name today. And here, in the old house where British Governors of Madras still dwell, hangs Elihu Yale's portrait, looking placidly out upon the scene of his labors.

French merchants, they also desirous of the trade of

[284]

India, during the latter half of the seventeenth century secured several small *points d'appui* along the southern coasts. Their commerce never equaled that of the English; but their aspirations and the national clashes in Europe alike led them into a series of anti-English intrigues with small Indian rulers, resulting in hostilities of varying result. So that while the English colonists of New England and New York, with the aid of Indian allies, were fighting "French and Indian Wars" for control of the future, English colonists on the other side of the world, with the aid of Indian allies, were fighting French and Indian wars for the same purpose. And with a comparable outcome.[13]

The struggle which began, openly, in 1746, when the French took Madras, came to its close in 1761, when the French unconditionally surrendered Pondicherry, their own headquarters, thus ending their effective career in India.

Until well into the eighteenth century, English holdings in India were limited to a few square miles in Madras, in the Island of Bombay, and at three or four other points; during this period the English representatives in India occupied themselves with trade alone, taking no hand in local wars or politics. But with the death of the Emperor Aurangzeb, the collapse of the Mughal Empire, and the chaos of freebooting

[13] As Americans we may here draw our critics' shot by admitting that while we have done much to exterminate our Indians and only in 1924 granted them citizenship though retaining guardianship over them (United States v. Nice, 241 U. S. 598, 1916), our British cousins have multiplied theirs, and have led them into a large and increasing measure of self-government.

wars that then broke over the land, the Company set up for the protection of its settlements a force of European troops, supplemented by Indian auxiliaries.

Thenceforward it grew toward the status of a governing corporation. In 1784 the British Government, by Act of Parliament, assumed a degree of control over the Company's procedure. With such authority behind it, the Company could enlarge its activities and proceed toward establishing peace in a country teeming with anarchy.

This meant reducing to order a host of robber gangs, of marauding chieftains, of captains of the old Mughal régime now out of a job and swarming like migrating bees looking for new kingdoms and new plunder. It also meant dissuading small reigning princes from their hereditary vocation of enlisting gangs of mercenaries and campaigning against their neighbors. And if these movements, which the princes themselves often requested, usually resulted in annexing more territory to the sphere of British influence or control, they also brought an increasing semblance of unity to the country.

Once the work of pacification was well in hand, began the attempt to build up civil institutions and public privileges and to introduce law, justice and order, a thousand years and more unknown in the land. The Company was still a trading company, with a trader's chief preoccupation. But it accepted the responsibility for the people's welfare implied in the authority it now held.

A human enterprise covering two centuries of human progress, the name of the East India Company was sometimes dimmed by mistaken judgment or by unfit agents. Some of these were overbearing, some tactless, some wavering, one or two were base and a few succumbed to the temptation to graft. Of their defects, however, not a little nonsense is spun.

The Company, on the whole, was honored in the quality of its officers. As time passed, a more sensitive public conscience at home made it increasingly alive to critical observation. Its affairs were reviewed by Parliament. And, with the general rise in world-standards, rose its standards of administration. Its inclusive achievement was courageous, arduous and essential towards the redemption of the country. Whatever its faults, it cleared and broke the ground for progress. And it lighted the first ray of hope that had ever dawned for the wretched masses of the Indian peoples.

The abolition of ancient indigenous horrors, such as the flourishing trade of the professional strangler tribes, the Thugs; the burning alive of widows; the burying alive of lepers, lie to the credit of the Company. And no briefest summary of the epoch-making elements of its concerns could be forgiven a failure to cite the gist of Section 87 of the Parliamentary Act of 1784, which reads:

No native of the said territories, nor any natural-born subject of His Majesty resident therein, shall, by reason only of his religion, place of birth, descent, colour, or any of them, be disabled from holding any place, office or employment under the Company.

A bomb, indeed, to drop into caste-fettered, feud-filled, tyrant-crushed India! Nor was this shock of free western ideas without its definitely unsettling influence. The Sikh Rebellion in 1845, the Indian Mutiny in 1857, were in no small degree direct fruits of that influence. And with the conclusion of the latter England felt that the time had come to do away with the awkward Company-Parliament form of government, to end the control of a great territory by commercial interest, however safeguarded, and to bring the administration of India directly under the Crown.

In the year 1858 this step was taken. Shabby, threadbare, sick and poor, old Mother India stood at last on the brink of another world and turned blind eyes toward the strange new flag above her head. It carried then, as it carries today, a pledge that is, to her, incredible. How can she, the victim and slave of all recorded time, either hope or believe that her latest master brings her the gift of constructive service, democracy and the weal of the common people?

Chapter XXII

THE REFORMS

The roots of the form of government now gradually working out in British India ramify into past centuries and are visible through continuous growth. For the purpose of this book they may be passed over, to reach the briefest outline of the present evolutionary phase.

The supreme power over India, today, is the people of Great Britain represented by the British Crown and Parliament, acting through the Secretary of State in Council of India, sitting in India Office, in London. The supreme government in India is that of the Governor-General-in-Council, commonly called the Government of India. The Governor-General, or Viceroy, is appointed by the Crown. His Council, similarly appointed, consists of seven Departmental heads—the Commander-in-Chief of the Forces, the Home Member, the Finance Member, the Member for Railways and Commerce, and the Members for Education, Health and Lands, for Industries and Labor, and for Law. Of this cabinet of seven members the three last named are Indians.

Next in the structure of the Central Government comes the "Indian Legislature," with its Upper Chamber or "Council of State," and its Lower Chamber or "Legislative Assembly."

[289]

The Council of State comprises sixty members, of whom thirty-four are elected, while twenty-six, of whom not over twenty may be government officials, are nominated by the Viceroy.

The Legislative Assembly consists of one hundred and forty-four members, of whom one hundred and three are elected. Of the remaining forty-one, all nominated by the Viceroy, twenty-six must be members of Government, while the rest are named to represent the minor interests in the country, as, the Christian Indian population, etc. Both chambers are heavily Indian, and both are constituted with a view to due representation of the several provinces into which, for purposes of administration, the country is divided.

British India is thus divided into fifteen provinces, each with its separate administration. Of the nine major divisions—Madras, Bengal, and Bombay Presidencies, the United Provinces, the Punjab, Behar and Orissa, the Central Provinces, Burma, and Assam— each is controlled by a Governor with his Executive Council. These act in conjunction with a Provincial Legislative Council, a legislature of which 70 per cent. (in Burma, 60 per cent.) at least must be elected by the people.

The electorate is intended to give fairly balanced separate representation to the various races, communities and special interests. The scale varies from province to province, with varying local conditions. In Madras, for example, it stands as follows:

[290]

Class of Constituency	Number of Members Returned
Non-Muhammadans (meaning Hindus, Jains, Buddhists, etc.)	65
Muhammadans	13
Indian Christian	5
Europeans (including British)	1
Anglo-Indian	1
Landholders [zemindars]	6
University	1
Commerce Industry	6

The qualifications for voters also varies in the several provinces. In general, however, the franchise rests on a minimum property qualification. The law, thus far, has given the vote to some seven-and-a-half million persons [1] and has conferred upon all the major provinces the right to enfranchise their women.[2]

The effort to decentralize—to magnify the responsibilities of provincial governments for the purpose of training and stimulating Indians to handle their own affairs, stands out preëminent in the present scheme. In part and as applied to the nine major divisions, this makes of the provincial government a two-branched machine operated from the office of the Governor. The Governor and his Executive Council, all Crown appointees, form one branch. Council membership is commonly divided between British and Indians. The Governor and his Ministers of Departments form the

[1] *The India Office,* Sir Malcolm C. C. Seton, Putnam, London, 1926, p. 59.
[2] See Appendix II.

second branch. These are appointed by the Governor from the elected members of the legislature and are themselves responsible to that body. All ministers are Indian. Between the two branches the various functions of government formerly handled by a single arm are now divided, under the heads of "reserved" and "transferred" subjects.

Reserved subjects, save for the ultimate power of the Central Government, lie in the hands of the Provincial Governor in Council. Transferred subjects are assigned to the provincial legislatures, and are operated by the Ministers.

The list of transferred subjects represents authority resigned by the British people in favor of the peoples of India. The intention of the plan is, if the experiment succeeds, to enlarge the list of subjects transferred. On the other hand, where the Ministerial machine fails to work, Governors-in-Council may resume control of a subject already transferred. Transferred subjects at present comprise Education, Public Health, Management of Public Works other than irrigation and railways, Development of Industries, Excise, Agriculture, Local Self-government and others. Reserved subjects include Maintenance of Law and Order, Defense of India, Finance, the Land Revenue system, etc.

Of the provincial legislatures, known as Legislative Councils, a recent authority [3] says:

The Councils have very wide powers of legislation and the annual provincial budgets are submitted to them. In Trans-

[3] *The India Office*, pp. 59-60.

ferred subjects they possess the power of the purse, but the Governor may restore grants for purposes of the Reserved side of the administration if he considers it essential to the discharge of his responsibility that money refused by the Council should be provided. He can disallow an Act or reserve it for the Governor-General's consideration, and has the exceptional right to enact on his own authority a measure (provided that it deals with a Reserved subject only) the passage of which he certifies to be essential to the discharge of his responsibility. This special power has hitherto been exercised only once.

Turning from provincial legislatures to that of the Central Government, the same authority summarizes: [4]

The Indian legislature, subject to the preservation of the powers of Parliament, has power to make laws "for all persons, for all courts, and for all places and things, within British India," for British officials and subjects in Indian States, for "native Indian subjects of His Majesty" beyond British India, and for officers, soldiers and followers of the Indian Army wherever serving. But it requires the sanction of the Governor-General for the introduction of measures affecting the public debt or revenues, religion, military discipline, foreign relations, or for measures treating on matters relegated to provincial governments. . . .

The power of the purse has been very largely entrusted to the Legislative Assembly. . . . The annual budget is laid before both Chambers, and the consent of the Legislative Assembly is sought for the grants required on most matters, though certain heads of expenditure are classed as "non-votable."

[4] *Ibid.*, pp. 60-2.

The Viceroy and the Crown hold the power of veto; and the former may enact a bill into law, subject to disallowance by the Crown, without the consent of either Chamber. An emergency measure, such a step would be taken only in extreme cases.

It will scarcely be necessary, in this place, to go further into the machinery of the present government of British India.

Commonly known as "Dyarchy," or "The Reforms," it is in essence no new thing, but merely an accelerated unfolding of the original British theme whose *motif* is the drawing of Indians into responsible participation in Government. India's outburst of loyalty in the World War, her whole-hearted contribution of men and means from every province and state save Bengal, prompted a responsive flood of feeling in Britain and a desire to requite one demonstration of confidence and sympathy with another in kind. But Parliament was, in reality, only re-phrasing the original principle embodied in the Proclamation of Queen Victoria in 1858, was only pursuing the line of the Indian Councils Act of 1909, when, in the Preamble of the Act of 1919, the Act now functioning, it declared its policy [5]

. . . to provide for the increasing association of Indians in every branch of Indian Administration, and for the gradual development of self-governing institutions, with a view to the progressive realisation of responsible government in British India as an integral part of the empire.

[5] Cf. pp. 193-4 and 287, *ante*.

The scheme in its shape of today has not the stability of the slow-growing oak, root for branch, balanced and anchored. Rather, it is a hothouse exotic, weedy, a stranger in its soil, forced forward beyond its inherent strength by the heat of a generous and hasty emotion. An outsider sitting today through sessions of Indian legislatures, Central or Provincial, somehow comes to feel like one observing a roomful of small and rather mischievous children who by accident have got hold of a magnificent watch. They fight and scramble to thrust their fingers into it, to pull off a wheel or two, to play with the mainspring; to pick out the jewels. They have no apparent understanding of the worth of the mechanism, still less of the value of time. And when the teacher tries to explain to them how to wind their toy up, they shriek and grimace in fretful impatience and stuff their butterscotch into the works.

As to the relation of these people to their supposed job, its most conspicuous quality, today, is its artificiality. Adepts in the phraseology of democratic representation, they are, in fact, profoundly innocent of the thought behind the phrase. Despotisms induce no growth of civic spirit, and the peoples of India, up to the coming of Britain, had known no rule but that of despots. Britain, by her educational effort, has gradually raised up an element before unknown in India— a middle class. But this middle class—these lawyers and professional men—are in the main as much dominated today as were their ancestors five hundred years ago by the law of caste and of transmigration—completest denial of democracy. They talk of "the people" simply because the word bulks large in the vocabulary of that western-born representative government which they now essay.

A village headman knows and feels infinitely more than do these elected "representatives" as to the duties and responsibilities of government. An Indian prince has the inherited habit of ruling, and, whatever his failings, whatever his purpose, keeps his people somewhere in mind. And an American unconscious of his own civic debt to his spiritual or blood-lineal ancestors, from Plymouth Rock to Runnymede, may be brought to a wholesome state of humility by a few days' watching of the anchorless legislators of India.

Off and on, during the winter session of 1926, in Delhi, I listened to Assembly debates. Hour after hour, day after day, the Swarajist bench spent their energies in sterile, obstructionist tactics, while for the most part the rest of the House sat apathetic save for an occasional expression of weary contempt from some plain fighting man out of the north. Little or nothing constructive emanated from party benches. The simplest piece of essential legislation proposed by Government evoked from the Swarajist orators fantastic interpretations as to sinister intent. The gravest concerns elicited from them only a bedlam of frivolous and abusive chatter. "We do not trust you," they would repeat in effect; "we know your motives are bad." "We believe nothing good of your thrice-damned alien government." And, coming down to specific arraignments, they could solemnly produce such theories as that the Supreme Court of the United States obeys, in its deci-sions, the will of the British Crown.[6]

Patient, unruffled, always courteous, the Government members answered back. Not once was there a sign of irritation or annoyance or fatigue, much less of despair of the situation thrust upon them.

One day I took up this subject with one of the most notable members of the Assembly, an Indian of superior abilities, whose dislike of Britain is probably as sincere as that of any of those who attack her on this floor.

"Your fellow-legislators of the opposition make terrible accusations against the good faith of Government," I said. "They impugn its honesty; they accuse it of trying to set Hindus and Muhammadans by the ears, on the principle of 'divide and rule'; they allege that it tramples Indian interests under foot, that it treats Indians themselves with disrespect, and that it sucks or cripples the resources of the country for its own selfish interests."

"Yes," he replied, "they say all that, and more."

"Do they mean it?" I asked.

"How could they?" he replied. "Not a man in the House believes anything of the sort."

To an American having America's Philippine experience fresh in mind, this repetition of history was infinitely saddening. One remembered the words of the King-Emperor's Message to the Indian Legislature

[6] *Legislative Assembly Debates,* Vol. VII, p. 278.

and Councils at the opening of the first Sessions held
under the Reforms Act:

On you, the first representatives of the people on the new
Councils, there rests a very special responsibility. For on you
it lies, by the conduct of your business and the justice of your
judgment to convince the world of the wisdom of this great
constitutional change. But on you it also lies to remember the
many millions of your fellow-countrymen who are not yet
qualified for a share in political life, to work for their uplift-
ment and to cherish their interests as your own.

What meaning had such language in the ears of
those to whom it was addressed? What relation did
they feel, between themselves and poor old Mother
India? What duty toward their own cause, to exhibit
capacity and thereby to command further concessions?

The history of British administration of India
shows that reactionary disorders follow attempts at
speeded progress. The East resents being hustled, even
in reforms. It was perhaps specially unfortunate for
"Dyarchy" that its birthday should fall in the season
of Mr. Gandhi's ill-starred adventure into politics,
when he could turn upon it the full fire of his non-
coöperative guns. His influence in Bengal and the
Central Provinces was enough at the time to stop the
experiment completely, and although that influence
has now everywhere lapsed into negligibility as a political factor, its crippling and embittering after-effects
still drag upon the wheels of progress.

Without presuming to offer a criticism of the Reforms Act, it would seem that its chief obstacle lies deeper in the roots of things than any enmity can reach. The whole structure of the Reforms is planned to rest on the foundation of a general electorate which, through its directly elected legislators, controls in each province the Ministers who handle the people's affairs. And the difficulty is that while the structure hangs waiting in midair, the foundation designed to sustain it yet lingers in the blue-print stage—does not in fact exist. India has no electorate, in any workable sense of the word, nor can have on the present basis for many generations to come. And of this statement the natural complement is also true: India's elected representatives are as yet profoundly unaware of the nature of the duties incumbent upon their office.

Reasons for the non-existence of an electorate will have been gathered in the foregoing pages of this book. One of the chief among them is, that while less than 8 per cent. of the peoples can read at all, that literate fraction is concentrated almost entirely in the large towns and cities, leaving the great masses spread over the great spaces of the land, unreached and un-reachable by the printed word.

This illiterate peasantry, these illiterate landholders, have no access to and no interest in the political game, nor in any horizon beyond that which daily meets their physical eyes. The town politician, the legislator actual or aspirant, rarely comes near them unless it be at election time or, as in the period of the "non-violence" agitations, to stir them with some report of evil to rise in blind revolt. When, recently, Swarajist members of the legislative councils decided to try to block the wheels of government by walking out, not one of them, as far as I was able to learn, took the previous step of consulting his constituents. The constituency is as yet too gauzy a figment, too abstract a theory, too non-oriental a conception, to figure as an influence in their minds.

No one who has studied the course of events in the Central and Provincial governments during the last six years can escape the conclusion that the British government officials charged with administering the new law have striven with honesty, sincerity and devotion, to make it a success. They work against great difficulties, straining their faith and power and patience to bridge wide voids of experience and development. Their success sometimes seems dim and slight. But one of the finest executives of them all used, in my hearing, these words:

"I would ask only this: 'Leave us alone. Don't always be resurveying, reinvestigating, pulling up the plant to look at its root. Each year that we get through is a gain, one year more of peace for the people, of public works protected and advanced, of justice given. The longer we can go on, now, without any great storm, the better the chance of Councils and Ministers discovering that when we oppose them it is in obedience to our conception of a law higher than that of personal ambition or clan advantage.'"

In the last clause of the paragraph just quoted lies

half hidden one of the greatest stumbling-blocks in the way to sympathy and just judgment between India and the West. To us it seems radically obvious that personal advantage and nepotism, as motives of the acts of public officials, can but mean, the world over, shame and disgrace. Therefore the suggestion that Indians find difficulty in sharing that view carries, to our ears, the taint of moral snobbery; and so we search our own minds for other explanations of certain phenomena that follow India's autonomization of Government.

But we should be fairer to the Indian as well as wiser ourselves if we looked in his mind, rather than in ours, for light on causes. Then we should see that no white man in office ever labors under such a handicap as does the average Indian official, or ever is so largely foredoomed to defeat, in effort toward disinterested public service.

With the Hindu comes, first, the ancient religious law of the family-clan; because of this system the public office-holder who fails to feather the nest of his kin will be branded by all his world not only a fool but a renegade, and will find neither peace at home nor honor abroad. No public opinion sustains him.

Second, beyond the family line comes the circle of caste. The Hindu office-holder who should forget his caste's interests for interests lying outside that circle would bring down upon his head the opprobrium, perhaps the discipline, of his orthodox fellow caste men. And this, be it remembered, means not only temporal discomfort, but also dire penalties inflicted upon his soul, determining the miseries of future incarnations.

Third, the political struggle between Hindu and Muslim, as will be seen in later chapters, brings tremendous pressure to bear upon the official from either camp, practically compelling him to dispense such patronage as he enjoys among his co-religionists only.

With these points in mind, one views with more charity and understanding the breakdown of allegiance to western ideals that generally occurs in even the staunchest of Indian public officials when the British superior officer who has backed him through thick and thin in free work for general good, is replaced by an Indian, himself subject to the ancient code.

It is stiff work to maintain, alone and accursed, an alien standard among one's own people.

Yet with all its increased expense and diminished efficiency, the new constitution is, somehow, turning the wheels. Taking the shorter view, it has improved the position of Indians in the services. It has opened to them the height of office along many lines. It has made Government more directly responsive to the sentiment of vocal India, to such an extent indeed that the onlooker is tempted to wonder whether Government's sense of proportion is not impaired, whether it has not been nervously stifling its conscience to save its ears, whether it is not paying more attention to the spoiled baby's shrieks for the matches than it is to the vital concerns of its whole big, dumb, helpless and infinitely needy family.

A "hard-headed American" long resident in India, himself a person of excellent standing, told me this incident:

One of the principal Swaraj politicians had just delivered himself of a ferocious public diatribe against the Viceroy.

"Now tell me, Pundit," said the American, privately, "how can you shout like that in view of the fact that only a few weeks ago this very Viceroy went far out of his way to be courteous and accommodating to you and to get you what you wanted?"

"How can I shout like that?" laughed the Indian. "Why shouldn't I shout? Of course I shout, when every time I shout he gives me something."

Thus in taking information from the Indian, at home or abroad, a vital preliminary step is to appreciate and keep always in mind the definition and value that he assigns to "truth."

The Indian may be a devoted "seeker after truth" in the sense of metaphysical speculation; he may be of a splendid candor in dealing with most parts of most subjects of which you speak together. And yet he may from time to time embed in the midst of his frank speech statements easily susceptible of proof and totally at variance with the facts.

Having repeatedly come across this trait, I took it up for examination with a distinguished Bengali, one of the most broad-minded of Indian public men. Said he:

"Our *Mahabharata* preaches truth above all. If we have deviated it is because of the adverse circumstances under which we long lived. If we lie it is because we are afraid to face the consequences."

Then I laid it before a great mystic, spiritual teacher of multitudes, who had favored me with a classic and noble metaphysical discourse. His reply was:

"What is truth? Right and wrong are relative terms. You have a certain standard; if things help you, you call them good. It is not a lie to say that which is necessary to produce good. I do not distinguish virtues. Everything is good. Nothing is in itself bad. Not acts, but motives, count."

Finally, I carried the matter to a European long resident in India, and of great sympathy with the Indian mind.

"Why," I asked, "do men of high position make false statements, and then name in support documents which, when I dig them out, either fail to touch the subject at all or else prove the statement to be false?"

"Because," he replied, "to the Hindu nothing is false that he wants to believe. Or, all materiality being nothingness, all statements concerning it are lies. Therefore he may blamelessly choose the lie that serves his purpose. Also, when he presents to you the picture that it suits him to offer, it never occurs to him that you might go to the pains of checking up his words at the source."

In the same line, a well-informed New York journalist, in the winter of 1926-27, asked certain Indians who had been publicly talking in the city: "Why do you make such egregiously false allegations about conditions in India?"

"Because," said one of them, speaking for the rest, "you Americans know nothing of India. And your missionaries, when they come back for more money, tell too much truth, and hurt our pride. So we have to tell lies, to balance up."

As his metaphysics work out, it is no shame to a Hindu to be "caught in a lie." You do not embarrass or annoy him by so catching him. His morality is no more involved in the matter than in a move in a game of chess.

Now, in the name of fair play, it cannot be too strongly emphasized that this characteristic, this point of view, this different evaluation, constitutes not necessarily an inferiority, but certainly a difference, like the color of the skin. Yet as a difference involved in the heart of human intercourse, it must constantly be reckoned with and understood; else that intercourse will often and needlessly crash.

Chapter XXIII

PRINCES OF INDIA

Thus far we have been dealing mainly with British India, as distinct from the Indian Empire composed of British India and the Indian States. Of the total area of the Indian Empire—1,805,332 square miles—39 per cent. belongs to the Indian States. Of the total population of the Empire—318,942,480—the Indian States hold 23 per cent., or about 72,000,000 persons.[1] Individually, the states vary in size from properties of twenty square miles or less to a domain as large as Italy. Each is governed by its own prince, or, if the prince be a minor, by his regent or administrator. Some of the ruling houses are Hindu, some Muhammadan, some Sikh, or, in accordance with their history.

The territorial integrity, as well as the sovereign rights of the princes within their territories, was made the subject of special pledge in Queen Victoria's Proclamation of 1858 on assumption of the Paramount Power. Laying down the principle that Britain not only desired no extension of territory for herself, but would permit no aggression from any quarter upon the domains of the Indian States, the Queen added:

We shall respect the rights, dignity and honour of the Native Princes as our own; and we desire that they, as well as

[1] See *Statistical Abstract for British India from 1914-15 to 1923-24,* pp. 3-5.

Photo by Harry Hubert Field

THE VILLAGE TANK

(See page 366.)

Photos by M. Moyca Newell

BENARES

Above: Sewage-seepage cracks in the Ganges wall, and bathers **and** drinkers below. (*See* page 357.)

Below: A temple courtyard. (*See* page 360.)

our own subjects, should enjoy that prosperity and that social advancement which can only be secured by internal peace and good government.

The relation between the British Government and the ruling chiefs is a treaty relation, not that of conqueror and conquered. It leaves the princes free to determine their own types of government, to levy their own taxes, and to wield the power of life and death within their territories. The basis of the relation, on the part of Britain, is (a) non-interference in the states' internal affairs, excepting in cases of grave need, while exercising such progressive influence as may be tactfully possible; and (b) the safeguarding of the interests of the country as a whole, in matters of an Imperial character. Foreign relations and negotiations between state and state, must, however, be conducted through the Paramount Power. A British political officer, called Resident, is stationed in each of the larger states, to advise the Ruling Chief. The small states, by groups similarly, have their British advisers, members of the political branch of the Viceregal Government.

Once a year the Chamber of Princes, under the chairmanship of the Viceroy, convenes at Delhi for discussion of common policies. This assembly is a brilliant, stately and dignified function. And if, in ordinary times, no great weight of business confronts it, owing to the self-contained nature of the elements represented, its convocation nevertheless serves a wise purpose. For it tends, through personal acquaintance under favorable auspices, to harmonize relations between the ruling houses, while affording a medium for rapid common action in case of need. Nevertheless to this meeting two or three of the greatest of the princes have never yet been persuaded to come, on the ground, it is said, that occasions would arise on which for mechanical reasons some one of their number must cede precedence.

In visiting Indian States it is extremely difficult to arrive at an idea of the actual nature of the administration. One is the guest of the prince, enjoying a lavish hospitality. Like any private host, the prince is showing off the estate, exhibiting those parts that are, to him, most noteworthy. From ancient palaces to modern improvements, there is much of great beauty and interest to occupy one's eyes. And one scarcely demands of one's host, East or West: "Now, where are the defects of the picture?"

Nevertheless, it is definitely visible that several states are well-governed, that most are fairly governed, including some that are backward, and that a few are governed badly. These last exhibit the famous "Golden Age," preserved like a fly in amber. Their court life and the life of the people are sections from the unexpurgated Arabian Nights. On the one side strange outbreaks of rage, jealousy, violence, the sudden and final disappearance over night of a favorite minister, lurid punishments and poisonings, and the endless mortal intrigues of the *zenana*. On the other side a populace too lifeless even to complain of the burden that crushes it.

The old normal relation of the prince to the people was the relation of a huge-topped plant to a poor, exhausted, over-taxed root. He squeezed his people dry, giving little or nothing in return. And under such a prince, unless he be too outrageous, the people may today be fairly content. For their whole historic experience tells them little or nothing of a possible other mode of existence. And they dearly love the parade, the great ceremonies and brilliant spectacles of birthdays, marriages and religious fêtes, that their princes so regularly provide but which, because of the tax burdens involved, are rarely afforded under British rule.

On the whole, however, it is obvious that the tendency of state government is to level up. This is largely due to the growing ambition of the chiefs for the condition of their properties. Or again, progress is effected when the removal of an unfit ruler leaves the administration of the state in the hands of the Resident, with, it may be, a regent, during the minority of the heir. A measure of comparison is thereby established, favoring the birth of active discontent if a retrograde government follows and tending gradually to force up its quality from below.

As a particular instance, one may cite the case of a certain prince whose minority lasted twenty years. During this period the British Resident administered the state, and, for the first time in its history, its revenues went to the service of the people. Good roads and bridges were built, schools were opened, a modern hospital was established and endowed with a competent staff; order was secured; trade and manufactures were fostered; the exchequer made solvent, the reserve funds built up, justice was put within the reach of all. And, all the years of this pleasant novelty, the people sighed for the day when their prince, not only dearly beloved but also ritualistically half-divine in their eyes, should come home and rule over them as his fathers had done over their fathers.

The day dawned. The boy took over. The wives and the concubines, the court officials, the dancing girls and the ambitious relatives at once laid hold on him, plying him with every soft temptation that could dissolve his energy and will-power, sap his manhood and make him easy to control. In three years' time he had ruined the work of the preceding twenty. The treasury reserves were gone. Taxes shot up. Public services went flat. The excellent doctor, who cost $500 a month, had been replaced by a sixteen-dollar dealer in charms and potions. The competent hospital staff was replaced by useless hangers-on. The hospital itself had turned into a kennel; and so on, through the departments, shabbiness and decay overwhelming them all. No justice was to be had and no appeal could be taken against bought decisions, for there was none who cared to hear, except at a price. Graft did everything, and the people were bled to provide money for their young ruler's extravagances and vices.

At last they came to their old friend, the Resident, pleading:

"We did long to have him come to live among us

and rule over us. But we knew not how it would be. We can bear no more. Let the Sahib return and give us peace and justice and the good life we had before."

The people had begun to think.

Scandalous tales are told of the cruelties and monstrous deeds of certain princes, and a measure of ground work probably underlies many such tales. But none of them can be accepted without specific proof, for the reason that the Indian anti-government press seizes upon every suggestion of such material, spreading it broadcast, elaborated and magnified without regard to facts. It provides a text to attack Government for laxness in permitting such things to be; although where Government intervenes the same elements are often quick to raise the cry of "alien despot."

The boy born to the throne comes into the world with a fearful handicap. All want his favor, and the ancient highroad thereto is the ministration to unbridled sensuality, arrogance and extravagance. But sometimes there is a strong and intelligent Queen-mother who defends her son. And sometimes the heir is sent to a public school in England; or, he may spend some years in one of the four Chiefs' Colleges in India, where, also, wholesome influences are brought to bear.

One of these influences is the give-and-take of life among his peers. In his home he has no equal within reach, and is, therefore, always with inferiors or elders. A second influence for good is the constant effort to rouse him from physical and mental sloth and to get him to work and to play active games, especially games such as tennis, which he can carry back to his home. Not the least factor that the school wields in his favor is the understanding friendship of the British head-master, his appreciation of the boy's difficulties, present and to come, and his quiet instillation of that active ideal of princely pride which is the pride to serve.

In some cases the work of education seems completely lost in the boy's later life. But the development of character in others is definitely lifting the whole standard of government in the Indian States.

An outstanding example is that of the State of Mysore, a principality of size nearly equal to that of Scotland, with some six million inhabitants. The father of the present prince was carefully trained for his duties under British guidance. Acceding to a government which, during his minority, had been set in order by British supervision, he proceeded, with the aid of a good Dewan,[2] to administer well and faithfully to the interest of his people. Dying in 1894, he left a minor heir, so that again the state, in the hands of the Queen-regent, came under British guidance, while again a young prince went into training for coming responsibilities. In 1907 this prince was enthroned. Since that time he has given a high example of un-selfish and intelligent devotion to his duties.

A devout orthodox Hindu, his recent choice of a Muhammadan Persian, Mr. Mirza Ismail, C.I.E., O.B.E., as Dewan, may be taken as a proof of his

[2] Premier.

single-eyed desire for the good of his state. The city of Mysore, with its wide, shaded avenues, its fine modern public buildings, its parks and gardens, and its floods of electric light, is a model town, clean and bright. A large technical college, a large University building with its separate library, an extensive hospital, are among the many conspicuous and handsome edifices. A big irrigation scheme is nearing completion. The state's rich mineral resources, its agriculture and its peasant industries and manufactures are being developed on progressive lines. Wages of both skilled and unskilled labor have doubled in late years. A system of bringing the people, through elected representatives, into periodic communication with the head of the state on the state's affairs, is in successful operation. And finally, to dismiss so pleasant a subject too briefly, two blots on the picture are being removed.

First; An Edict has gone forth that, as between two candidates for administrative office, the office shall go to the better qualified man rather than to the man of higher caste. And, second, the state's health record being too low, the prince, through his Dewan, has not stopped short of reaching for the best the world affords. He has asked the International Health Board of the Rockefeller Foundation to help him make Mysore the cynosure of India.

The request, the second [3] of its sort to come from any part of the Indian Empire, has been gladly hon-

[3] The first request to the Rockefeller Foundation to advise a government in India came from that of the Madras Presidency. An officer of the Foundation is now stationed there.

ored. The outcome will be of extraordinary interest.

All of the princes keep armies, according to the needs of their domains. Thus the Nizam of Hyderabad, with his state of nearly 83,000 square miles maintains an army of about twenty thousand men, while the Maharaja of Datia, with but 911 square miles, commands a full company of Infantry and a battery of seven field guns. Infantry, cavalry, artillery, and transport corps compose the larger commands.

Here is a story, from the lips of one whose veracity has never, I believe, been questioned. The time was that stormy period in 1920 when the new Reforms Act was casting doubt over the land and giving rise to the persistent rumor that Britain was about to quit India. My informant, an American of long Indian experience, was visiting one of the most important of the princes —a man of great charm, cultivation and force, whose work for his state was of the first order. The prince's Dewan was also present, and the three gentlemen had been talking at ease, as became the old friends that they were.

"His Highness does not believe," said the Dewan, "that Britain is going to leave India. But still, under this new régime in England, they may be so ill-advised. So, His Highness is getting his troops in shape, accumulating munitions and coining silver. And if the English do go, three months afterward not a rupee or a virgin will be left in all Bengal."

To this His Highness, sitting in his capital distant

from Bengal by half the breadth of India, cordially agreed. His ancestors through the ages had been predatory Mahratta chiefs.

The Swarajists, it would appear, forget that, the moment government were placed in their hands, the princes would flash into the picture as powers in the land, severally to be reckoned with exactly as they were a century ago; and that the Indian Army, if it hung together at all, might be more likely to follow one of the outstanding princes rather than the commands of a Legislative Assembly composed of a type that India has never known or obeyed.

The Indian mind is cast in the mould of autocratic aristocracy. A natural war means a princely leader and unlimited loot. If His Highness above had set out for Bengal, the manpower of the countrysides, barring Britain's presence, would surely have romped after him.

But the princes know well that if Britain were to withdraw from India, they themselves, each for himself, would at once begin annexing territory; that all would be obliged to live under arms, each defending his own borders; and that the present-day politician would in the first onset finally disappear like a whiff of chaff before flame.

The princes, however, want no such issue. They frankly say that they enjoy the *pax Britannica*, which not only relieves them from the necessity of sustaining larger military establishments, but which gives them the enjoyment of public utilities, as railroads, good highroads, ports, markets, mail, and wires, while permitting them to develop their properties in peace. Their attitude during the War was wholly loyal, and they contributed munificently of money, men and goods to the Empire's cause. In a word, they are a company of high-spirited, militant aristocrats strongly interested that the British Crown shall remain suzerain in India, but absolutely refusing to carry their complaisance so far as to admit the Indian politician of the Reforms Government as an agent to their courts.

Their supreme contempt of that class is not unmingled with distinct irritation that the Power to which they acknowledge fealty stoops to parley with what seems to them an impudent and ridiculous *canaille*.

"Our treaties are with the Crown of England," one of them said to me, with incisive calm. "The princes of India made no treaty with a Government that included Bengali *babus*. We shall never deal with this new lot of Jacks-in-office. While Britain stays, Britain will send us English gentlemen to speak for the King-Emperor, and all will be as it should be between friends. If Britain leaves, we, the princes, will know how to straighten out India, even as princes should."

Then I recall a little party given in Delhi by an Indian friend in order that I might privately hear the opinions of certain Home Rule politicians. Most of the guests were, like my host, Bengali Hindus belonging to the western-educated professional class. They had spoken at length on the coming expulsion of Britain from India and on the future in which they themselves would rule the land.

"And what," I asked, "is your plan for the princes?"

"We shall wipe them out!" exclaimed one with conviction. And all the rest nodded assent.

PART V

Interlude

INTO THE NORTH

Kohat, guarding the mouth of Kohat Pass—just
one little post on the long line of the North-West
Frontier defenses. All compact and tight-set, fit for
the grim work it faces. Beds of blue violets along its
streets. Beds of blue violets in gardens, for somehow
your Briton will have flowers, wherever you strand
him. Barbed wire entanglements girdling the town.
Lights every hundred paces, and heavy-armed sen-
tries. Big arc searchlights at each corner of each house,
turned on full blaze at dusk. No shrubs, no trees or
other cover for skulkers, allowed too near a dwelling.
No white woman permitted outside the wire after day-
light begins to fail; not because of fears, but because
of things that have happened. Army officers' wives
they are, the few white women in Kohat; the quiet,
comradely sort that play the whole game to the finish.

And not one moment of any day or night, in this or
any Frontier post, is free from mortal danger.

Under the wing of the Post, an Indian town, ringed
about by high mud walls. Bazaars, mosques, temples,
blind-faced houses in pinched and tortuous streets,
where hawk-nosed men in sheepskin coats, with rifles
lying in the crook of their arms, shoulder bullocks and
asses for passage. Hundreds of little stalls, like booths

[321]

in a country fair, reflect the Afghan boundary. Wonderful shining slippers, heelless and curly-toed, for the little feet of Muslim ladies; Persian bed-posts, gayly lacquered; beautiful gauzes; block-printed silks and cottons; vessels inlaid in tin and brass or copper; peacock pottery; fine fox-skins from the mountains; red rugs from Bokhara; meat, for this is a Muslim country; rice and curry and sugar, because certain Hindus have ventured in, lending money while they sell their wares and getting always richer with their money-lending.

Getting too rich, maybe, and a little too confident. For though the hawk-nosed man in the big sheepskin coat may not be their match in playing with money, that lurks in his half-humorous, wholly piercing hawk-eye that should warn the boldest.

Besides, this hawk-nosed, hawk-eyed citizen is here in his own country. And no more than a revolver-shot away, in the gray, impending crags of the Frontier mountains lurk his brother Muslims, the wild tribes who call no man king or master, who know no business other than that of raiding, and whose favorite year-round sport is the kidnapping of Hindu money-lenders to hear the queer sounds they emit in the course of the subsequent entertainment.

In all this world, say the men who, day and night, year in, year out, guard the frontier of India—in all this world are no fighters better than the tribesmen. Also, behind them lies Afghanistan, like a couchant leopard, green eyes fixed on the glittering bait of

India. And behind Afghanistan—nay, in Kabul itself, lurks "the Man that walks like a Bear," fingering gold and whispering ceaselessly of the glories of a rush across the border that shall sweep the Crescent through the strong Muslim Punjab, gathering Islam in its train; that shall raise the Muslims of the South and so shall close from both sides, like a tide, forever, over the heads of the Hindus.

"Why not?" asks the Bear. "Are you feebler men than your fathers? What stops you? The English? But look! I worry them on the other flank, stirring up the silly Hindus, North and South, against them. Already these English relax their hand, as the councils of their home-country weaken. And, I, the Bear, am behind you. Look at the loot and the killings! Drive in your wedge! Strike!"

Chapter XXIV

FIREBRANDS TO STRAW

Roughly speaking, three-quarters of the population of British India are Hindus, if the 60,000,000 Untouchables be computed with the Hindus.[1] Roughly speaking, one quarter of the population of British India is Muhammadan. And between the two lies a great gulf whence issues a continuous threatening rumble, with periodic destructive outbursts of sulphur and flame.

This gulf constitutes one of the greatest factors in the present Indian situation.

Its elements formed integral parts of the problem that the British Crown assumed in 1858. And if for the first half-century of Crown rule they remained largely dormant, the reason is not obscure. During that half-century, Government was operated by British officers of the Civil Service, both in the administrative and in the judicial branches. These officers, in the performance of their duties, made no difference between Hindu and Muhammadan, holding the general interest in an equal hand. Therefore, being in the enjoyment of justice and of care, man by man, day by day, and from an

[1] The Census of India of 1921 shows about three and a quarter million Sikhs and about one and a sixth million Jains, of both of which sects many members call themselves Hindus. The Buddhists, numbering eleven and a half millions, are largely confined to the Province of Burma, outside the Indian Peninsula.

outside authority that neither Hindu nor Muhammadan could challenge, neither party was roused to jealousy, and religious communal questions scarcely arose.

In 1909, however, the wind switched to a stormy quarter. The Minto-Morley scheme was enacted by Parliament as the "Indian Councils Act."

The effect of this measure was instantly to alarm the Muhammadan element, rousing it into self-consciousness as a distinct and separate body, unorganized, but suspicious, militant in spirit and disturbed about its rights. For it saw, clearly enough, that in any elected legislature, and in any advantages thereby to be gained, the Hindu was practically sure to shoulder the Muhammadan out of the path.

Now in order to understand how this situation came about, it is necessary to recall that Muhammadanism first came to India as the religion of the conqueror; that for five hundred years its arm controlled the greater part of India, during which period Persian was the language of the court, the language of literature and verse, the language of the law. But the Muhammadan, though he learned his Koran and his Persian verse, was as a rule an open-air sort of man who would rarely bother his own head with pens or books if he could find another to do the job for him. Therefore, whenever some Brahman, with his quick brain and facile memory, acquired a knowledge of Persian and thereby released his further store of learning for the master's use, he was apt to find a desirable niche in government service.

Consequently, for five centuries or so, the Brahman did much of the paper work, while the Muhammadan commanded the country.

The history of the interval between Islam's effective dominance and the assumption of direct administration by the British Crown has been elsewhere outlined.[2] It was twenty-one years previous to the latter event—back in the days of the East India Company—that a little seed was sown with whose fruit we now deal.

This was the changing of the language of the Courts of Justice from Persian to English.

The change took place as a logical part of the westernizing of Indian education. It looked simple. Its results have been simple, like the results of a clean stroke of the ax. The Calcutta University Commission thus suggests the initial process: [3]

The influence of the Act of 1837 and the Resolution of 1844 [giving preference in government appointments to Indians who had received a Western education] upon the Hindu *bhadralok* [4] from among whom all the minor officials had long been drawn, was bound to be decisive. They had long been in the habit of learning a foreign language—Persian—as a condition of public employment; they now learnt English instead. It was, indeed, the Hindus who alone took advantage of the new opportunities in public education in any large numbers. The Musalmans naturally protested strongly against the change; which was, indeed, disastrous for them. Hitherto their

[2] *See* pp. 283 *et seq., ante.*
[3] *Report,* Vol. I, Part I, pp. 37-8.
[4] Professional classes.

knowledge of Persian had given them a considerable advantage. They refused to give up learning it. It was for them the language of culture. To take up English in addition would be too heavy a burden; moreover, they had learnt to think of English as associated with Christian teaching, owing to the activity of the missionaries, and they were less willing than the Hindus to expose their sons to missionary influences. Their pride and their religious loyalty revolted; and they stood aloof from the movement.

Literate or illiterate, the Muhammadan is a passionate monotheist. "There is but One God." His mosques are clear of images. His frequent daily prayer is offered straight to the invisible One Omnipotent. And although he respects Christianity as a revealed religion and reverences Christ as an inspired teacher, the doctrine of the Trinity constitutes an impossible heresy. His faith is his highest possession, and he would not willingly open the door to what he considered impure doctrine by learning its vehicle, the English tongue.

Deeply hurt by the alternatives forced upon it, Islam withdrew into itself, little foreseeing the consequences of its withdrawal.

As long as British officials administered the affairs of India in town and village, the potentiality of the situation thus created remained obscured. But the first gun of the Minto-Morley "Reforms," rent the curtain, and the startled Islamic chiefs, their hands on the hilt of the sword a-rust in the scabbard, peered forth half-awake upon a world dark with shapes of ill-omen.

And so, greatly at a disadvantage, the Muslims as

[327]

a political entity reappeared in the field. Yet over the wide country, in the villages and the hamlets, the stir scarcely reached. For there, still, the British official alone represented Government, dealing justice and favor with an even hand, and Muslim and Hindu, side by side, lived at peace.

Then came 1919, the extension of the "Reforms" of 1909, the transfer of much power, place and patronage from British into Indian hands, and the promise, furthermore, of a reviewal of the field at the end of a third ten-year interval, with an eye to still further transfers.

From that moment, except in country districts unreached by agitators, peace between the two elements became a mere name—an artificial appearance maintained wholly by the British presence. And now, as 1929 draws nigh, the tension daily increases, while the two rivals pace around each other in circles, hackles up, looking for first toothhold.

For a time during the political disturbances that followed the War a brief farce of unity was played by the leaders of that day. Mr. Gandhi embraced the Khilafat [5] agitation as embodied in those picturesque freebooters, the Ali brothers, if thereby the Muhammadan weight might be swung with his own to embarrass the British administration. But the Khilafat cause itself died an early death. And a single incident of the

[5] An Islamic movement aiming at the restoration of Turkey to prewar status, including her reconquest of the emancipated Armenians and Arabs, and her recovery of Palestine, Syria, Thrace, and the Dardanelles.

[328]

Gandhi-Ali alliance may be cited to illustrate the actual depth of the brotherhood it proclaimed.

Up on the mountains overlooking the Malabar coast, among a population of about two million Hindus, live a people known as the Moplahs, descendants of old Arab traders and the women of the country. The Moplahs, who themselves number about a million, live in surprisingly clean and well-kept houses, have often intelligent, rugged faces and, according to my own experience, are an interesting and friendly primitive folk.

But, zealot Muhammadans, they have ever been prone to outbreaks of religious passion in which their one desire is to be sent to Paradise by a bullet or a knife, first having piled up the longest possible list of non-believers dead by their hands.

Among these simple creatures, in the year of disorders 1921, the political combination above indicated sent emissaries preaching a special edition of its doctrines. Government's hand, these proclaimed, was raised against the holy places of Islam. Government was "Satanic," an enemy of the Faith. Government must and would be driven out of India and that right soon. Swaraj must be set up.

From mosque to mosque, from hamlet to hamlet, from cocoanut grove to cocoanut grove, the fiery words passed. And, whatever meaning they might bear for an abstract philosopher, to the simple Moplah, as, in those miserable years, to so many millions of simple

Hindus all over the land, they meant just what they said—War.

But, the point that Mr. Gandhi missed, whatever the humorous Ali brothers may privately have thought about it, was this: Swaraj, to a Moplah, could only mean the coming of the earthly Kingdom of Islam, in which, whatever else happened or failed to happen, no idol-worshiping Hindu could be tolerated alive.

So the Moplahs, secretly and as best they could, made store of weapons—knives, spears, cutlasses. And on August 20, 1921, the thing broke loose. As if by a preliminary gesture of courtesy to the sponsors of the occasion, one European planter was murdered at the start. But without further dissipation of energy the frenzied people then concentrated on the far more congenial task of communal war. First blocking the roads, cutting the telegraph wires and tearing up the railway lines at strategic points, thereby isolating the little police stations scattered through the mountains, they set to work, in earnest and in detail, to establish a Muslim Kingdom and to declare a Swaraj after their own hearts.

Their Hindu neighbors, though outnumbering them two to one, seem to have stood no chance against them. The Hindu women, as a rule, were first circumcised— "forcibly converted," as the process is called—and were then added to Moplah families. The Hindu men were sometimes given the choice of death or "conversion," sometimes flayed alive, sometimes cutlassed at once and thrown down their own wells. In one district, the

Ernad Taluk, over nine hundred males were "forcibly converted" and the work spread on through the mountain-slopes.

As rapidly as possible police and troops were thrown into the country, by whose work, after six months of trying service, the disorders were quelled. But not until some three thousand Moplahs had cast away their lives, without reckoning the Hindus they accounted for, not until much property had been destroyed and many families ruined, and not until a long list of prisoners awaited trial for guilt that certainly belonged on heads higher than theirs.

Meantime, the circumcised male Hindus wandered up and down the land calling upon their brethren to take warning.

A trained American observer, agent of the United States Government, chanced to be in the region at the time. His statement follows:

"I saw them in village after village, through the south and east of Madras Presidency. They had been circumcised by a peculiarly painful method, and now, in many cases, were suffering tortures from blood poisoning. They were proclaiming their misery, and calling on all their gods to curse Swaraj and to keep the British in the land. 'Behold our miserable bodies! We are defiled, outcasted, unclean, and all because of the serpents who crept among us with their poison of Swaraj. Once let the British leave the land and the shame that has befallen us will assuredly befall you also, Hindus, men and women, every one.'

[331]

"The terrors of hell were literally upon them.

"And the Brahman priests were asking one hundred to one hundred and fifty rupees a head to perform the purification ceremony which alone could save the poor creatures' souls.

"This ceremony consisted in filling the eyes, ears, mouth and nose with soft cow-dung, which must then be washed out with cow's urine, after which should be administered *ghee* (clarified butter), milk and curds. It sounds simple, but can only be performed by a Brahman, and with proper rites and sacred verses. And the price which the Brahmans now set upon their services was, to most of the needy, prohibitive. Their distress was so desperate that British officials, for once interfering in a religious matter, interceded with the Brahmans and persuaded them, in view of the large number concerned, to accept a wholesale purification fee of not over twelve rupees a head."

I have not verified the final item in this statement. My informant, however, besides having been on the spot at the time, is professionally critical as to evidence.

If there was anything particularly Muhammadan in this outbreak, it was in the feature of "forcible conversion" rather than in the general barbarity educed. Less than six months before the Moplah affair began, occurred the Chauri Chaura incident in the United Provinces, far away from Malabar.

An organization called the "National Volunteers" had lately been formed, more or less under pay, to act as a militia for the enforcement of the decrees of the

Working Committee of the Indian National Congress. This "Congress" is a purely political organization, and was, at the time, under the control of Mr. Gandhi.

On February 4, 1921, a body of National Volunteers, followed by a mob whom their anti-government propaganda had inflamed, attacked the little police station at Chauri Chaura, within which were assembled some twenty-one police constables and village watchmen, the common guardians of the rural peace. The peasantry and the "Volunteers," numbering altogether some three thousand men, surrounded the police station, shot a few of its inmates dead, wounded the rest, collected the wounded into a heap, poured oil over them, and fried them alive.

This was as Hindu to Hindu.

Again, in the Punjab during the disorders of 1919, anti-Government workers launched a special propaganda for the violation of foreign women.

Its public declarations took the form of posters such as these: "Blessed be Mahatma Gandhi. We are sons of India . . . Gandhi! We the Indians will fight to death after you;" and "What time are you waiting for now? There are many ladies here to dishonor. Go all around India, clear the country of the ladies," etc., etc.[6]

This was as Indian to white man.

Such language, to such a public, could carry neither a figurative nor a second import. Had time been given it to do its work, had a weak hand then held the helm

[6] See *Disorders Inquiry Committee, 1919-20, Report,* Chapter VII, for placards posted in and around Lyallpur, in April, 1919.

of the Punjab, an unbearable page had been written in the history of India.

And if these three instances are here brought forward from among the scores of grim contemporaneous parallels with which they can be diversified and reënforced, it is not for the purpose of shaming the Indian peoples, but rather to point out the wild, primitive and terribly explosive nature of the elements that politicians and theorists take into their hands when they ignite those people's passions.

In most rural regions even now no developed Hindu-Muhammadan animosity exists, and the two elements live together amicably enough as neighbors, unless outside political agents have disturbed them.

Instances occur, to be sure, such as that in the District of Bulandshahr, near Delhi, in the year 1924, when the Ganges flooded. It was a disastrous flood, sweeping away whole villages and their inhabitants, man and beast. Upon certain Hindu ferrymen and fishermen, the local owners of boats, depended the first work of rescue. And these made use of the opportunity to refuse to take a single drowning Muhammadan out of the water.

But, on the other hand, I recall visiting a village night-school, set up by Muhammadans for their own boys, which was in part supported by contributions from the Hindu neighbors. This was in Nadia District, in Bengal, where the villagers of the two religions seemed to bear no sort of ill-will toward each other, and where an ever-active British Deputy Commissioner was their confidant and chosen counsellor in all their affairs.

Something, again, is to be learned from the simple history of a park designed for the city of Lucknow. When the ground came to be surveyed, it was found that a little Hindu temple lay in one corner of the allotted area. Following their established policy in such matters, the British authorities left the temple undisturbed.

Then came the Muhammadans of the city, saying: "We, too, desire a place in this fine new park wherein to say our prayers."

So the Municipal authorities arranged that a suitable open space be set aside at the opposite corner of the park for the Muhammadans. And the Hindus worshiped in their temple, and the Muhammadans worshiped in their open space, both quite happily and innocently, for a matter of eight years.

In the interval came the "Reforms," came the fruit of the "Reforms," came a tension, stiffening steadily.

For Lucknow is a Muhammadan city, in the sense that all the important people, all the old families, all the great buildings and monuments, are of the ancient Muhammadan kingdom of Oudh. Wherefore the Muhammadans felt that if the control of India was about to revert to Indians' hands their city of Lucknow ought to revert to them.

But, though the history and the aristocracy of Lucknow are indubitably Muhammadan, in the population of Lucknow the Hindu outnumbers the Muhammadan three to one. Wherefore the Hindus, filled with sudden fear of the future, now asked each other:

"If this Swaraj is indeed coming, where will it plant us Hindus of Lucknow? Under Muhammadan masters? Better were we all dead men!"

Upon which they began to organize, to assert themselves, perhaps rather aggressively and offensively, and particularly to do so each evening, toward sunset, in that little old temple by the park.

Now, sunset is an hour appointed for Muslim devotion. For eight years the Muslim prayer-rugs had been spread, five minutes before sunset, in that same little park, and the faithful, kneeling in rows, had said their vespers there. Nor would they submit to interruption by obstreperous Hindus now. So, they issued an edict: The Hindus, hereafter, must choose for their temple meeting a time that did not clash with the Muhammadans' evening prayer.

The Hindus resented the edict of the Muhammadans. The Muhammadans resented the resentment of the Hindus. Tinder smoldered up to flame. And presently big gangs of each religion gathered in the park at one and the same hour to fight the thing to a finish.

In the matter ensuing, the Muhammadans seem to have been the more skillful, since they swept the field quickly of human impedimenta and were about to smash the offensive temple itself, when a detachment of police, reënforced by British troops, intervened.

Thus this particular incident came to a standstill, **such** of the combatants as were able dispersing to their homes. But an intense and really dangerous feeling, bred of the battle and of the fear and jealousy in the air, survived in full vigor. If a small lurking party of the other side saw a Hindu or a Muhammadan pass in the street, that party would dash out, seize and beat him. To restore confidence it was necessary for two or three days to patrol the city streets with British cavalry.

Enter, then, the British District Commissioner—for cities, as well as rural parts, have their commissioners. And the Commissioner, obviously, must "arrange." For the quarrel was literally ruining the town. Trade was suffering, small shops were failing, the people were boycotting each other, and fresh broils and violence, promising any eruption, disfigured every day.

So the Commissioner invited the leaders of the factions to come to his house and talk it over—because his house was the only place where they would meet in peace. They came, and sat, and came again. They sat and talked and talked again. And neither party would yield an inch.

The Hindus insisted that they must begin to beat their prayer drums five minutes before sunset. The Muhammadans as firmly maintained: "At exactly five minutes before sunset we must begin our evening worship, which you Hindus shall not disturb."

Yet at last the Commissioner prevailed. For he elicited from the Hindus a concession of five minutes, and from the Muhammadans a concession of five minutes. Then, with his combined winnings safe under his feet, he proceeded to extract from the Hindus a promise that, during the last ten minutes before sunset, they would not play music in their temple; and from the Muhammadans a promise that on the dot of the first of the silent ten minutes they would begin their ten-minute vesper prayer.

For, during the conferences in the Commissioner's drawing room, the fact had developed that the Muhammadans' objection lay, not to the Hindus' praying, but to the din they made at their prayers, hammering temple gongs and drums.

Those joint conferences in the Commissioner's drawing room lasted, altogether, fifteen hours. As the fifteenth hour closed, the Commissioner's dinner-gong rang in the hall. Whereupon one of the Hindus pondered aloud:

"That gong's voice, over in our temple, wouldn't reach so far."

"Will you try it and see?" asked the Commissioner, quickly. And to this day the Hindus of that Lucknow temple worship to the low and mellow voice of the British Commissioner's dinner-gong.

But that experienced official is by no means deluding himself with the notion that he can now go to sleep on his post.

Photo by M. Moyca Newell

THE PLAGUE VILLAGE

"Sahib, what shall we do?" (*See* page 376.)

Photos by M. Moyca Newell

A MAHRATTA GYPSY FISHER-GIRL   A SHEPHERDESS OF GUJERAT

Chapter XXV

SONS OF THE PROPHET

In December, 1916, a political body called the All-India Muslim League united with the Indian National Congress already mentioned, in proclaiming the identity of Muhammadan and Hindu interests, and in asserting their common desire for Swaraj.

The white light of the Moplah uprising remained yet veiled on the knees of the future, but at the joint act of the two organizations, the Muhammadans' instinct of self-preservation, far and wide over India, took alarm. So that when, in the autumn of 1917, Mr. Montagu, Secretary of State for India, sat in Delhi to receive from Indian interests their views on the subject of his proposed Reforms, association after association came forward to deplore or to repudiate the act of the All-India Muslim League; and the language they used was simple enough. Said the United Provinces Muslim Defence Association: [1]

. . . any large measure of self-government which might curtail the moderating and adjusting influence of the British Government could be nothing short of a cataclysm.

Said the Indian Muslim Association of Bengal: [2]

[1] *Addresses Presented in India to His Excellency the Viceroy and the Right Honourable the Secretary of State for India,* London, 1918, p. 10.
[2] *Ibid.,* p. 30.

[339]

In the existing backward condition of the majority of
Hindus and Muslims, with their divergent creeds, castes, institutions and clashing interests, the differences which separate
the Hindu from the Muslim cannot but be reflected in their
dealings and relations with each other. . . . No careful observer will be deluded by the deceptive unanimity of the National Congress and the Muslim League . . .

The Indian Muslim Association . . . does not agree to
the wisdom of any catastrophic changes likely to weaken the
permanance and stability of British rule in India, upon the
broad foundations of which rest all our hopes and aspirations
of constitutional and administrative progress.

Said the Association to Safeguard the Muslim Interests in the Province of Bihar and Orissa: [3]

We cannot deprecate too strongly the want of foresight
displayed by some of our co-religionists in endorsing in their
entirety, the views and claims of the Congress. Already
there is strong tendency visible in certain quarters to oppress
and terrorise the Musalmans and ignore . . . their interests.
The guiding principle of the English rule up to now has
always been to administer the affairs of Indian Empire with
impartiality in the presence of diverse religions and nationali-
ties of which it is composed. . . .

The South India Islamia League [4] presented a plea
in which they reminded Mr. Montagu that, being a
minority community, they

. . . realise the value of the British Government in holding
the scales even between different classes in this country . . .

[3] *Addresses Presented in India to His Excellency the Viceroy and
the Right Honourable the Secretary of State for India,* p. 40.
[4] *Ibid.,* pp. 62-3.

[and] are opposed to any scheme of political reconstruction which tends to undermine the authority of British Govern‍ment in India, but are strongly in favour of gradual progres‍sive political development.

The Muttialpet Muslim Anjuman, a Muhammadan educational society of Madras, implored Mr. Montagu to stay his reforming hand: [5]

The Britisher alone can hold the scales even between the various communities. Whenever our interests collide with those of other communities, it is to him we look up as the embodiment of justice and fair play. Whatever reforms may be introduced, we trust that nothing will be done to undermine the authority of the British Government in India.

The Muhammadans of the Bombay Presidency presented an anxious appeal which read in part: [6]

It is freely asserted that in no distant future the English bureaucracy will disappear and an Indian majority in the Councils will take its place. Whatever may have been the defects of that much abused bureaucracy in the past, it must be admitted that it has had one redeeming merit, viz., that of holding the balance even as between the two principal communities in India, and thus protecting the weak against the strong.

But in view of the nature of Muhammadan thought, a more ominous weight lay in a simpler pronouncement. The Ulema is the body of official interpreters of the Koran which, on occasion of doubt, delivers deci-

[5] *Ibid.*, p. 63.
[6] *Ibid.*, pp. 78-9.

sions that guide the Muslim world. The solemn verdict of the Ulema of Madras, now laid before the British Secretary of State for India, was expressed in three closely similar dicta, one of which follows: [7]

"Verily, Polytheists are unclean." In case the British Government were to hand over the administration, as desired by the Hindus, it would be contrary to the Sacred Law of Musulmans to live under them, Polytheists.

Saiyid Muhi-ud-din
Trustee of the endowments of the
Amir-un-Nisa. Begum Sahiba Mosque
One who is forgiven!

The comparative numbers of the Hindu and the Muhammadan element in the major provinces of British India may be seen from the following table: [8]

Province	Hindus	Muhammadans
Madras	88.64	6.71
Bombay	76.58	19.74
Bengal	43.27	53.99
United Provinces	85.09	14.28
Bihar and Orissa	82.84	10.85
Central Provinces and Berar	83.54	4.05
Assam	54.34	28.96
Punjab	31.80	55.33
North-West Frontier Province	6.66	91.62

[7] *Addresses Presented in India to His Excellency the Viceroy and the Right Honourable the Secretary of State for India*, pp. 63-4.
[8] *Statistical Abstract for British India, from 1914-15 to 1923-24*, pp. 14-5.

[342]

Now, in view of the militant character developed in any people by the Islamic faith, it appears that British India's Muhammadan factor, even where it is weakest, is strong enough to make trouble. Always an international rather than a nationalist, all over India the Muhammadan is saying today: "We are foreigners, conquerors, fighting men. What if our numbers are small! Is it numbers, or men, that count? When the British go, *we* shall rule India. Therefore it behooves us quickly to gain such ground as we can."

The Hindu, on his side, wittingly misses no step to consolidate his own position. And so wherever choice rests in Indian hands, every office must be filled, every decision taken, every appropriation spent, on religious communal lines, while the other side fights it, tooth and nail, and the actual merits of the matter concerned disappear from the picture.

Heavily as this condition in all directions handicaps the public service, nowhere is its influence more stultifying than in the judiciary. Always an eager litigant, the Indian finds in his religious quarrels endless occasions for appeal to law. But, if the case must be tried before an Indian judge, one side or the other is in despair. For, though he were, in fact, a miracle of rectitude, he is expected to lean, in his verdict, to the side of his own creed, and nothing can persuade the litigant of the other faith that he will not do so.

The bench of India has been and is graced by some native judges of irreproachable probity. Yet the Indian is traditionally used to the judge who accepts a fee from either side in advance of the trial, feeling that probity is sufficiently served if, after the verdict, the fee of the loser is returned. Bought witnesses are also a matter of course; you may see them today squatting before the court house waiting to be hired. "Theoretically I know it is irregular," said one western-educated barrister of Madras, "but practically I cannot leave that advantage entirely in my opponent's hands. It is our custom."

But when the matter of the Hindu-Muslim conflict enters in, all else as a rule gives way. "How shall any judge decide against his gods?" moans the unfortunate. "And does he not hold court in the midst of my enemies? Take me, therefore, before an English judge, who cares naught for these matters but will give me upright judgment, though I be right or wrong."

A freakish case was that of an old, experienced Muhammadan District Magistrate of the United Provinces before whom, last year, were brought certain police officers of his district. These men had grossly failed in their duty during certain religious riots, entailing thereby the death of several persons. They richly deserved a severe sentence. But they were Hindus. Therefore the judge, fearing the accusation of religious animosity, let them off with a sentence so light as to amount to an unjust award and an offense against the public service.

More usual is the spirit illustrated in another incident, which occurred in February, 1926. An old Muhammadan assistant engineer who had long served in the Irrigation Department under a British superior, suddenly found himself taking orders from a Hindu. This young man, just out of college and full of new ideas, set himself to worry his senior, baiting and pin-pricking till his victim could bear no more.

So, accompanied by his son, the old Muslim sought out a major British official, asking for counsel.

"Sahib, can't you help my father? Surely it is a shame, after all his years of service, to treat him so!" exclaimed the son, at the end of the story.

But the Briton could not resist his opportunity. "Mahmoud," said he. "You have always wanted *swaraj*. You see, in this, what *swaraj* does to you. How do you feel about it?"

"Aha!" replied the youngster. "But I've got a Deputy Collectorship now. I take office shortly, and when I do, God help the Hindus I get my hands on!"

The Muslim comprises but a bare quarter of the population of British India. But that percentage is growing. His gains indicate both superior fecundity and superior vitality. His brain is not quick, but he has often a gift of horse sense. He is beginning to see that he must go to school. Granted time, opportunity and a sense of security, he may wipe out his handicaps and fit himself for full participation in the administration of the country. Thrown into the arena today, he would see but one recourse—the sword.

And it should never for a moment be forgotten that when the Muslims of India draw the sword, it will not be as an isolated body but as the advance line of an

[345]

energy now banked up, like the waters of a brimming reservoir, by the Frontier Defense of the Army.

A glance at the map shows a strip of territory some three hundred and fifty miles long by from twenty to fifty miles wide, lying along the northern boundary of the Punjab. This strip is the North-West Frontier Province. Beyond it lies a parallel strip of similar dimensions, tribal territory occupied by independent Muhammadan clans, superb fighters whose sole business, since time began, has been the business of raiding. Behind this, again, lies Muhammadan Afghanistan and Muhammadan Asia, a huge primeval engine always to be swung as one great hammer by the call to loot and a Holy War.

To release that force needs at any moment but a word. Its ceaseless pressure along the thin steel line of the frontier, its tenseness, its snapping, stinging electric current, is scarcely realizable until one sees and feels it for one's self.

Few Hindu politicians do realize it. "The Afghan has kept off us these many long years. Why should he come through now? Bah! It is a child's bogey!" they say with dull eyes, as unaware of their own life-long protected state and how it is brought about as the oyster on its sea-bed is unaware of the hurricanes that blow.

The North-West Frontier Province, 95 per cent. Muhammadan, lies today quiet and contented with its government, a buffer state between, on the one hand, the rich, part-Hindu Punjab and the vast soft Hindu South, and on the other hand, the hungry Muslim fighting hordes whose fingers twitch and whose mouths water to be at them. The contentment of the North-West Frontier Province with things as they are is invaluable to the peace of India.

I talked with many leading men of that province. All seemed of one mind in the matter. Here, therefore, are the exact words of a single representative—a mountain-bred man of Persian ancestry some generations back—big, lean, hawk-nosed, hawk-eyed, leader of many, sententious until his subject snatched the bridle from his tongue:

"The whole province is satisfied now and desires no change. As for those little folk of the South, we have never called them men. There is far more difference between us and them than between us and the British. If the British withdraw, immediate hell will follow, in the first days of which the Bengali and all his tribe will be removed from the earth. I can account for a few, myself, with much pleasure. Coöperation between the British and us is our one course. They have given us roads, telephones, good water where no water was before, peace, justice, a revenue from trade made possible only by their protection, safety for our families, care for our sick and schools for our children. None of these things did we have till they came. I ask you, is it likely we shall throw them all away because a coward and a sneak and our own inherited enemy calls for 'boycott,' and 'non-coöperation'? Nothing was ever gained and much lost by that stupid 'non-coöperation.' India is a big country and needs all our united strength can do for it. Muslims and British and even Hindus. But without the British no Hindus will remain in India except such as we keep for slaves."

On December 26, 1925, over eight years after the Indian National Congress and the All-India Muslim League proclaimed their united demand for the self-government of India, the former, or Hindu body, assembled for its annual session. Its president, this time a woman, a product of European life and education, opened the proceedings with an address that deplored the

. . . sharp and importunate sense of aloofness on the part of my Muslim brothers, which, to the profound alarm and resentment of the Hindu community, manifests itself in a growing and insistent demand for separate and preferential rights and privileges in academic, official, civic and political circles of life.

A few days later the All-India Muslim League convened. And the address of its president, Sir Abdur Rahim, coming as a tacit reply to the earlier pronouncement, was so clean-hewn as to constitute a landmark in Indian history. It repays study at length.[9]

Hindus and Mussalmans are not two religious sects like the Protestants and Catholics in England but form two distinct communities or peoples. . . . Their respective attitudes towards life, their distinctive culture, civilisation and social habits, their traditions and history no less than their religion,

[9] Sir Abdur Rahim's address was published in pamphlet form by Karim Bux Brothers, Calcutta.

divide them so completely that the fact that they have lived in the same country for nearly a thousand years has contributed hardly anything to their fusion into a nation.

Referring to recent Hindu movements set on foot to proselyte Mussalmans, and to train Hindus in the arts of self-defense, the speaker said:

The Muslims regard these movements . . . as the most serious challenge to their religion which they ever had to meet not even excepting the Christian crusades whose main objective was to wrest back from the Muslims some places sacred to both. . . . In fact, some of the Hindu leaders have talked publicly of driving out the Muslims from India as the Spaniards expelled the Moors from Spain. . . . We shall, undoubtedly be a big mouthful for our friends to swallow. . . .

Any of us Indian Mussulmans travelling, for instance in Afghanistan, Persia, Central Asia, among Chinese Muslims, Arabs, Turks . . . would at once be made at home and would not find anything . . . to which we are not accustomed. On the contrary, in India, . . . we find ourselves in all social matters total aliens when we cross the street and enter that part of town where our fellow Hindu townsmen live. . . .

It is not true that we Muslims would not like to see a self-governing India provided the Government . . . is made as much responsible to the Muslims as to the Hindu. . . . Otherwise, all vague generalities such as swaraj, or commonwealth of India, or home-rule for India have no attraction for us. . . . But as a first step we must . . . definitely check the baneful activities of those Hindu politicians who under the protection of Englishmen's bayonets and taking advantage of their tolerance and patience are sowing trouble in the land to attain swaraj, the full implications of which they do not understand and would never face. . . .

The real solution of the problem . . . is to bring about a state of things in which the conditions of life of the entire population—Hindus, Muslims, Sikhs, Parsis and Christians, the peasants, labourers and Hindu untouchables—will be so improved economically and intellectually and the political power so distributed in the general population, that domination by a class of monopolists and intelligensia, will have disappeared and with that all strife between the different communities.

It has been my lot to be in daily contact with educated Englishmen, for nigh upon 35 years as practising barrister, as Judge, . . . and last of all as Member of the Executive Council of Bengal. . . .

I wish to acknowledge without reserve that I found that I had much to learn from my English colleagues at every stage of my career. . . . I have also been associated with many eminent countrymen of mine in the discharge of public duties and I believe they will admit that most of the progressive measures were originated by the initiative of Englishmen. . . . In the Government, I cannot recall even a single occasion when there was agreement on any question among us Indians that our opinion was disregarded. . . . I have not known any one who has seriously suggested that the people of this country left solely to themselves would be able at present to set up a government of their own and maintain it against outside attacks. . . . It is best for us all to recognise frankly that the presence of the English people . . . is justified by necessity. . . . England owes a great moral debt to India and the only way she can discharge that debt is by taking all possible measures to help her to become self-reliant and strong.

The best men of England recognise this obligation. . . . I do not know whether the revolutionaries have any political programme; if they have, they have not divulged it. Their immediate objective, apparently, is to overthrow the British régime, and with it the entire present system of Government. We can, however, dismiss the revolutionaries because there is not the least possible chance of their success.

We Muslims whose history for 1300 years and more has been one of constant struggles and wars, spreading over Asia, Africa and Europe, cannot but regard as extremely foolish and insane the men who think that by throwing a few bombs now and then, or shooting one or two Englishmen from behind, or by rasing and looting the houses of unsuspecting and defenceless Indian villagers and by killing and torturing them, they are going to shake the foundations of British power in India. . . . We Muslims cannot regard boys or men suffering from hysteria as serious politicians and the fact is significant that not a single Muslim has joined them. . . .

Political measures are not the sole means of building up a nation. At present we have not even a vernacular name for the people of India including Hindus, Muslims and others, nor a common language. . . . It is neither by the English alone nor by the Hindus or the Mussalmans acting singly, but by the earnest and united efforts of all that the 300 millions of India's population can be led to a higher destiny.

Sir Abdur Rahim's plain words brought down a storm of accusation from the Hindu leaders and their press, while the rancor between the two camps grew stronger.

Meantime, grim potentialities were beginning to be dimly perceived. The Calcutta Riots broke out. By midsummer, 1926, thirty-one murderous explosions had occurred since the beginning of the year, some with heavy casualties.[10] It was already evident that both sides, Muslim and Hindu, were becoming sobered by the situation into which their mutual fears had brought them. The old Gandhi-ist accusation that the secret hand of Britain bred their dissensions still found its mouthpieces; but these, commonly, were of the irresponsible firebrand type who had no stake in the country save such as might best be served under cover of smoke. Thinking men of either party saw the untenability of the idea and began, however reluctantly, to declare the need of a strong and impartial suzerain to give them security in the advantages already in their possession; advantages which, they now saw clearly enough, had their roots in the British presence and would be drowned in blood on the day that presence was withdrawn.

The Summer Session of the Indian Legislative Assembly met in a mood to talk reason. Said Maulvi Muhammad Yakub, a Muhammadan member, speaking on the twenty-fourth day of August: [11]

I do not agree with those who think that the Government have a hand in fomenting communal riots and communal feelings. I also do not think that the Government of India have ever shown partiality towards any community in dealing with communal matters.

[10] For the list, see *Legislative Assembly Debates,* Vol. VIII, August 18, 1926, p. 12.
[11] *Ibid.,* August 24, 1926, pp. 280-3.

There can be no two opinions that communal bitterness
. . . has now assumed an all-India importance. . . .

Sir, we are fed up with these communal frictions, and the
situation has become so very difficult that we cannot enjoy our
home life happily, nor do our festivals bring any joy to us.
. . . Is not the time ripe, . . . when we should ask the Government to come forward and help us, since we could not
solve the question ourselves?

A few months earlier such words could scarcely have
been spoken on that floor without rousing a flurry of
rebuttal. Today not a voice opposed them. Instead rose
that king-pillar of orthodox Hinduism, our old friend
the Dewan Bahadur T. Rangachariar of Madras, not
to rail at an "alien government," not to accuse it of
clumsy or arrogant interference in Indian affairs, but
to acknowledge that [12]

. . . facts are facts, and they have to be faced by us like men.
. . . I admire the sincere spirit in which my Honourable
friend Maulvi Muhammed Yakub has come forward. He
feels the soreness of this disgraceful position . . . and I feel
it likewise. I am glad, and the whole country is glad, that His
Excellency Lord Irwin has taken it up in right earnest. . . .
We cannot achieve the results which we have at heart without
the co-operation of all people, official and non-official alike.
I want a majority of the people whose hearts are really bent
upon changing the situation.

The doctrine of non-coöperation with the established
Power led nowhere, as all now see. The mystic doctrine

[12] *Legislative Assembly Debates,* August 24, 1925, pp. 283-4.

of spiritual war, a war of "soul-force," that uses the language of hate while protesting theories of love, had logically and insistently projected itself upon the material plane in the form of the slaughter of men. The inability of individuals to subordinate personal, family or clan interests and to hold together for team-work, had been demonstrated. And the fact had been driven home to the hilt that neither Hindu nor Muhammadan could think in terms of the whole people.

For the moment, some of them see it. Can they hold the vision? To have seen it at all marks gain.

Chapter XXVI

THE HOLY CITY

Edwin Arnold has written beautifully about Benares. Hundreds of people have also written about Benares. Tourists, enraptured with its river-front panorama, have exhausted their vocabulary in admiration.

And small wonder, for the scene is beautiful, instinct with color and grace and with that sense of souls' uplifting that surrounds the high altar of any part of the human race.

Benares is the Sacred City of the Hindu world. Countless temples adorn it, set like tiers of crowns above and among the broad flights of stairs that ascend from the Ganges, Holy River. Chains of yellow marigolds are stretched across that river to welcome Mother Ganges as she comes. And as the worshipers, clad in long robes of tender or brilliant colors, bearing their water-jars upon their heads or shoulders, trail up and down the high gray steps, they seem so like figures in the vision of a prophet of Israel that one almost hears the song they sang as "they went up by the stairs of the city of David, at the going up of the wall."

But my visit to Benares was made in the company of the Municipal Health Officer, a man of whom no artist-soul is apt to think.

This gentleman is an Indian. Before taking up his

present duties, he made preparatory studies in America, in the enjoyment of a Rockefeller Foundation Scholarship in Public Health. Without attempting to convey an idea of his whole problem, one may indicate here a few of its points.

The normal stationary population of Benares is about two hundred thousand, of whom some thirty thousand are Brahmans connected with the temples. In addition, two to three hundred thousand pilgrims come yearly for transient stays. And upon special occasions, such as an eclipse, four hundred thousand persons may pour into the city for that day, to depart a few days later as swiftly as they came.

To take care of all this humanity the Municipality allows its chief Health Officer an annual sum equal to about ten thousand dollars, which must cover his work in vaccination, registration of births and deaths, and the handling of epidemics and infectious diseases.

Much of his best work lies in watching the pilgrims as they debark from the railroad trains, to catch cholera patients before they disappear into the rabbit-warrens of the town. Let that disappearance once be effected and the case will lie concealed until a burst of epidemic announces the presence of the disease. For, although the municipality pays the higher officials and the foremen of the Public Health Department fairly well, it allows a mere pittance to its menial staff, with the result that, if contagion is reported and disinfection is ordered, the subordinates harass the people for what they can wring from distress.

Benares is an old city. Some of its drains were built in the sixteenth and seventeenth century. No one now knows their course except that, wherever they start, their outlets give into the river. Constructed of stone, their location is sometimes disconcertingly revealed by the caving-in of their masonry beneath a building or a street. Sometimes, silt-choked at the outlet, their mouths have been unwittingly or unthinkingly sealed in the course of river-wall repairs. Not a few still freely discharge their thick [1] stream of house-sewage into the river, anywhere along its humanity-teeming front. But most, having become semi-tight cesspools, await the downpours of the rainy season, when their suddenly swollen contents will push into the city's sub-soil with daily increasing force.

The city stands on a bluff, her streets about seventy-five feet above river level. The face of the bluff, for a distance of three miles or more along the river front, is buttressed by stairs and by high walls of stone. These, because of their continuity, back up the sub-soil water, which, from time to time, bursts the masonry and seeps through into the river, all along its famous templed front. There, among the worshiping drinkers and bathers, among the high-born pilgrim ladies, the painted holy-men, the ash-pasted *saddhus* and *yogis*, you may see it oozing and trickling down from those long zigzag cracks that so mellow the beauty of the venerable stones.

[1] "Thick" in particular because of the little water used in Indian houses.

[357]

Against bitter religious opposition, the British, in 1905, succeeded in getting a partial sewage system and water pipe-line into the city. Its main pumping station is at the south end of the town, not much habitation lying above it. The water is settled in a tank, filtered, and then put into general distribution, the Municipal Health Officer himself doing a weekly chemical and bacteriological analysis from each filter.

But the devout will not drink this filtered water. Instead, they go daily to the river, descend the stairs of some bathing-ghat, scoop up a vesselful in the midst of the bathers under the seepage-cracked wall, and carry it home to quench the thirst of the household. All warnings and protests of the Health Officer they meet with supreme contempt.

"It lies not in the power of man to pollute the Ganges." And "filtering Ganges water takes the holiness out," they reply, firmly.

Now, whoever bathes in the Ganges at Benares and drinks Ganges water there, having at the same time due regard to the needs of the priests, may be cured of the worst disease that flesh is heir to. Consequently upon Benares are deliberately focused all the maladies of the Hindu millions. Again, whoever dies in Benares, goes straight to heaven. Therefore endless sick, hopeless of cure, come here to breathe their last, if possible, on the brink of the river with their feet in the flood.

Many of the incidents connected with this tenet are exquisitely beautiful and exalted in spirit. But the threat to public health needs little emphasis.

[358]

One such has to do with the over-burdened burning-ghats.

The main burning-ghat lies directly in the middle of the populous waterfront. "Nothing on earth can move it from there," says my conductor, "because the place is of particular sanctity. So all I can do is to try to see that all bodies are completely burned."

But complete burning takes a lot of wood. Not every heir will or can face so heavy a cost. And the Indian-run municipality, thus far, has been unable to interest itself in the matter to the extent of giving an additional quantity of wood when necessary to complete incineration.

"See those dogs nosing among the ashes. There—one has found a piece!" said I to the doctor, as we stood looking on.

"Yes," he answered. "That happens often enough. For they burn bodies here, sometimes rather incompletely, at all hours of day and night. Still, if the dog hadn't got that bit, it would simply have got into the river, to float down among the bathers. As the dead babies do, in any case. No Hindu burns an infant. They merely toss them into the stream."

There are no latrines along the water-front. The people prefer to use the sandy places at the water's brink among the bathing stairs. Thus and otherwise one typhoid or cholera carrier may, during his stay, infect ten thousand persons. The river banks are dried sewage. The river water is liquid sewage. The faithful millions drink and bathe in the one, and spread out their clothes to dry upon the other. Then in due time, having picked up what germs they can, they go home over the length and breadth of India to give them further currency, carrying jars of the precious water to serve through the year.

Also, the beautiful and picturesque temples do their part. This may be sufficiently indicated in the words of a distinguished Brahman pathologist, educated in European universities and an annual visitor to London and Paris. Said he, with deep feeling:

"The temples of Benares are as evil as the ooze of the river-banks. I myself went within them to the point where one is obliged to take off one's shoes, because of sanctity. Beyond lay the shrines, rising out of mud, decaying food and human filth. I would not walk in it. I said *No!* But hundreds of thousands do take off their shoes, walk in, worship, walk out, and put back their shoes upon their unwashed feet. And I, a Hindu and a doctor, must bear witness to that!"

The position of Public Health Officer of Benares, one key to the health of India, means so large and difficult a task that it would seem to confer honor and distinction upon any man to whom it is entrusted. The present incumbent appeared to be confronting his job in a good spirit, determined to piece out his little means with his wits. But I found in the attitude of an Indian brother doctor a differing view. This man, also a Rockefeller Foundation scholar, said: "That fellow has a rotten job."

"Why rotten?" I asked, sincerely surprised.

[360]

"Because it is so hard. But chiefly because of the indignity that he, a Rockefeller scholar, should have to serve under a white man. The Minister is an Indian, of course. But the immediate superior, the Director of Public Health, is a Briton. It is a miserable shame!"

Curiously enough, this remark was made while, with the speaker, I was visiting an Indian attempt at sanitary self-help. The attempt was not brilliant, but at least it was a beginning, and the workers were simple, eager, unpretentious little folk hungry and thirsty for encouragement. Seeing which hunger, our Rockefeller scholar, now an official and to them a great luminary, slowly, thoroughly, and without a glimmer of sympathy, impaled them on the toasting-fork of his laughing scorn.

Other holy cities exist in India, other centers of pilgrimages. Each, automatically, is a reservoir and a potential distributing point of disease, demanding the utmost vigilance and the utmost tact in handling.

But the public health problem presented by an ordinary Indian city is stiff enough. Take, for example, Lahore. The European section of the town has something about it of western America—all of one age, new, roomy, airy, with certain of its good modern buildings erected by the public spirit of that fine old Punjabi, Sir Ganga Ram. But Kim's Lahore, the old Indian quarter, where the crowds live and move, and in particular its bazaar, where the crowds adore to congregate, is the danger-point that keeps the Director of Health awake at night.

Streets about eight feet wide, twisting like earth worms after a rain, straight up from whose edges rise solid lines of dwelling houses sometimes several stories high. At their base, on either side, a row of little open-fronted shops, their cottons, brasses, holy pictures, embroideries, silks, grain-piles, jewelry, exposed on their floors or walls. Many rickety wooden platforms, built of intermittent slats, project from the front edge of the shop floors, at street level, to the edge of the street. Close under these platforms, on both sides of the road, runs an open gutter about a foot wide. The gutter is in steady and open use as a public latrine. Heaped on the slats of the wooden platforms, just escaping the gutter, are messes of fried fish, rice cakes, cooked curry, sticky sweetmeats, and other foods for sale. All the food-heaps lie practically underfoot, exposed to every sort of accident, while flies, dirty hands, the nosing of dogs, cows, bulls and sheep, and scurrying rats constantly add their contributions; as do the babies and children with sore eyes and skin diseases, pawing and rolling in the midst of it all, enveloped in clouds of dust and of acrid smoke.

And you must be careful, in walking, not to brush against the wall of a house. For the latrines of the upper stories and of the roofs drain down the outside of the houses either in leaking pipes or else from small vent-holes in the walls, dripping and stringing into the gutter slow streams that just clear the fried fish and the lollypops.

Mr. Gandhi, whose early sojourn in England has

influenced his general point of view in more ways, perhaps, than he knows, has repeatedly written on this subject. He says, for example: [2]

Some of the [Indian] national habits are bad beyond description, and yet so ingrained as to defy all human effort. Wherever I go this insanitation obtrudes itself upon my gaze in some shape or another. In the Punjab and Sind, in total disregard of the elementary laws of health we dirty our terraces and roofs, breeding billions of disease-producing microbes and founding colonies of flies. Down south we do not hesitate to dirty our streets, and early in the morning it is impossible for any one in whom the sense of decency is developed to walk through the streets which are lined with people performing functions of nature which are meant to be performed in seclusion and in spots which human beings need not ordinarily tread. In Bengal the same tale in varying form has to be told; the same pool in which people have washed their dirt, their pots, and in which cattle have drunk, supplies drinking water. . . . These are not ignorant people; they are not illiterate; many have travelled even beyond the borders of India. . . . No institution can handle this problem better and more speedily than our Municipalities. They have . . . all the powers they need in this direction, and they can get more if necessary. Only the will is often wanting.

And again: [3]

[2] *Young India,* October 29, 1925, p. 371.
[3] *Ibid.,* November 19, 1925. Mr. Gandhi on "Our Insanitation," p. 399. In its issue of January 21, 1926, *Young India* all too clearly shows that the sanitary habits of the body of Hindu political delegates just assembled at Cawnpore in the Indian National Congress are identical with the worst that Mr. Gandhi elsewhere describes.

Whilst the Government has to answer for a lot, I know that the British officers are not responsible for our insanitation. Indeed if we gave them free scope in this matter, they would improve our habits at the point of the sword.

Mr. Gandhi's judgment of the attitude of Indianized municipal governments was corroborated by my own observations in big and little towns in many parts of India.

The city of Madras, for example, the third largest city in the land, completed its present water system in 1914. The catchment area, in the hills, includes several villages. The water, as it reaches the city plant, is about as foul as water can be. By the design of the system it is here passed through slow sand-filters into a pure-water tank at the rate of 10,000,000 gallons a day.

But the population of Madras has increased and the capacity of the plant is now 4,000,000 gallons short of the daily needs of the town. Detailed plans for the construction of adequate new filters, backed by British experts, have been laid before the Municipal Council. But these sixty leaders and guardians of the public weal, Indians all, have adopted a simpler scheme. As I saw and heard for myself from the Indian Superintendent on the spot, they now filter 10,000,000 gallons of water a day, run it into the pure-water tank, then add 4,000,000 gallons of unfiltered sewage, and dish the mixture out, by pipes, to the citizens of the town.

In judging this performance, one must remember that it takes longer to outgrow race thought and habits of life than it does to learn English. The well-dressed man who speaks with an easy Oxford accent may come from a village where, if they desire a new well, they do today what their fathers did a thousand years ago; they choose the site not by the slope of the land but by throwing a bucket of water over a goat. The goat runs away. The people run after. And where the goat first stops and shakes himself, though it be in the middle of the main street, just there the new well is dug.

Chapter XXVII

THE WORLD-MENACE

British India has half a million villages made of mud. Most of them took all their mud from one spot, making thereby a commensurate hole, and built themselves on the edge of the hole.

The hole, at the first rains, filled with water and became the village tank. Thenceforward forever, the village has bathed in its tank, washed its clothes in its tank, washed its pots and its pans in its tank, watered its cattle in its tank, drawn its cooking water from its tank, served the calls of nature by its tank and with the content of its tank has quenched its thirst. Being wholly stagnant, the water breeds mosquitoes and grows steadily thicker in substance as it evaporates between rain and rain. It is sometimes quite beautiful, overgrown with lily-things and shaded by feathered palms. It and its uses pretty generally insure the democratization of any new germs introduced to the village, and its mosquitoes spread malaria with an impartial beak—though not without some aid.

Witness, small Bengali babies put out to lie in the buzzing grass near the tank's edge.

"Why do you mothers plant your babies there to be eaten alive?"

"Because if we protect our babies the gods will be jealous and bring us all bad luck."

[366]

One of the most popular and most glorious gifts that a liberal rich man can make to his own village is the digging of an extra tank. One of the fondest dreams of the British Public Health official is to get all tanks filled up.

Nobody knows the exact incidence of malaria in India, for village vital statistics are, perforce, kept by primitive village watchmen who put down to "fever" all deaths not due to snake-bite, cholera, plague, a broken head or the few other things they recognize. But a million deaths a year from malaria may be regarded as a conservative estimate of India's loss by that malady.

Malaria originates in many places aside from tanks. There is, for example, the water-front of the city of Bombay, needless and deadly poison-trap for the sailors of the world. There are railway embankments built without sufficient drainage outlets, asking for remedy. There is the water-logged country in the Punjab; there is the new farm-land of the United Provinces, cut out of the tiger haunts of the Himalayan foot-hills—both by nature heavily malarial, but both being ditched and drained as a part of the huge agricultural irrigation schemes now under development by Government.

Malaria, altogether, is one of the great and costly curses of the land, not alone because of its huge death-rate but even more because of the lowered physical and social conditions that it produces, with their invitation to other forms of disease.

Under present conditions of Indianized control, governmental anti-malarial work, like all other preventive sanitation, is badly crippled. Yet it generally contrives to hold its own, though denied the sinews of progress.

And one recognizes with satisfaction, here and there, a few small volunteer seedlings springing up, strangers and aliens to the soil. Preëminent among these is the Anti-Malaria Coöperative Society of Bengal, an Indian organization now trying to bring control of malaria into the lives of the people, through educating the villagers in means of protecting their own health. Much praise is due to the enthusiasm of its chief exponent, Rai Bahadur Dr. G. C. Chatterjee, with his ardent co-adjutors, Dr. A. N. Mitra and Babu K. N. Banerjee. Not only are these gentlemen, whom I visited at their center in Nimta, trying to do anti-malaria work, but also they are raising funds to make available to the Bengali villagers the services of Indian doctors properly trained in western medicine.

Aside from its precious tank a village may have a well. The depth of the wells averages from twenty to forty feet. Their content is mainly surface seepage. A little round platform of sun-dried brick usually encircles the well, a log lying across the orifice. Squatting on that platform and on that log at all hours of the day you may see villagers washing their clothes, taking their baths, cleaning their teeth and rinsing their mouths, while the water they use splashes back over their feet into the pit whence they drew it.

Also, each person brings his own vessel in which to draw the water he wants—an exceedingly dirty and dangerous vessel from a doctor's point of view—which he lowers into the well with his own old factotum rope. When he returns to his house, he carries his vessel with him, filled with well-water for the family to drink.

One of the great objectives of the British Sanitary Administration is to put good wells into the villages and to educate the people in their proper use. Now, not infrequently, one finds such *pucca* wells. But, exactly as in the Philippines, the people have a strong hankering for the ancestral type, and, where they can, will usually leave the new and protected water-source for their old accustomed squatting- and gossiping-ground where they all innocently poison each other.

As for pumps, the obvious means to seal the wells and facilitate haulage, some have been installed. But, as a rule, pumps are impractical—for the reason that any bit of machinery is, to the Indian, a thing to consume, not to use and to care for. When the machine drops a nut or a washer, no one puts it back, and thenceforth that machine is junk.

Now, this matter of Indian wells is of more than Indian importance. For cholera is mainly a water-borne disease, and "statistics show that certain provinces in British India are by far the largest and most persistent centers of cholera infection in the world."[1]

The malady is contracted by drinking water infected with the fæces of cholera patients or cholera carriers, or from eating uncooked or insufficiently cooked in-

[1] *The Prevalence of Epidemic Disease . . . in the Far East,* Dr. F. Norman White, League of Nations, 1923, p. 24.

[369]

fected food. It finds its best incubating grounds in a population of low vitality and generally weak and unresisting condition.[2] There is a vaccine for preventive inoculation but, the disease once developed, no cure is known. Outbreaks bring a mortality of from 15 to 90 per cent., usually of about 40 per cent. The area of Lower Bengal and the valley of the Ganges is, in India, the chief cholera center, but "the disease is very generally endemic in some degree throughout the greater part of the whole [Indian] peninsula."[3]

Since the year 1817, ten pandemics of cholera have occurred. In 1893 the United States was attacked, and in this explosion the speed of travel from East to West was more rapid than ever before.[4]

In ordinary circumstances, in places where the public water supply is good and under scientific control, cholera is not to be feared. But the great and radical changes of modern times bring about rapid reverses of conditions; such, for example, as the sudden pouring in the year 1920 of hundreds of thousands of disease-sodden refugees out of Russia into Western Europe.

Without fear of the charge of alarmism, international Public Health officers today question whether they can be sure that local controls will always withstand unheralded attacks in force. With that question in

[2] Cf. *Philippine Journal of Science,* 1914, Dr. Victor G. Heiser.

[3] *A Memoranda on the Epidemiology of Cholera,* Major A. J. Russell, Director of Public Health in Madras Presidency, League of Nations, 1925, which see, for the whole topic.

[4] *Recent Research on the Etiology of Cholera,* E. D. W. Grieg, in *The Edinburgh Medical Journal,* July, 1919.

Photos by M. Moyca Newell

HINDU HOLY MEN

"Their enormous mops of long, snarled hair."   (*See* page 405.)

MORE HINDU HOLY MEN

The nearest is a Brahman. (*See* page 405.)

mind, they regard India's cholera as a national problem of intense international import.

In estimating the safety of the United States from
infection, the element of "carriers" must be considered.
Each epidemic produces a crop of "carriers" whose
power to spread the disease lasts from one hundred and
one days to permanency.[5] Moreover, the existence of
healthy carriers is conclusively proved. And India is
scarcely a month removed from New York or San
Francisco.

"Whenever India's real condition becomes known,"
said an American Public Health expert now in international service, "all the civilized countries of the
world will turn to the League of Nations and demand
protection against her."

Bengal, one of the worst cholera areas, is about the
size of Nebraska. It has a village population of over
43,500,000 persons, living in 84,981 villages. In the
year 1921, a mild cholera year, the disease was reported
from 11,592 of these villages, spread over 26 districts,
the reported deaths totaling 80,547.[6] Imagine the task
of trying to inoculate 43,500,000 persons, scattered
over such an area, in advance of the hour of need;
bearing always in mind the fact that the virtue of a
cholera preventive inoculation lasts only ninety days.
Imagine also the task of disinfecting all these village

[5] E. D. W. Grieg in *Indian Journal of Medical Research,* 1913,
Vol. I, pp. 59-64.
[6] *Statistical Abstract for British India, 1914-15 to 1923-24,* pp. 2
and 382; and *54th Annual Report of the Director of Public Health
of Bengal,* Appendix I, p. xxviii.

wells, when first you must persuade, not compel, the incredulous, always fatalistic and often resisting people to permit the process.

In the winter of 1924-5 sporadic cases of cholera appeared in the Indian state of Kashmir. The British authorities did what they could to induce those of Kashmir to act, but the latter, Indian fashion, could see no point in disturbing themselves about ills yet only in bud. Consequently, in April, came an explosion, killing in a single month 2 per cent. of the entire population of the State. Across the border of British India, in the Punjab, the hasty Indianization of the Public Health Service had already so far proceeded that only one British officer remained in the department. Result: for the first time in thirty years the deadly scourge overflowed the Kashmir border and reaped a giant harvest among the Punjabi peasantry.

In the normal course of events, however, the main danger source for widespread cholera epidemics is the periodic concentration of great masses of people in fairs and festivals and in pilgrimages to holy cities. During the past twelve years or more, the British sanitary control of the crowds, in transit and also in concentration, where temporary latrines are built, pipe-lines for water laid, wells chlorinated and doctors and guards stationed, has been so efficient as greatly to lessen the risks. Of the possibilities of the future the Kashmiri incident speaks.

Hookworm, an intestinal parasite, saps its victim's vitality, eventually reducing him, body and mind, to a

useless rag not worth his keep to himself or any one
else. Hookworm is contracted by walking with bare
feet on ground contaminated with the fæces of persons infected. The procedure against hookworm is
(a) to have the people use proper latrines, and (b) to
have them wear shoes.

As Mr. Gandhi has shown, Hindus, anywhere, dispense with latrines, but are not, beyond that, always
greatly concerned as to what they use. In one town I
found from the municipal chairman that latrines had
been built obediently to the Health Officer's specifica-
tions and desire; but the people, he said, were leaving
them strictly alone, preferring to do as they had always
done, using roads, alleys, gutters and their own floors.

This was in part because the town was short of outcastes and therefore had no one to remove night-soil—
a thing which no caste man would do though he smoth-
ered in his own dirt; and in part because it was easier
so to observe the Hindu religious ritual prescribed for
the occasion concerned.[7] Villagers, in any case, always
use the open fields immediately surrounding their village, fields over which they continually walk.

To sum up in the words of Doctor Adiseshan, Indian, Assistant Director of Public Health of Madras:
"How are you to prevent hookworm when people will
not use latrines, and when no orthodox Hindu, and
certainly no woman, will consent to wear shoes?"

Under such circumstances it appears that, although
the cure for hookworm is well established, absolute,

[7] See *Hindu Manners, Customs and Ceremonies,* pp. 237-40.

simple and cheap, it would be an indefensible waste of public monies to administer that cure to patients sure to be immediately re-infected.

It is estimated that over 80 per cent. of the people of Madras and 60 per cent. of those of Bengal, harbor hookworms. And in this connection Dr. Andrew Balfour makes an interesting calculation. As to India, he says: [8]

A conservative estimate shows that 45,000,000 wage-earners in that country are infected with hookworm. In 1915 the Statistical Department calculated the average wage of an able-bodied agricultural labourer in Bengal at 10 rupees monthly. . . . Assuming that the average yearly wage of the 45,000,000 infected labourers is 100 rupees each, these men are at present earning Rs. 4,500,000,000 annually. Now the managers of tea estates in the Darjeeling district estimate that the Rockefeller anti-hookworm campaign there . . . has increased the labour efficiency of the coolies from 25 to 50 per cent.

Suppose that in India generally only 10 per cent. increased efficiency is achieved. Even so the Rs. 4,500,000,000 [$1,500,000,000] become Rs. 4,950,000,000 [$1,650,-000,000].

Bubonic plague was first introduced into India in 1896, coming from China. Today India is the world's chief reservoir of infection,[9] and has lost, since 1896, some 11,000,000 lives by that cause alone. The case

[8] *Health Problems of the Empire*, pp. 193-4.
[9] *Prevalence of Epidemic Disease in the Far East*, Dr. F. Norman White, p. 21.

mortality is about 70 per cent. Of pneumonic plague, which sometimes develops in conjunction with the other form, only an occasional case survives.

Plague uncontrolled at its source may at any time become an international scourge, a danger to which international health officers are the more alive since latter-day observations continue to show the disease breaking out in regions where its occurrence has been unknown before.

Plague, unlike cholera, is not communicated by man to man, but to man by fleas from the bodies of sick rats. The flea bites the man and leaves a poisonous substance around the bite. Man, scratching the bite, scratches the poison into his skin and the deed is done. When plague breaks out in a village, the effective procedure is to evacuate the village at once and to inoculate the villagers with plague vaccine.

In most countries you simultaneously proceed to real control by killing the rats. But this, in a Hindu land, you cannot effectively do, because of the religion.

The constant obstacle in the Public Health Officer's path is, characteristically, a negative one—the utter apathy of the Indian peoples, based on their fatalistic creed. The intermittent obstacle, acute of latter years, is the political agent who runs here and there among the villages, whispering that an evil Government is bent on working harm. To such a pitch have these persons from time to time wrought their victims, that the latter have murdered the native health agent entrusted with the task of getting them out of an infected site.

With repeated examples, however, of the results of following Government's behests, a degree of improvement has taken place. In some parts where plague has struck often, the people have begun to evacuate of themselves, when rats begin to die, and to flock into the nearest dispensary begging for inoculation. But in general the darkness of their minds is still so deep that the agitator can easily excite them to resistance, even to violence, by some tale of wickedness afoot.

When the first Indian lady of the district can say to the English lady doctor brought to her bedside: "Why should I show you my tongue when the pain is so much lower down? And besides, if I open my mouth like that a lot more devils will jump in"; or when the chief landlord of the district will tie a great ape just beyond claw-reach of his ten-day-old son and then torment the ape to fury to make it snatch and snarl at the child, to frighten away the demon that is giving him convulsions, what is to be expected of the little folk squatting by the tank?

In the winter of 1926 I went through a plague-infested district in company with a British Public Health officer on tour. The first village that we visited was a prosperous settlement of grain-dealers—shop-keepers and money-lenders—the market town for the surrounding farmers. Each house was stored with grain in jars and bins, and rats swarmed. The rats had begun to die. Then two men had died. And on that the British District Commissioner had ordered the people out.

Now they were all gathered in a little temporary

"straw village" a few hundred yards beyond their town gate, there to await spring and the end of the scourge. As the doctor, a Scotchman thirty years in the Indian Medical Service, approached the encampment, the whole lot, men, women and children, rushed forward to greet him and then to ask advice:

"Sahib, if we build fires here to cook our food, and the wind comes, it will blow sparks and burn these straw houses we have made. What, then, shall we do to cook our food? Please arrange."

"Build your fires over yonder, behind that mound."

"Ah, yes, Sahib, to be sure."

"Sahib, if while we sit here, outside our gates, bad folk creep into our houses and steal our grain, what then?"

"Even so, is it not better that bad men die of the plague than that the plague kills you? Also, you may set watchmen at a distance."

"The Sahib is wise. Further: there is, in a tent near by, a stranger of no merit who wishes to push medicine into our skins. Is it good medicine? Shall we listen to him? And what is the right price?"

"The man in the tent is sent by Government. The medicine is necessary to all who wish to live. It is free medicine. There is no price."

A pause, while the people exchange glances. Then the headman speaks:

"It is well, indeed, that the Sahib came."

"It looks," says the doctor, as we move on, "as if my little dispenser fellow had been squeezing those people for money before inoculating them. They *will* do that! And then, if the people won't satisfy them, they report that inoculation is refused. Except in the case of soldiers and police, we have no authority to compel inoculation. It is a risky business, this fighting wholesale death with broken reeds!"

Later we find the "stranger of no merit" squatting in his tent, a traveling dispenser of the Public Health Department trained and charged to do minor surgery, well disinfection and plague inoculation, to give simple medicines for simple ailments, to lecture, and to show lantern slides on health propaganda. By his own showing he had sat in this tent for a month.

"I call the people every day to be inoculated, but they refuse to come forward," he complained. "'Plague-doctor,' they say, 'now that *you* are here the plague *must* come!' and they laugh at me. They are a backward and an ignorant people."

The doctor inspects his equipment. On the inner lid of his plague box the dosage is written. Within are the serum tubes, the needles, the disinfectant equipment, undisturbed. Also his medicine chest—"Dyspepsia Powders," "Country Medicines," simple drugs in tablets.

"Let me see your instruments," says the doctor. All are rusty, several are broken and useless.

"You should have sent those in, each one as soon as you broke it. You know it would have been replaced at once," says the doctor, patiently. "Now you have nothing to work with."

"Ah, yes, I meant to send them. I forgot."

Chapter XXVIII

"QUACKS WHOM WE KNOW"

"It is better to sit than to walk, to lie down than to sit, to sleep than to wake, and death is the best of all," says the Brahman proverb.

Taking into consideration the points with which the preceding chapter is concerned, the question naturally arises as to how the Indian is affected by his own peculiar sanitary habits. That question may be answered in the words of an American scientist now studying in the country:

"From long consumption of diluted sewage they have actually acquired a degree of immunity. Yet all of them are walking menageries of intestinal parasites, which make a heavy drain upon their systems and which inevitably tell when some infection, such as pneumonia or influenza, comes along. Then the people die like flies. They have no resistance."

These conditions, added to infant marriage, sexual recklessness and venereal infections, further let down the bars to physical and mental miseries; and here again one is driven to speculate as to how peoples so living and so bred can have continued to exist.

A reply is thus couched by one of the most eminent of European International Public Health authorities:

"It is a question of adaptation, and of the evolution

[379]

of a sub-grade of existence on which they now survive. The British are to blame for the world-threat
that they constitute. If the British had not protected
them, the virile races of the north would have wiped
them out."

The superior virility of the northern races—including the Sikhs, and more especially the Pathans and
other Muhammadan stocks—is favored by their superior diet. These hardy out-door folk are all large meat-
eaters, and consume much milk and grain. The diet of
the southern Hindu has little in it to build or repair
tissue. He subsists mainly on sweets and carbo-hydrates,
and, to the degree that he is able, he leads a sedentary
life. Diabetes is often the incident that brings to its
early close the career of the southern Indian public
man.[1]

Lieutenant-Colonel Christopher, I.M.S., Director of
the Central Research Institute of the Government of
India, in a paper called "What Disease Costs India,"
has said:[2]

The deaths in India annually number about 7,000,000,
i.e., very nearly the population of greater London. . . . Now
all men must die, but it is to be hoped that each will have a
run for his money. . . . During the first year of life, the
[Indian's] expectation of life is . . . about twenty-three
years. At the age of five it is thirty-five years, the highest
expectation at any age."

[1] For an extended exposition of this subject see *The Protein Element in Nutrition,* Major D. McCay, I.M.S., London, Edward Arnold,
1912.
[2] *Indian Medical Gazette,* April, 1924, pp. 196-200.

And Colonel Christopher further points out that so heavy a mortality inevitably indicates a background of widespread and continuous sickness, of reduced productivity, of enhanced costs of administration, and of penalized trade, whose combined tax upon the resources of the country, though difficult to calculate, cannot but be an enormous moral and economic burden to support, a heavy drag upon prosperity.

For this great field of need the lack of means is always conspicuous. For 1925-26, some of the provincial budgets showed the following items: [3]

	Education	Public Health
Bombay Presidency	$6,959,700.	$ 964,700.
Madras Presidency	6,211,100.	1,054,500.
United Provinces	5,713,000.	493,700.
Bengal	4,322,000.	880,000.

The open road to better conditions is clear, and, alas, untrodden. One finger-post reads thus: [4]

The necessary preliminary to any satisfactory advance . . . is the growth among the educated classes of a missionary and humanitarian spirit which will lead them to consecrate time, money and energy to the task of ameliorating the conditions in which their less fortunate brethren live. . . . India can never be safeguarded from a disastrous death rate, punctuated by heavy epidemics, until her people can be weaned from their tenacious adherence to social observances which are as diametrically opposed to public health as they are to economic prosperity.

[3] *Indian Year-Book*, 1926, pp. 89, 97, 107, 118.
[4] *Statement Exhibiting the Moral and Material Progress . . . of India During the Years 1923-24*, London, 1924, pp. 211-12.

[381]

But that humanitarian spirit does not today exist.
Curiously lucid contributions on this line come from
Mr. Gandhi; speaking as of Hindu medical men, he
says: [5]

It is worth considering why we take up the profession of
medicine. It is certainly not taken up for the purpose of serving humanity. We become doctors so that we may obtain
honours and riches.

After which he affirms:

European doctors are the worst of all.

Amplifying his accusation, Mr. Gandhi continues:

These [European] doctors violate our religious instinct.
Most of their medical preparations contain either animal fat
or spirituous liquors; both of these are tabooed by Hindu and
Mahomedans.

And again, more specifically:

I overeat, I have indigestion, I go to a doctor, he gives me
medicine. I am cured, I overeat again, and I take his pills
again. Had I not taken the pills in the first instance, I would
have suffered the punishment deserved by me, and I would
not have overeaten again. . . . A continuance of a course
of medicine must, therefore, result in loss of control over the
mind.

"In these circumstances," he concludes, "we are unfit
to serve the country." And therefore "to study European medicine is to deepen our slavery."

[5] Mr. Gandhi's statements quoted in this chapter will be found in
his *Indian Home Rule*, Ganesh & Co., Madras, 1924, pp. 61-2.

[382]

Whatever may be thought of Mr. Gandhi's judg‚ ment, his sincerity is not questioned. Holding such an opinion of the motives and value of western medical men in India, it is scarcely surprising that, in the period of his "non-coöperation" campaign against Government and all its works, not excepting its educational efforts, he should have exhorted medical and public health students to desert their classes and to boycott their schools.

Boy-fashion, they did it—for a time—and at what a cost to India!

The other side of this phase of Indian nationalism is its enthusiasm for the Aruvedic or ancient Hindu system of medicine under which a large part of the native population is today being treated, more particularly in Bengal and in central and southern India.

This system is held to have been handed down from the gods in earliest times, and to be of spiritual and inspired nature. Some hint of its quality may be gathered from an excerpt from the Sushruta Samhita, one of the two venerable works on which the system is based.[6]

The favourable or unfavourable termination of a disease may be predicted from the appearance, speech, dress and demeanour of the messenger sent to call a physician, or from the nature of the asterism and the lunar phase marking the time of the arrival, or from the direction of the wind blowing at the time, or from the nature of omens seen by him on the road, or from the posture or speech of the physician him-

[6] Translation of Kaviraj Kunja Lal Bishagratna, p. 270.

[383]

self. A messenger belonging to the same caste as the patient
himself should be regarded as an auspicious omen, whereas one
from a different caste would indicate a fatal or an unfavourable termination of the disease.

Several works on modern Aruvedic practice have
been published. These make the claim that the Sushruta anatomy and surgery of two thousand years ago
were far superior to those of modern western science,
and deduce that as Aruvedic methods have undergone
no serious change since that time, they must be practically perfect. Says Sir Patrick Hehir: [7]

One of the principles of the system is that diseases are the
result of the operations of evil spirits who have to be pacified
by various offerings and propitiated by incantations. Regarding the diseases of children it is stated [8] that these "are due to
the action of certain spirits who were belated in obtaining
lucrative posts in the retinue of the Destroyer and were compelled, to secure power, to tax sorrowing parents, who might
have committed any of the hundred-odd ritual faults by af-
flicting their offspring." One searches in vain for anything
approaching definite and rational therapeutics in this system.
We have [here] in a *modern* Aruvedic work a complex combination of drugs extolled as being able to cure such diverse
conditions as obesity and gonorrhea, and another extensive
combination alleged to effect a cure in all diseases of women
however caused.

[7] *The Medical Profession in India,* Major-General Sir Patrick
Hehir, I.M.S., Henry Frowde and Hodder and Stoughton, London,
1923, p. 104.
[8] Quoted from Kaviraj Nagendra Nath Sen Gupta, *The Ayurvedic
System of Medicine,* 3 vols., Calcutta, 1909.

My personal enquiry into Aruvedic surgical cases was limited to two instances. The first was that of a little boy who walked into a Madras Presidency hospital one day in 1925, carrying his own forearm as a parcel, with a request to the British surgeon in charge, from a well-known Aruvedic doctor, to sew the forearm in place.

The history of this case was that the arm had sustained a compound fracture, the bone sticking through the flesh in an open wound. The Aruvedic doctor had first applied cow-dung to the open wound and then had clapped on splints, which he bound tight with strips of freshly-peeled tree-bark. The weather being hot and dry, the bark had contracted rapidly and produced extreme pressure. The circulation stopped, dry gangrene set in and the arm sloughed off at the elbow. Seeing which, the Aruvedic man thought it time to invoke the courtesies of the profession and to suggest the western needle.

The second case occurred in 1926, in the same province. An Aruvedic doctor attempted to operate according to his code upon a man having an enlarged gland in the groin. Holding his patient down, and without an anæsthetic, he opened the gland. As the knife went in, the patient jumped, an artery was cut and the peritoneal cavity slit open. The doctor, knowing no anatomy, then took his patient to a near-by government dispensary. But there the little dispensary man in charge, an Indian, out of sheer terror pushed the risk away.

"I am not meant for this sort of thing," he protested. "I am only meant for minor surgery. Take the man on to a hospital."

But before reaching the hospital the man died.

Action for manslaughter was brought by the police against the Aruvedic physician. But an association of Indian doctors holding western degrees, many of whom were in Government employ, defended his case and paid the expenses. "Our fine old Indian system must not be attacked," they said. Their lawyers first got the defendant off on a technicality; and then secured the prosecution of the little dispensary man for criminal delay.

The common arguments in favor of the old system are that it is cheaper for the people, that it particularly suits Indian constitutions and that it is of divine sanction and birth. Leaving the last tenet aside, as not in the field of discussion, we find that the cost of running an Aruvedic dispensary is much the same as that of running a dispensary on western lines; [9] and that no material difference has ever been discovered between white man and brown, in the matter of reaction of medicines upon the system.

The Montagu-Chelmsford Reforms, however, have occasioned a great recrudescence of native medicine. Provincial ministers dependent on popular vote are prone to favor spending public money to erect Aruvedic and Unani [10] colleges, hospitals and dispensaries. With the Indian National Congress claiming that Aru-

[9] *The Medical Profession in India,* p. 116.
[10] The ancient Arabic school of medicine.

vedic medicine is "just as scientific as modern western medicine," with such men as Sir Rabindranath Tagore, the poet, fervently declaring that Aruvedic science surpasses anything the West can offer; and with Swarajists in general pushing it forward on patriotic grounds, you get the melancholy spectacle of the meager appropriations allotted to medicine and public health, in this most disease-stricken of lands, being heavily cut into to perpetuate a "science" on the same level as the "voodoo doctoring" of the West Indian negro.

That the old native systems still exert a strong hold on the imaginations of the masses cannot be questioned. Also, like the voodoo doctors, they teach the use of a few good herbs. These two points enable their practitioners to induce enough "cures" to keep their prestige alive.

But once upon a time it chanced that Mr. Gandhi, having widely and publicly announced that "hospitals are institutions for propagating sin"; [11] that "European doctors are the worst of all," and that "quacks whom we know are better than the doctors who put on an air of humaneness," [12] himself fell suddenly ill of a pain in the side.

As he happened to be in prison at the time, a British surgeon of the Indian Medical Service came straightway to see him.

"Mr. Gandhi," said the surgeon, as the incident was

[11] *Indian Home Rule,* p. 61.
[12] *Ibid.,* p. 62.

reported, "I am sorry to have to tell you that you have appendicitis. If you were my patient, I should operate at once. But you will probably prefer to call in your Aruvedic physician."

Mr. Gandhi proved otherwise minded.

"I should prefer not to operate," pursued the surgeon, "because in case the outcome should be unfortunate, all your friends will lay it as a charge of malicious intent against us whose duty it is to care for you."

"If you will only consent to operate," pleaded Mr. Gandhi, "I will call in my friends, now, and explain to them that you do so at my request."

So, Mr. Gandhi willfully went to an "institution for propagating sin"; was operated upon by one of the "worst of all," an officer of the Indian Medical Service, and was attentively nursed through convalescence by an English Sister whom he is understood to have thought after all rather a useful sort of person.

Chapter XXIX

PSYCHOLOGICAL GLIMPSES THROUGH THE ECONOMIC LENS

The welfare of any people, we are wont to agree, must finally rest upon economic foundations. In the foregoing pages certain aspects of economic conditions in India have been indicated. To these indications I should like now to add a few more, disclaiming any pretense that they constitute a survey, and offering them merely for what they are worth as scattering observations made in the living field, entirely non-political both in character and in purpose.

The Indian, aside from his grievances earlier described, has other explanations of what he calls his depressed status, in large part covering them with the elastic title of "economic drains" upon the country. Compared with the matters already handled, these considerations seem superficial, serving mainly to befog the issue. The principal drains, as they appear to me, have been shown in the body of this book. But the Indian native politician's category comprises none of them. He speaks, instead, under such headings as cotton, tea, interest on Government bonds, export of grain, army maintenance, and the pay of British Civil Servants in India.

The attempt carefully to examine these or any comparable point with the Indian intelligentsia is likely to end in disappointment and a web of dialectics—for the reason that, as the question grows close, the Indian, as a rule, simply drops it and shifts to another ground where, for the moment, he has more elbow-room. To touch briefly on the items just enumerated will, however, illustrate his mode of thought.

Of cotton, his persistent statement is that the country's raw crop, selfishly cornered, is sent to England to give employment to Lancashire spinners, and then, brought back as cloth, is forced upon Indian purchasers.

The facts are: (a) The English market stands sixth on the list of purchasers of the Indian cotton crop.[1] (b) Indian cotton, being of poor quality, irregular, short of staple and persistently tampered with, to make weight, does not meet the requirements of English cotton cloth manufacturers. (c) The cotton for the looms of Lancashire is supplied from America and the Sudan. (d) The little Indian cotton used in the United Kingdom goes chiefly to making lamp-wicks, cleaning cloths and other low-grade fabrics.

As affecting the present status of India's cotton import trade, two mutually countervailing influences must be mentioned: On the one hand stands the recent handling by Government of the old excise duty on Indian-milled cotton goods—an imposition which no Briton today defends; that excise duty is now wiped out, and its disappearance would naturally serve to diminish importations and to stimulate sales of home manufac-

[1] See Appendix III A.

ture. On the other hand stand the facts that the people of India acquire, year by year, a little more money to spend and a little more habit of spending it; that they like fine cloths; and that the cloth from Indian mills is mostly coarse. Therefore, in spite of free markets, in spite of Japan's growing competition in fine goods, in spite of Mr. Gandhi's cottage spinning campaign and its rough product, India still chooses to indulge in a considerable amount of Lancashire's sheer fabrics.

Government, meantime, has been sparing no pains to improve the quality of the cotton crop. In the endeavor to induce the growers to put more intelligence into the work, experimental farms and model stations have been established in the cotton areas, inspectional teaching has been set up, and improved implements[2] and good seed[3] provided, with an active propaganda as to the feasibility of higher prices.

"India is actually a better cotton country than is the United States," an American authority has said, "but the people will not put their backs into the work, and the Swaraj politician does what he can to discourage improved production, on the ground that 'India must not help England by growing cotton that Lancashire will use.' "

Whether unaware or regardless of the facts just recounted, the foremost of Indian politicians repeatedly assured me that "England takes our raw cotton away to give work to her own unemployed, brings the cloth back

[2] Originally imported from America, but now made by Indian labor in the Government agricultural stations.
[3] From American stock.

here and foists it upon us. So all the profit is hers and India is robbed. No country can stand such a drain."

"But America raises cotton, some of which England buys, makes into cloth and sells to America again. We gladly sell to our best bidders, and we buy where we find what we want. Also, we make some cloth ourselves. Where is the difference," I asked, "between your case and America's?"

"But consider the question of tea," replies the Indian economist quickly. "We raise great crops of tea, and almost the whole is swept out of India—another exhausting drain upon the country."

"Do you sell your tea, or give it away?"

"Ah, yes—but the *tea*, you perceive, is *gone*."

The third "drain" upon the country, as named above, is the interest upon Government's Public Utility bonds, paid to London. The caliber of the complaint may briefly be shown through the single instance of railways.

The first line of railway in India was finished in 1853. At the end of March, 1924, India had a total length of 38,039 miles of open system,[*] which in 1925 carried over four and a half times as many passengers per mile of steel as did the railways of the United States.

Taking the respective viewpoints of Americans and of Indians in the matter now in hand, we get further light on the Indian economist. When America built her railways, she had not sufficient means to do so without

[*] *Statistical Abstract,* p. 413. See also Appendix III B.

borrowing. Consequently she borrowed from Europe, largely from Great Britain, about half the money that built her railway system, well content to pay what it cost in view of benefits expected from the opening of the country. These costs, in the normal course, continued until about 1914. When India built her railways, she also failed to find the money at home; yet in her case not because money was lacking, but because Indian capitalists would lend only at huge rates of interest. Consequently India borrowed from her cheapest market, London, practically all the money that built her railways, paying from 2.5 to 5 per cent., with an average of 3.5 per cent. on the loans—the lowest rates that the world knows.

It is the payment of the annual interest on these loans that the Indian critic is constantly describing as an insupportable grievance, "a drain" of the country's resources.

But the net profits to the Government of India brought in by the railways after payment of interest, sinking funds, annuity charges, etc., were, in 1924-25, $58,736,000.[5]

Mr. Gandhi's views on railways, being a conspicuous feature of his anti-British propaganda, may be noticed here:[6]

Good travels at a snail's pace—it can, therefore, have little to do with the railways. Those who want to do good . . . are not in a hurry. . . . But evil has wings. . . . So

[5] *Statesman's Year Book,* 1926, p. 139.
[6] *Indian Home Rule,* pp. 45-8.

the railways can become a distributing agency for the evil one only. It may be a debatable matter whether railways spread famines, but it is beyond dispute that they propagate evil. . . . God set a limit to man's locomotive ambition in the construction of his body. Man immediately proceeded to discover means of over-riding the limit. . . . Railways are a most dangerous institution.

Yet Mr. Gandhi himself sets the example of braving that danger, in his many political tours about the country. And, despite his doubts on the point, one effect of the existence of the railroads has certainly been to wipe out the mortal terror of famine in India. Whereas in the old days that threat hung always over the land, waiting only the failure of a monsoon to reap its human harvest, deaths from this cause are now almost unknown; because Government's systematized famine scheme is sustained by means to transport (a) men from famine areas to areas where labor is wanted, and (b) food and fodder whence both exist in plenty to places where, to save life, both are needed.

Beyond the railheads runs the British-built network of good highroads, speeding motor traffic where bullock carts alone used to creep and wallow.

"And every time I think of famine and the desperate work and the wholesale death it used to mean," said one old Deputy District Commissioner, "I say, 'God bless Henry Ford!'"

It is scarcely necessary to point out the further practical uses of the railways, whether in equalization of prices, in opening of markets, or in development of trade with its consequent increase of individual prosperity and of Government revenues.

Turning now to the fourth item listed for consideration, one finds Mr. Gandhi and other Indian critics pointing to the exportation of grain from a country where many regions are from time to time short of food, as an intolerable "drain" due to administrative ill will, greed, or mismanagement. However elaborately this idea is clothed, its bare bones tell a plain story.

No man sells grain today that he needs today to put into his mouth. If he sells grain, it is to get something that he holds more necessary or more desirable. Government, in the last thirty years, has created great areas of rich grain land where only desert existed before. Millions of Indians are raising on these lands quantities of grain far beyond their own consuming power or that of the regions in which they live. Roads, railways, and ships have brought the markets of the world to their doors. They sell to the highest bidder. If Government should clap an export duty on their produce to keep it at home, what shame would then be cried upon the despot whose jealous grip denied to labor the fruit of its toil! Grain travels to and from India as it does everywhere else—in obedience to the currents of world trade.

For our fifth point: The cost of the army is always alleged to be monstrous in proportion to the country's revenue. "The army is too big," says the politician.

"Is it too big for the work it has to do in keeping your safety and peace?"

"I don't know. I have not looked into that," is the usual reply. "But anyway, it costs an outrageous percentage of India's revenue."

In presenting this view of the subject it is the custom to speak as of the Indian central budget only, which gives a figure of expenditure on defense amounting to about 59 per cent. of the total. To arrive at a just statement, the provincial budgets, which are entirely free from defense items, must be reckoned in; it is then found that the proportion of governmental revenues assigned to defense is about 30 per cent.[7]

The Indian peoples are taxed about $.58 per capita for the defense of their country.[8]

The people of Great Britain pay about $13 per capita on that count, the people of America about $5; those of Japan pay for defense six times as much as the people of India, implying a per capita tax on that score of over $3.50.[9]

India possesses 1,400 miles of constantly dangerous frontier, always actively threatened, and three times in the last century ablaze with open war. She also has an enormous and extremely vulnerable coast line, which without extra cost to her is defended by the British fleet. And finally, she has a population which, time and again, in its sudden outbursts of internecine fury,

[7] *Defence of India,* "Arthur Vincent," Humphrey Milford, Oxford University Press, 1922, p. 94.
[8] *India in 1924-25,* p. 31.
[9] *The Statesman's Year Book,* 1926, p. xix.

needs protection against itself. Taxes are light because
the people are poor. Revenues are small because taxes
are light. Costs of national defense look large because
revenues are small. The maintenance of order and
peace is the prime duty of Government. On that duty
any Government must spend what it must. If the total
revenue be small, the less is left for other activities.
The obvious solution is to increase the revenue.[10]

But the great weakness in the Indian's reasoning that
the costs of the army constitute a "drain" out of India
of India's wealth lies in the fact that practically all the
pay of the Army stays in India. The pay of the great
body of troops, which is Indian, naturally does so.
That part of British soldiers' pay that goes home to
Britain is scarcely large enough to waste words upon.
British Army officers in India in practically all cases are
spending their private means there, over and above
their pay. Equipment and stores, by order, are bought
in India whenever Indian firms can provide them in
suitable quality and at a reasonable competitive price.
Otherwise they are bought abroad, by the High Commissioner for India stationed in London, who is himself an Indian. In this matter of governmental purchase of stores, in whatever department, a frequent
disparity exists between the actual records and the
statements of the Indian politicians who, as my own
research proved, are wont to suit their allegations to
their convenience rather than to the facts.

The sixth conspicuous channel of "drain" upon the

[10] See Appendix III C.

country's resources is the pay of the British members of the Indian Civil Service. Here the relevant facts are that in the beginning it was necessary to offer good pay to get good men to take on the job; and that, with all the upward rush of prices in the last quarter century, no comparable increase has taken place in that pay. India, today, is a costly place to live in, as any sojourner will find. She is not a white man's country, in the sense that she frequently robs him of his health if not of his life. In committing himself to her service he must resign all home associations and privileges for long periods of time. If he marries he must part early with his children, and maintain them separated from their parents by a journey three weeks long. When he retires, after twenty-five to thirty-five years of active service, his pension of £1,000 per annum loses 25 per cent. by taxes; and, last but not least, the salaries paid to all but the few highest officials are large only from the point of view of the Indian, with his greatly differing standard of living which few white men would accept. The married British Civil Servant in India, if he has children to educate and no private resources on which to draw, must live with watchful economy to make both ends meet. And he can save little or nothing for a rainy day.

Nevertheless, the unhappy peoples of India, says Sir M. Visvesvaraya,[11] speaking as does many another prominent Indian, "have not only to feed and clothe

[11] *Reconstructing India*, p. 7.

[398]

themselves, but also to support one of the costliest administrations in the world."

To dissect this statement were, after one glance at the Tax Table, a waste of time. "One of the costliest administrations in the world" cannot be supported from such resources. Including land revenue, which is properly to be listed as rental rather than taxation, the total per capita tax paid by the inhabitants of British India in 1923-24 was five and a half rupees [12] or nearly $1.82 in United States currency at the then rate of exchange. The per capita taxation in the Philippines for the year 1923, as shown in the Annual Report of the Insular Auditor, was $3.50.

Even such a sum may seem large, in comparison with the general poverty of the Indian people. Costs of Government reduced to the irreducible are still high to a pauper. But observers are not wanting who believe that among the causes of India's poverty is this very lightness of taxation, which deprives the Administration of means with which to work.

Now, leaving matters of argument, let us face about and look at indisputable wastages of India's vital resources. The major channels have been shown in earlier pages, but these leave untouched a list of points only second in importance, such as caste marriage costs, the usurer, the hoarding of treasure, and mendicancy.

Caste laws strictly limit the range of possible marriages, sometimes even to the confines of half-a-dozen

[12] *Statistical Abstract, 1914-15 to 1923-24,* p. 190.

families, so that, despite his dread of sonlessness, a man may be forced to wait till he is old for the birth of a girl within the circle wherein he may marry,[13] and then may be forced to pay ruinously to secure her. Or again, there is such a scramble for husbands of right caste that, rather than sacrifice their own souls by leaving a girl unmarried, fathers strain their credit to the snapping point to secure eligible matches for their daughters.

In Bengal, of late years, several cases have become public of girls committing suicide at the approach of puberty, to save their fathers the crushing burden of their marriage dowry.[14] And the chorus of praise evoked from Bengal youth by this act has stimulated further self-immolations. Nor do the father's finances greatly affect the case. Though a man prosper and take in much money, marriages in his family still pull him down to ruin, for the reason that pride and custom forever urge him ahead of his means.

Marriage expenses and funeral expenses, love of litigation, thriftlessness and crop failures are among the chief roads that lead the Indian into debt. The Indian money-lender, or *bania*, is the same man as the usurer of the Philippines. And, exactly as in the Philippines, the average Indian having a little money laid by, even though he be not a *bania* by caste and calling, will, if he be minded to lend, lend to his neighbors at 33 per cent. and up, rather than to Government at a miserable

[13] *Reconstructing India,* Visvesvaraya, p. 241.
[14] *Legislative Assembly Debates,* 1922, Vol. II, Part II, p. 1811.

3.5 per cent. so that Government may build him a railway. Let the silly folk in London do that.

The *bania* is the man who, foreseeing a short crop, corners all the grain in his region, and at sowing-time sells seed-grain to his neighbors at 200 per cent. profit, taking the coming crop as security.

Once in debt to a *bania,* few escape. Clothing, oxen, and all purchased necessities are bought of the same wise old spider. Compound interest rolls up in the good old way as the years pass, and posterity limps under the load unto the third and fourth generation.

"The assumption that debt is due to poverty cannot be entertained. Debt is due to credit and credit depends upon prosperity and not poverty," writes Calvert. Credit, in India, is the creation of the British Government by the establishment of peace and security of property, coupled with public works that increase production and the value of land. The *bania* in his fullest glory is therefore a by-product of British rule. In the Punjab, rich among provinces, we find him in his paradise, 40,000 strong, collecting from the people annual interest equaling nearly three times the total sum that they annually pay to Government.[15]

Everywhere, whether openly or covertly, the usurer opposes the education of the people, because a man who can read will not sign the sort of paper by which the *bania* holds his slave, and a man who can figure will know when his debt is cleared. As two Indian members of the profession warmly told me, the *bania* hates "this

[15] See Appendix III D.

meddlesome and unsympathetic foreign government that has introduced a system of coöperative credit, which, wherever a Briton directs it, is ruining our good old indigenous banking business. Moreover, not content even with that mischief, it is pushing in night schools and adult-education schemes to upset the people's mind."

Intimately powerful as he is throughout the country, the *bania* exercises a strong undercurrent of influence in the Swarajist party, making it generally hostile to labor interests and currency reforms.

A third actual drain upon prosperity, seldom advertised, yet affecting not only India but the rest of the world, is India's disposition of bullion. Since the early days of the Roman Empire, western economists have been troubled over India's intake of precious metals, rather than of foreign goods, in payment for her produce. These metals she has always swallowed up.[16]

In 1889 it was estimated that India held imprisoned "a stock of gold bullion wholly useless for commercial purpose and increasing at the rate of nearly 3 million sterling [$14,000,000] annually, of the value of not less than two hundred and seventy million pounds sterling [$1,312,000,000]."[17] This ever-accumulating treasure lies in the hands of all conditions and orders

[16] See Appendix III E.
[17] *The Industrial Competition of Asia. An Inquiry into the Influence of Currency on the Commerce of the Empire in the East,* Clarmont John Daniell. Kegan Paul, Trench, Trubner and Co., Ltd., London, 1890, p. 249.

Photo by M. Moyca Newell

IN THE STREETS OF BOMBAY

OLD SOLDIERS OF THE NORTH

One day in 1914 he on the right appeared in the District Commissioner's office: "Sahib, is it true that the King-Emperor makes war?" "Yes." "And Indian troops may be wanted?" "Yes." "Sahib, I came to town to get my boy out of school and thrash him. Will the Sahib thrash him for me and let me get back to my village to gather the men?"

of men, from the poorest laborer to the most eminent prince.

In 1927, Mr. D. C. Bliss, American Trade Commissioner in Bombay, wrote of treasure in India: [18]

Vast reserves have been accumulated, . . . estimated as amounting to more than five billion dollars—but they have been jealously hoarded in the form of unproductive precious metals. Put to productive uses, or loaned out in the world's money-markets, they would suffice to make India one of the powerful nations of the world. The traditional "wealth of the Indies" is there, but in such a form that it yields nothing to its possessors.

From time immemorial it has been considered improper for any great heir to draw upon his father's hoard of precious treasure and equally improper for him not to build up a hoard of his own. The late Nyzam of Hyderabad collected in his vaults jewels to immense values. The present prince is understood to prefer bullion, of which his own accumulations are said to reach to between 150 and 200 million dollars. Equally, every peasant in the land secretly buries silver in the earth, and loads it upon his women's necks and wrists and ankles, for safe-keeping. Forty per cent. of the world's total gold production, and 30 per cent. of the world's silver, is thus annually absorbed by India. None of this gold is coined or goes into currency, and,

[18] *The Bombay Bullion Market,* Don C. Bliss, Jr., U. S. Bureau of Foreign and Domestic Commerce, Trade Information Bulletin No. 557, pp. 5-6.

says Mr. Bliss, of silver: "All of the absorption is in
response to the demand for bullion for . . . orna-
mental uses." "Undoubtedly," he adds, "an enormous
quantity of bullion has been buried and forgotten."
The man heavily in debt to the *bania* commonly possesses a store of hidden coin, yet continues borrowing.
This custom rests on the idea of being prepared for
the rainy day and on a profound distrust of the human
element in any scheme of banking.

The tendency of the world's gold and silver to con-
centrate in India and there to disappear from action
tells its own story. On the one hand, an essentially
poor country could not bring such a thing about. On
the other hand, no country that buries its wealth and
then lies down and sleeps on the grave can be really
prosperous.

Turning now to the drain incurred through robbing
the soil: India, as we know, is preëminently an agricultural country. But she has never fertilized her soil.
Continually taking from it, she puts nothing back—
and yet laments the thinness of her crops. Having but
little firewood, she burns her cow-dung for fuel. And,
being under religious taboo against the handling of
dead animal substance, the Hindu majority will not
use for bone-manure the cattle bones of which they
have such store, but, instead, sell them to be exported
to foreign parts. And they cultivate with a little wooden
plow that barely scratches the surface of the ground.

Suppose that, still respecting the taboo, they used
some of their idle buried cash, or the interest it would

bring, put to work, to buy fertilizer and machinery; what far-reaching profit might not that one step effect, did but their general way of life permit enduring prosperity!

The fragmentation of property through the ancient laws of inheritance, until a man's holding is so split up into absurdly shaped and widely scattered splinters that its useful cultivation is impossible, is another formidable obstacle to the people's welfare. Those interested in the subject will find it well developed in Calvert's *Wealth and Welfare of the Punjab*, where also is treated the great restriction of potential revenue through lack of women's work.[19]

And here, too, though at cost of repetition, must be recalled the enormous dead loss incurred by the country through the maintenance of its seventy-odd millions of unprofitable cattle, which, because of religious inhibitions, may but rarely contribute even hides and bones to the country's profit.

Last on our list of draughts upon the wealth of India, we find the item of mendicancy.

The Brahmanic code commends renunciation of active life and the taking up of a life of contemplation and beggary as the proper terminal half of man's earthly career. At the same time it teaches that he who gives to the beggar is in reality a debtor to that beggar, in that he who receives affords the giver a priceless opportunity to establish credit in the life to come.

[19] See Appendix III F.

[405]

Therefore neither shame nor gratitude attaches to the beggar's part.[20]

In the Indian Legislative Assembly, on February 2, 1926, Sir Hari Singh Gour said: [21]

> In the last Census Report . . . we find recorded as beggars, vagrants, witches and wizards . . . altogether 58 lakhs [5,800,000]. . . . But in point of fact their number is still greater as to that class must be added saints and fakirs who live by beggary.

Government's estimate of 1921 put the saints and fakirs then living by beggary at 1,452,174.

Now and again these privileged ones gather in groups of hundreds and stream across country feeding off the populace as they go. The disciple that follows each holy man holds out his master's begging bowl. And rarely is he denied. One sees their encampments in moving about the country. One meets them on the road, almost or quite naked except for their coat of ashes, their enormous mops of long snarled hair bleached to the color of ginger, their eyes reddened with drugs. At great fairs they turn out in multitudes. A competent witness informed me that at the latest twelfth-year fair of Madras, the two and a half miles of road from the city to the bathing place was lined on both sides with religious beggars sitting shoulder to shoulder, each with an attendant squatting in front, calling out his master's claims to alms.

[20] See Appendix III G.
[21] *Legislative Assembly Debates*, Vol. VII, No. 8, pp. 435-6.

And now we come to a more obscure question, that of the present economic status of the peoples in comparison with their condition in past eras. Mr. Gandhi and his school affirm that the peoples of India have been growing steadily poorer and more miserable, as a result of British rule. To form a close surmise of the facts is difficult indeed. The masses have, as a whole, little ambition to raise or to change actual living conditions. Their minds as a rule do not turn to the accumulation of things. They are content with their mud huts. Given windows and chimneys, they stop them up. Given ample space, they crowd in a closet. Rather than keep the house in repair, they let the rains wash it away, building a new one when the old is gone. Rather than work harder for more food, they prefer their ancient measure of leisure and just enough food for the day.[22]

But their margin of safety is indubitably greater, their power of resistance to calamity increased, and, allegations to the contrary notwithstanding, means of enlarging their income lie at all times, now, within their hands. In just such measure as desire for material advance awakens, one sees this demonstrated in individual lives.[23] The question whether or not such desire is good underlies one of the prime differences between eastern and western thought and practice.

Now in assigning value to these factors, one must remember that the soil of India is today supporting the

[22] *Census of 1921,* Vol. I, Part I, p. 54.
[23] See Appendix III H.

pressure of over 54,000,000 more human beings than it sustained fifty years ago, plus an increase of 20 per cent.[24]

This, again, is a result of freedom from wars and disorders and from killing famines; of the checking of epidemics; and of the multiplied production of food—all elements bound to produce ever greater effect as essential features of an established government. And the prospects it unfolds, of sheer volume of humanity piling up as the decades pass, is staggering. For, deprived of infanticide, of *suttee*, and of her other native escape-valves, yet still clinging to early marriage and unlimited propagation, India stands today at that point of social development where population is controlled by disease, and disease only.[25]

---

[24] *Census of India, 1921*, pp. 7, 48. These figures of increase are reached after allowing for the factor of population added by annexation of territory.

[25] *Ibid.*, Vol. I, Part I, p. 49.

Chapter XXX

CONCLUSION

The preceding chapters of this book state living facts
of India today. They can easily be denied, but they
cannot be disproved or shaken. That there are other
facts, other columns of statistics, other angles left untouched by this research I do not contest.

Neither do I wish to imply that some of the most
unflattering things here affirmed of India are without
counterpart in character and tendency, if not in degree,
in certain sections of our western life. But India has
carried the principles of egocentricity and of a mate-
rialism called spirituality to a further and wider conclusion than has the West. The results, in the individual, the family and the race, are only the more
noteworthy. For they cast a spotlight toward the end
of that road.

Some few Indians will take plain speech as it is
meant—as the faithful wounds of a friend; far more
will be hurt at heart. Would that this task of truth-
telling might prove so radically performed that all
shock of resentment were finally absorbed in it, and
that there need be no further waste of life and time
for lack of a challenge and a declaration!

Appendix I

MEDICAL EVIDENCE

In the Indian Legislative Assembly of 1922, the following evidence, introduced from the floor of the House as descriptive of the conditions of the day, aroused neither question nor opposition from any one of the assembled Indian legislators. The fact that, although thirty-one years old, it still remained beyond challenge, carries a contributing significance. The evidence submitted consists of a list, compiled in 1891 by the western women doctors then practicing in India, and by them laid before the Viceroy, with a petition for intervention on behalf of the children of India. It is made up, they affirm, entirely of instances that have come under the hands of one or another of their own number, and whose like are continually revealed in their ordinary professional experience.

A.—Aged 9. Day after marriage. Left femur dislocated, pelvis crushed out of shape, flesh hanging in shreds.

B.—Aged 10. Unable to stand, bleeding profusely, flesh much lacerated.

C.—Aged 9. So completely ravished as to be almost beyond surgical repair. Her husband had two other living wives and spoke very fine English.

D.—Aged 10. A very small child, and entirely undeveloped physically. This child was bleeding to death

[411]

from the rectum. Her husband was a man of about forty years of age, weighing not less than eleven stone [154 lbs.]. He had accomplished his desire in an unnatural way.

E.—Aged about 9. Lower limbs completely paralyzed.

F.—Aged about 12. Laceration of the perineum extending through the sphincter ani.

G.—Aged about 10. Very weak from loss of blood. Stated that great violence had been done her, in an unnatural way.

H.—Aged about 12. Pregnant, delivered by craniotomy with great difficulty, on account of the immature state of the pelvis and maternal passage.

I.—Aged about 7. Living with husband. Died in great agony after three days.

K.—Aged about 10. Condition most pitiable. After one day in hospital, was demanded by her husband, for his "lawful" use, he said.

L.—Aged 11. From great violence done her person, will be a cripple for life. No use of her lower extremities.

M.—Aged about 10. Crawled to hospital on her hands and knees. Has never been able to stand erect since her marriage.

N.—Aged 9. Dislocation of pubic arch, and unable to stand or to put one foot before the other.

The list will be found in the *Legislative Assembly Debates* of 1922, Vol. III, Part I, p. 919, Appendix. See also p. 882 of the *Debates*.

Appendix II

ENFRANCHISEMENT OF WOMEN

In framing the Reform Bill of 1919, the British Parliament decided that the question of enfranchisement for the women of India could properly be determined only by the Indian peoples themselves. Parliament accordingly allowed the old sex disqualification to remain in the Bill; but at the same time so shaped the electoral rules as to leave it in the power of each province's Legislative Council to place women on the provincial electoral register by passing a resolution to this effect.

Pursuant of this power, the Provinces of Madras, Bombay, Bengal, United Provinces, Punjab and Assam have removed their sex disqualifications, granting the vote to women on the same terms as to the male electorate. Further, the Central Legislative Assembly having passed a similar resolution, women may now vote not only for their Provincial Councils but also for the Legislative Assembly. Under the present general qualifications, however, the total number of women entitled to vote throughout India does not exceed 1,000,000, or about 17 per cent. of the total electorate.

Sir Alexander Muddiman's Reform Enquiry Committee of 1924, in opening the consideration of a further step—that of women's candidature for elective office—reaffirmed that [1]

the question went deep into the social system and susceptibilities of India, and . . . could only with any prudence be settled in accordance with the wishes of the Indians themselves as constitutionally expressed.

It was, however, upon the Muddiman Committee's recommendation that the rules of candidature for Provincial Councils were lately amended, enabling the removal of the sex disqualification by vote of Provincial Council. To this invitation Madras and Bombay have already responded.

The Muddiman Committee next recommended that the electoral rules of both chambers of the Indian Legislature—the Council of State and the Assembly—be amended by the removal of the sex disqualification, so that constituencies in provinces that have enfranchised their women might at will elect women to both Chambers. On September 1, 1926, the Indian Legislature so voted.

Thus far, however, it seems to be the British Provincial Governor rather than the Indian electorate that uses the new privilege. From 1922 to 1926, twenty-two women had become Municipal Councilors or Members of Local Government Boards, of whom only four were elected, the rest being nominated by Government.[2]

The following statement is that of an Englishman

[1] *Report of the Reforms Enquiry Committee*, 1924, p. 57.
[2] *Indian Year Book*, 1926, p. 511.

[414]

deeply conversant with Indian affairs, one who wields much moral influence in India, and who vigorously used that influence to advocate the changes above indicated. It was elicited by my request for the grounds of his position and his view of the present status, and was elsewhere confirmed by ranking Indians.

As for the reason for enfranchising Indian women, I can give you my own reasons, which I put before the Parliamentary Committee which framed the Act. In some places women had long enjoyed the municipal franchise, especially in Bombay. There were a considerable number of women, in Bombay, who took a very useful part in our social work. Therefore I pressed for the enfranchisement of women, both to encourage and hearten these where actually so engaged, and to give others inducements to come forward. The *purdah* must be broken as fast as it can . . . its influence on the health of Indian women is disastrous. I looked on the franchise as another nail in the *purdah* coffin.

As for the effect of enfranchisment in the Bombay Presidency, so far as I can see, it has been slight; the women in public life are the women who were there in one way or another before enfranchisement took place. In other parts of India I should say the effect was smaller still. Until the social conditions have improved, the franchise can mean nothing to the Indian woman, for she dares not use it.

In observing the position of the women of Bombay, outstanding in India, one heavily contributing factor appears: This city is the great Parsi center. Out of the total number of Parsis in all India—101,778—nearly 93,000 are domiciled in Bombay Presidency.[3] Descend-

[3] *Census of India, 1921,* Vol. I, p. 118.

ants of old Persian stock, the Parsis are practically all either merchants or bankers. Eight hundred per 1,000 of their men are literate, as against the 115 literates per 1,000 of male Hindus. The Parsis neither sequester nor suppress their women, but favor their adequate education. Thus 672 per 1,000 [4] of the women of the Parsis are literate, as against the 14 per 1,000 female literates of the Hindus.

The presence of such a body, occupying conspicuous positions, cannot but influence the whole upper-class population.

[4] *Census of India, 1921,* p. 180.

Appendix III

A

INDIAN COTTON

The record of raw cotton exported from India in the years 1924-25 is as follows, the unit being bales of 400 pounds: [1]

Japan	1,671,000
Italy	485,000
China (excluding Hong Kong)	284,000
Belgium	201,000
Germany	174,000
The United Kingdom	162,000

Of the raw cotton exported to England the Lancashire looms use little because of its inferior quality, buying, rather, in Egypt and in America.

India's total raw cotton export, in 1924-25, was 3,326,400 bales.[2] Her consumption in Indian mills during that period was 2,050,891 bales.

Japan's purchase is mostly of the poorer grades of cotton and is mainly used in competing in China with the product of India's mills. In 1924 there were 337 cotton mills in British India. These are nearly all

[1] *Review of the Trade of India in 1924-25,* Calcutta, Government of India Central Publication Branch, 1926, p. 73.
[2] *Ibid.,* pp. 21-2.

[417]

Indian-owned and as a rule have British superintendents and foremen, with Indian labor. The following figures [3] will further clarify the situation:

	1913–14 Million Yards	1922–23 Million Yards	1923–24 Million Yards	1924–25 Million Yards
Production in Indian mills of cotton piece goods	1,164.3	1,725.2	1,701.6	1,970.5
Export of Indian-milled piece goods	89.2	157.0	165.3	181.5
Imports of foreign-made cotton piece-goods, from all countries, including the United Kingdom, Japan, Italy, Netherlands and the United States.	3,197.1	1,593.3	1,485.8	1,823.2

It will thus be seen that while the production and the export trade of India have been rising, the import trade is about half what it was before 1914.

B

RAILWAY STATISTICS

The following figures as of the year 1925 are based on statistics contained in *The Statesman's Year Book* of 1926:

[3] *Review of the Trade of India in 1924-25,* p. 23.

	India	Argentine	United States	Canada
Mileage open per 1,000 square miles of territory in	21	19	88	15
Number of passengers carried per mile of open railway	15,834	5,966	3,550	814
Tons of goods carried per mile of open railway	2,785	2,042	8,277	2,019
Total value of imports and exports carried per mile of open railway	$56,929	$73,092	$33,116	$35,647

C

MILITARY EXPENDITURE

An acknowledged authority thus puts the frame of the matter: [4]

The safe figure of a nation's military expenditure . . . is fixed by considerations almost entirely beyond the country's control; by her geographical and ethnological boundaries, by the power and attitude of her neighbours, by her national resources in men and material, by her racial unity or disunity, and so on. . . . What requires investigation is whether [India's] total budget . . . is worthy of her immense territories and their prosperity. Were that total to be increased largely, the defence item would remain virtually stationary,

[4] *The Defence of India,* "Arthur Vincent," pp. 93-4.

and the disproportion would disappear to the point of making India one of the best-placed nations in the world for protective expenditure.

D

THE USURER

Of the Punjab *bania* Mr. Calvert writes:[5]

He represents the richest single class. His profits probably exceed those of all the cultivators put together. Beside him, the professional class is inconsiderable; the industrial class is insignificant, even trade and commerce take second place.

But the usurer is by no means peculiar to the Punjab. The total rural debt of British India is estimated at approximately $1,900,000,000, in the main unproductive. This burden is largely due to the vicious usury and compound interest system, a trifling percentage is incurred for land improvement, and the rest may be mainly attributed to extravagant expenditures on marriages.

E

BULLION

The export of merchandise from India, in the year 1924-25, exceeded the import to the value of over $500,000,000.[6] During that year the import of private treasure totaled $328,000,000.[7]

---

[5] *The Wealth and Welfare of the Punjab,* H. Calvert, Lahore, 1922, p. 130.
[6] *Review of the Trade of India,* p. 47.
[7] *Ibid.,* p. 48.

America, during 1924-25, imported Indian goods [8] to the value of $117,000,000. Yet she sold to India only $46,900,000 worth of goods and exported to India bars of silver on private account of approximately the same value and gold to the value of $67,700,000. This process is steadily increasing as the years pass, raising the world's price of bullion.

F

LOSS OF WOMEN'S LABOR

Calvert says, in his *Wealth and Welfare of the Punjab*, p. 207:

If there were in Western countries a movement aiming at the exclusion of female labour from all except purely domestic tasks, that movement would endanger the whole economic fabric, and, if successful, would involve those countries in ruin. . . . The fact that there are [Indian] tribes . . . which do not allow their womenfolk even to work in the fields is alone sufficient to explain their poverty.

The same point is recognized by the Hindu writer, Visvesvaraya, in his *Reconstructing India*, p. 246:

The time has come when Indians must seriously consider whether the passive life, to which they condemn women with a view of preserving the so-called proprieties and decencies of life, is worth the appalling price the country is forced to pay in the shape of loss of work and intelligent effort from half the population of the country.

[8] *Ibid.*, pp. 48, 60-1, 76.

G

MENDICANCY

On February 2, 1926, Mr. Abdul Haye, Muhammadan member from the East Punjab, introduced into the Indian Legislative Assembly a resolution looking to the prohibition of beggary and vagrancy in India. Supporting it, he said in part: [9]

> One wonders whether the stars in heaven are more in number or the beggars in this country. . . . Barring agriculture there is no other profession in India which can claim more followers. . . . I make bold to say and without any fear of contradiction that every twenty-fifth man in this country is a beggar.

Of these mendicants Lala Lajpat Rai says in his *National Education in India*, p. 37:

> We find that today a good part of the nation (sometimes estimated at one-fourth), having abandoned all productive economic work, engages itself in . . . making the people believe that next to becoming a Saddhú [a begging ascetic] himself, the best thing for man to do to avoid damnation is to feed and maintain Saddhús.

H

ECONOMIC CONDITION OF THE MASSES

As general circumstantial evidence of increased means, one sees the consumption by the peasants of

[9] *Legislative Assembly Debates*, Vol. VII, No. 8, p. 627.

non-essentials, once beyond their dreams. Thus, at the fair at Aligarh, in February, 1926, the turnover of cheap boots in one week amounted to $5,000, netting a profit of 20 per cent. Boots, to the sort of people who snapped these up and put them on their own feet, were, twenty years ago, an unheard-of luxury. Big stocks of umbrellas, lamps, and gayly painted iron trunks were sold out and renewed over and over again, on the same occasion, the buyers being the ordinary cultivators. Tea, cigarettes, matches, lanterns, buttons, pocket-knives, mirrors, gramophones are articles of commerce with people who, fifteen years ago, bought nothing of the sort. The heavy third-class passenger traffic by rail is another evidence of money in hand. For railway travel, to the Indian peasant, takes the place that the movie fills in America. In 1924-25, 581,804,000 third-class railway travelers, as against 1,246,000 of the first-class, proved the presence of money to spare in the peasants' possession. "Where are they all going?" I repeatedly asked, watching the crowds packing into the third-class carriages.

"Anywhere. Visiting, pilgrimage, marriage parties, little business trips—just 'there and back,' mostly for the excitement of going," was the answer.

Index

[425]

INDEX

Dutch witness to, 278; Peter Mundy on, 278

Capitalists, Indian, demand exorbitant rates, 393; and public utility bonds, 393; *see also* Bania

Caste System, 151; inflammatory effect of any attack upon, 155; British East India Company and British Crown on, as to educational rights, 156-7; not to be confused with snobbery, 156, 169; creates in higher castes aversion to useful pursuits, 185; higher castes averse to education of lower, 214; in relation to working of democracy, 295-6; demands nepotism and class favoritism, 301-2; and removal of night soil, 373; caste-marriage laws economic drain on country, 399 *et seq.*

Cattle, India devoured by, 223; number of, 223; estimated annual loss by, 223; going to pasture, 226; tranquillity of, 226-7; pasturage absorbed by Government's greed, 227; deteriorated through Government's policy, 227-8; unintelligence and callousness of Indian toward, 229-30; pasturage of, past and present, 230; "selection by starvation," 231; selection and use of bulls, 231; Higginbottom on, 232; pasturage in Bengal, 232; depredations of hungry, on crops, 232; fodder, 232; starvation of, laid to British, 233; British responsible for over-burden of, 233; Government's experimental work in, Chap. XVIII; America's breeding, in Philippines, 235; American Holstein-Friesians imported by British Government, 236-7; native milch breeds, 236-7; milk production of half-breeds, 236; "dual purpose," 238; beef, price of, 238; fodder-growing on Government farms, 238; traveling lecturers, 238; indifference of Indian to development of, 239; gvalas, 239; maltreatment of herd bulls offered by Government, 238-40; slaughtered, by Hindu collusion, 241-2; tail-breaking justified, 243; other method of speeding, 243; *see also* Cruelty to Animals

Census of India, quoted, 22, 44

Census, of the United Provinces, quoted, 70

Chakravarti, Brajalal, quoted, 124-5

Chandragupta, Emperor, 270-1

Chandravarkar, Sir Narayan, quoted, on British origin of Indian awakening as to Untouchability, 165-6

Chowdri, Mrs., sub-assistant surgeon, on mid-wifery, 95

Chatterjee, Rai Bahadur, Dr. G. C., his anti-malarial work, 368

Chauri Chaura, massacre of Hindus, by Hindus, 332-3

Chetty, Shanmukhan, quoted, condemning infant marriage, 38

Chiefs' Colleges, 311-2

Children, condition at birth, 23; taught to dwell on sex relation, 23; made prostitute, 25; mortality, 35; effect of child motherhood on, 45; feeding at birth, 97

Child-birth, deaths in, 44; instance of Zemindar's wife, 78; ritualistic uncleanness of mother at, 92-3, 98, 105; no preparations made for, 92; handling by native midwives, 91 *et seq.*; confinement of a princess, 102-3; fate of woman dying in, 104; conducted from cow's back, 106-7

Child-marriages, abstract uneasiness concerning, among Hindus; orthodox insistence on, 27; attitude of Government of India on, 33, *et seq.*, impossibility of control by law, 33; *et seq.*; arguments for and against, 33 *et seq.*; disputes concerning, 44; universality of, among Hindus, 44; Captain Hira Singh Brar on, 45; instances of effect, 53-6; defended, 60

Child mother, 16; age of motherhood, 22; ignorance of the, 23, 131-2

Cholera, transmitted from holy places, 359, *et seq.*; and village well, 369-72; India the greatest cholera center of world, 369; how transmitted, 369-70; no cure known, 370; mortality, 370; pandemics of, 370; United States attacked, 370; relation of United States to cholera threat of India, 371; cholera in Bengal, 371-2; in Kashmir and the Punjab, 372; fairs and pilgrimages the great danger source, 372

Christian converts, persecution of, 160; rating of, 164, 169; furnish large part of teachers, 207-8

Christopher. Lieut.-Col., I. M. S.,

[427]